Be Good, Love Brian

Be Good, Love Brian

Growing up with
Brian Clough

CRAIG BROMFIELD

with Tim Rich

MUDLARK

Mudlark
HarperCollins*Publishers*
1 London Bridge Street
London SE1 9GF

www.harpercollins.co.uk

HarperCollins*Publishers*
1st Floor, Watermarque Building, Ringsend Road
Dublin 4, Ireland

First published by Mudlark 2021

1 3 5 7 9 10 8 6 4 2

A catalogue record of this book is
available from the British Library

ISBN 978-0-00-846686-2

Printed and bound in the UK using 100%
renewable electricity at CPI Group (UK) Ltd

MIX
Paper from
responsible sources
FSC™ C007454

This book is produced from independently certified FSC™ paper
to ensure responsible forest management.

For more information visit: www.harpercollins.co.uk/green

Dedicated to Brian Clough, Barbara Clough,
Gerald Bromfield and Aaron Bromfield

If you love me, send me flowers when I'm alive,
not when I'm dead.

Brian Clough

Map of the North-East

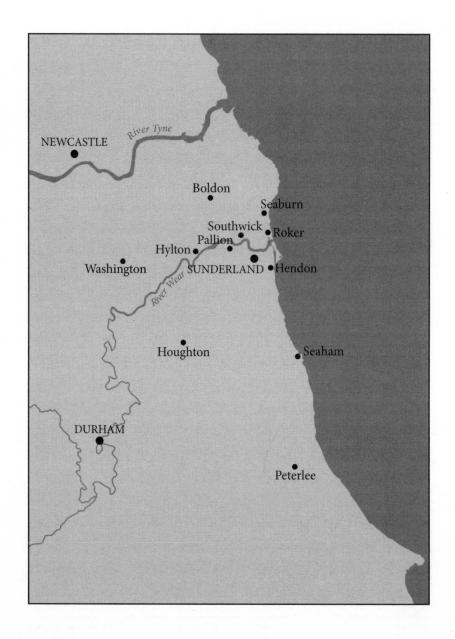

Contents

1.

On the Beach

20 October 1984

He is walking towards me, his collar turned up against the autumn chill that whistles across the beach from the North Sea.

He is wearing a green and purple jacket and tracksuit bottoms. Both have seen better days. His white trainers look a hundred years old. He is the most famous manager in English football.

It hadn't been much of a summer for English football. We don't watch a lot of telly because ours runs off a meter but we couldn't watch the European Championship from France even if we wanted to. It wasn't on because England hadn't qualified.

All summer there has been a ferocious campaign to remove the England manager, Bobby Robson, by any means necessary, including running stories about his marriage, and put this man in charge.

The *Sun* has been handing out 'Clough for England' badges with every copy of the newspaper. Only Brian Clough, they say, has the personality to make the England team work.

He has the personality. He has the ego. He once said of Frank Sinatra: 'He met me, you know.' He has shared a stage with Muhammad Ali. Mike Yarwood impersonated him on TV every Saturday night.

One of Yarwood's favourite routines is that a gunman comes to kill Brian Clough. He gives Clough the option of where he'd like to be shot.

'Anywhere except in the mouth,' comes the reply.

The gunman, realising the impossibility of this task, throws away his weapon and walks off.

Right now, he doesn't look in the mood for talking – he's head down and there are people around him, walking with him. His staff, his entourage.

I am going over to talk to Brian Clough but not for the reasons most 11-year-old boys want to talk to the most famous manager on the planet. I don't want his autograph and I don't want to wish him luck for this afternoon's game against Newcastle even though, like everyone in Sunderland, we'd like Newcastle United to be thrashed every single Saturday of our lives. I want to ask him if he knows where Kenny Swain is.

Kenny plays full-back for Nottingham Forest. I met him last night when we were doing 'Penny for the Guy' outside the hotel opposite, the one where the team is staying. He gave us five pounds. We didn't know who he was but no one in Sunderland would give you a five-pound note when you were out Guying. Ever.

Kenny told my brother, Aaron, and me that if we came back to the hotel the next morning, he'd give us all the players' autographs. So here we are. Only we can't find Kenny. It was then that Aaron spotted Brian Clough walking along the beach. Aaron's older than me by a couple of years and he's also got a different dad. It's complicated. I'm Craig, by the way.

I've another brother, Darren. He's the oldest and he's got the same mam and dad as me. He's had to do more looking out for me and Aaron than any brother should. When I was being bullied, our Darren would always say: 'Hit the biggest one first, the others will stop and think about it.'

So, instead of going to the edge of the group and asking one of the entourage where I could find Kenny Swain, I go right to the middle. I didn't even think why I wouldn't ask him. Without Darren, I might have lived my whole life as a mouse.

'Excuse me, but hello, Mr Clough. Can you tell me if Kenny Swain is up yet, please?'

'Hello, beauty. I'm not sure, why do you ask?'

'We met him last night and he told us that, if we came back this morning, he would get some players' autographs for us.'

'Well, we'd better go and have a look then, hadn't we? He's probably having breakfast with the lads.'

And he marches us off towards the revolving doors of the Seaburn Hotel, where he and the rest of the team are staying, and in that moment, one month and three days from my twelfth birthday, my life will change utterly and forever. Brian Clough will become part of my life and even now, 17 years after his death, he is still a part of my life. A part I have never been able to let go.

Looking back, I often wondered why he would let these two ruffians from Sunderland into his life and would make me part of his family for the next nine years – 'Rag-tags,' he called us.

He wasn't wrong. We *were* rag-tags. When I was at primary school, we had to build a model ship from cardboard. You needed a toilet roll for the funnel. I didn't have a toilet roll because we didn't use toilet paper, just ripped-up newspapers nailed to a wall.

Sunderland boasted that it had once built more ships than anywhere else in the world, but even Austin & Pickersgill, whose cranes we could see from the shops near our house, would struggle to construct a seagoing vessel from copies of the *Daily Star*.

We were nice kids, though. Good kids. We made people laugh. We were polite. We stood up for old folk on the bus. We called him 'Mr Clough' not 'Cloughie' or 'Brian' or 'marra', the North-East word for 'mate'.

We were from Sunderland. That mattered. He was from Middlesbrough but he said he preferred Sunderland people. They talked more, they were friendlier and, more importantly, when he transferred from Middlesbrough to Sunderland in 1961, they seemed to appreciate him more.

When he lived here, he would walk this beach, sometimes stopping to pick up sea coal, washed up from the collieries along the Durham coast. He was Sunderland's highest-paid player, the quickest to score 250 goals in the history of the Football League, but he still recognised the value of free coal, even though it spat when you burned it.

Later, when his cruciate ligaments were ruined by a tackle on a Boxing Day match at Roker Park on a pitch strewn with snow and straw, he would run endless miles along the beach at Seaburn, sometimes shirtless. He would run repeatedly up and down the Cat and Dog Steps that link the beach to the promenade – so-called because that was where Sunderland people supposedly hoyed their unwanted pets into the sea at high tide.

Everything was done to make the knee right, but the knee was never right, and in 1964 he accepted his career was over at 29. Sunderland collected on the insurance, worth about a million pounds now. They gave one of the finest strikers ever to wear their colours one fortieth of that. However, they also offered him a job in management, looking after the youth team. It seemed a decision motivated by pity because nearly everyone who had played with Brian Clough thought him too self-obsessed, too vindictive and too bloody rude to men in authority – men he would need – ever to be a football manager.

He always promised he would come back. 'I would crawl over broken glass to manage Sunderland, son,' he would say whenever he took his team to Roker Park. He was asked – he was *always* asked.

It was all for show. He came to the Midlands in 1967 to manage Derby. He never left, apart from a few months at Brighton, which he did for the money, and the 44 days at Leeds, which he did to prove a point to his great rival, Don Revie, who was also from Middlesbrough. He was never happy working from a hotel and he has no intention of asking the Seaburn for its long-term rates.

The place still had a pull because the other thing that strikes me now is that the Seaburn was an odd choice of hotel. It was logical if you were playing at Roker Park, half a mile down the road, but Forest were playing Newcastle and, for St James'

Park, most teams either stayed near the racecourse at Gosforth Park or at the Post House at Washington, a new town on the A1 built around the old colliery halfway between Sunderland and Newcastle. Perhaps he just wanted to walk the beach again.

He is 49 now, three years younger than Alex Ferguson will be when he wins his first title at Manchester United. He can and does reel off the trophies he has won. The league title with Derby – the first in their history. The league title with Nottingham Forest – the first in their history. Two European Cups. Two League Cups.

It is more than four years since he last won something and he is probably more alone than he has ever been. Jimmy Gordon, the wizened Scottish trainer who coached his players at Derby and Forest and even during the 44 days at Leeds, has retired.

Peter Taylor, one of the very few who played alongside Brian Clough and thought he had the makings of a great manager, left two years ago. He and Clough moulded teams together. They were the Lennon and McCartney of football and, like John and Paul, they ended up hating each other. They will never speak again.

One of the things he misses about Peter Taylor is his ability to make him laugh. 'Ooh,' he'll say to me over the next few years, 'Pete knew how to make me laugh.'

Why did he take to us? We were from Sunderland; that helped. He felt sorry for us – even in his final interview as manager of Nottingham Forest he described himself first and foremost as a socialist. He wanted to give us something more precious than money: he wanted to give us memories. But we also made him laugh and, looking back, you wonder how much laughter there was in Brian Clough's life in the autumn of 1984.

Ronnie Fenton, from up the coast in South Shields, has been promoted from reserve-team coach to assistant manager but the rest are new men. Nottingham Forest are still a force in football – they finished third in the season just gone and reached the semi-finals of the UEFA Cup – but the club is being strangled by debt.

Thinking they would forever be competing for European Cups, the club built a vast new stand. They now had one of the most beautiful grounds in the First Division but one they could not afford. They could not fill it either.

From the Tyne to the Trent, the heavy industries that sustained the working man's game are collapsing and football is collapsing with them. Crowds at the City Ground, Nottingham, are now 45 per cent lower than they were when Forest won the league six years ago. Clough will write the club a cheque for £56,000 so they can keep the Inland Revenue at bay.

Sunderland, too, is dying.

The town – and it is the largest town in England – is in a state of siege. If you go back from the beach where I've just been talking to Mr Clough, you come to the seafront. Seaburn and Roker … People used to come here on holiday, though they don't any more. Package holidays to places like Majorca, a destination Brian Clough popularised in the 1970s, have seen to that.

If you go down the seafront and turn left, you come to the great, green girders of the Wearmouth Bridge. It was opened in 1929, a year after the Tyne Bridge, which it looks like. The Tyne Bridge is more famous and it really pisses off people in Sunderland if you confuse the two. Newcastle is bigger, more glamorous. The Tyne Bridge featured in *Get Carter* and *The Likely Lads*. Nobody saw Sunderland as a film set.

The town centre is on the south side of the river. The main drag is called Fawcett Street, where the Town Hall with its Victorian colonnades and clock tower stood. They tore it down in 1971, the year before I was born. When an older generation of Sunderland people list their grievances, they always end with: 'and they pulled the Town Hall down'.

On the north bank of the Wear, just before it meets the sea, the towers of the huge Monkwearmouth Colliery stand over Sunderland like a fortress. The colliery and the shipyard cranes are the guardians of the river, the guarantees of Sunderland's future but Monkwearmouth, where my uncle works, has been silent for seven months because of the miners' strike. The *Sunderland Echo* is telling the miners to get back to work.

We live on the north side of the river in Southwick. They build ships here but the ships are leaving the Wear. One by one, the yards are closing. In four years' time, they will all be gone.

I live at 91 Shakespeare Street, Southwick, Sunderland SR5 2PG. As you walk through the front gate and in through the front door, facing you is a staircase of 15 steps, 12 straight and then three turning the corner on to the landing. I loved those stairs. I'd spend ages trying to long-jump the whole 15 steps in one go and never quite made it. So many times I'd get down-stairs with a bumped head after holding onto the banister and vaulting 12 of them, then hitting the front door sprawling. Or I'd bite my tongue bum-sliding down the 12 straight steps.

Through the door on the right, you'd come to the sitting room. It was lovely at times, with a proper coal fire. Through the sitting room there was a small door leading to the kitchen. On the left-hand side of the kitchen was another small door leading to the bathroom and downstairs toilet. We had three bedrooms upstairs: one for Mam and Dad, one for Joanne, my older sister, and one for Darren, Aaron and me (or Dazzy and Azzy as they were always called).

We had a back garden, a side patch that was always flooded from the kitchen sink overflow and a tiny front garden. Mam made sure the downstairs was kept spotlessly clean and, when we had money, she decorated it beautifully.

Dad did the decorating whenever he was home long enough. He'd usually start something while he was drunk and it would take ages to finish it. He was a sign writer, though he was never, as he claimed, a professional sign writer. Mam's dad worked at the pit at Houghton, a village to the south of Sunderland, and was a non-commissioned officer in the National Union of Mineworkers. He never went out without a tie.

Dad wrote the gold lettering on the purple velvet banner that the Houghton branch of the NUM carried to the Durham Miners' Gala every July. Alongside the flags from every colliery in the North, it was paraded past the balcony of the County Hotel, where the men who ran the National Union of Mineworkers and the Labour Party stood like lords.

He spent most of his spare time building things from matchsticks. He would put them in the oven so they were easier to bend and would burn some of them to change the colour of whatever it was he was making. His speciality was probably wishing wells but he also made pool tables, caravans and windmills, purely out of matches. We never kept any of them – he'd either make them to order or we'd have to go round trying to sell them. A lot of houses in Seaburn had one of Dad's matchstick ornaments.

When we were skint, he made us sell all the lovely stuff Mam had bought when she had money, until the walls were bare and we had to start again. It was stupid really and I bet he lost a lot of money doing it like that. When we needed money, we had to go around Southwick, knocking on strange people's doors and asking them if they wanted to buy some brass plaques or some furry drums that we got from Nana. We sold so much stuff for 'thirty bob' but we also sold some expensive stuff. We could easily raise 20 quid in one night, selling pictures and a big brass and wood clock and weather measurer, or a *barometer*, as our Dazzy called it. Why the hell would someone want a clock that would tell you if it was going to rain? We got a tenner for it.

Mam's favourite story was how she once turned down Bryan Ferry. He was from Washington, where his dad looked after the pit ponies at the colliery, and one night he found himself at the social club in Houghton. He went over to Mam and asked her out. She said no. There was a bloke who ran the amusement arcades in Houghton and Mam thought he was the better option.

We dined out on that story or we would have done if we ever went to a restaurant. The nearest we came to dining out was takeaways of chips and gravy from the New Jade on Southwick Green.

The more I thought about that story, the more obsessed I became with the idea that Bryan Ferry could have been my dad and every time 'Dance Away' or 'More Than This' came on the radio I hated him for not being my dad. If he had been, we'd have been in Bel Air or the South of France by now and the more I looked around, the more I realised that, without something dramatic happening, Southwick was a place I might never escape from.

The man who I was following through the revolving doors of the Seaburn Hotel would help me escape. Not to Cannes or Los Angeles but to somewhere I had never heard of.

A village called Quarndon.

2.

The Running Boy

Bryan Ferry was not my dad. My real dad was called Colin. My first memory of him dates from when I was two: he was smashing a mirror over Mam's head. Out in the street where everyone could see.

A few years later, they split up, leaving three children aged 10 or under – Darren, Joanne and me. Mam said she couldn't cope. Colin said he didn't want us (you won't be hearing anything more from Colin).

We were taken into care on a big council estate called Thorney Close. The social services file said we were 'resilient children', which was just as well. They had tried to separate my sister Joanne from the rest of us to begin with but they relented, and when we saw her again she was weepy, upset and afraid. On our first night together, she clambered into my bed. Then she wet it and went back to her own bed.

The care home was run by women in their fifties and sixties, who we called 'auntie'. When Auntie Audrey saw my bed was wet she ordered me to wear nappies – 'You've got to wear them until you can prove you are dry, Craig.'

For the next three months I wore nappies. I was six, I was going to school. There were 10 other kids in the home. They couldn't stop laughing.

While we were in the clutches of the 'aunties', Mam had got a job in a factory down the coast at Seaham, whose one great claim to fame was that it was where Lord Byron had lived. Sadly for the County Durham Tourism Board, he loathed the place. He kept complaining that all he could see from his front window were ships wrecked on the rocks below. Now, it was where they made Sara Lee frozen gateaux and it was while working here that Mam started seeing Jerry Bromfield, who played rugby for Seaham Harbour. He had a son called Aaron, whom everyone called 'Azzy' and who was a year and a half older than me and a few months younger than Joanne.

They actually met in the Silver Dollar, a bar in the Galleries, a big concrete shopping centre in Washington. It wasn't a romantic date. The Silver Dollar was opposite Savacentre, one of the biggest supermarkets in the North-East. People like Mam and Jerry used to go to the Silver Dollar to sell the stuff they nicked from it. Where they met was a pretty good guide to how the rest of their relationship would pan out.

One thing Jerry did insist on was that they went to Thorney Close to fetch us. When he and Aaron started living with us, Darren said we should show Jerry some respect and call him 'Dad'. What Dazzy said went. From then on, he was only ever 'Dad'.

We were happy for a while. Mam's job meant that every night she would bring in a lovely cake from the factory. Soon, we were eating more Black Forest gateau than anywhere outside south-west Germany.

One morning, we're getting ready to go to school and a song comes on the radio called 'I Can't Stand Losing You' by The Police. Mam starts hugging us all and crying. Something's wrong because she never cries just because we're going to school.

I run off – I want to get a bottle of milk from someone's doorstep so she can have a cup of coffee. I'm gone ages. When I came back, Mam was gone. She didn't return that evening and not the day after. Eventually, I went up to our Dazzy and said: 'Where's Mam? What's happened to her?'

'I didn't want to tell you this, Craig, but she's in prison.'

He'd lied to me. I punched him in the face. Dad told us she had gone to prison for not paying the TV licence but when we thought about it – and we thought about it *a lot* – we decided they wouldn't send you to prison for not paying to watch *Blue Peter*. We found out later that it had been for something called 'fraud'.

For the six months Mam was at Low Newton prison near Durham, Dad looked after us. I don't think he ever beat us, but he did like to knuckle our knuckles if we hadn't washed our hands. He would occasionally test how long he could squeeze my finger with a pair of pliers – jocular stuff like that.

Once, he came home and said we had left the house a pigsty – 'If you kids want to live like animals, you'll be bloody tret like animals.' He marched into the kitchen, furiously opened a couple of tins of beans and made some toast. Then he put it on four plates and put the plates on the floor – 'You'll all eat off the floor like the bloody dog.'

We knelt down.

It's 1983. I'm wearing an England shirt from last summer's World Cup in Spain. I'm a normal 10-year-old with big teeth and fluffy hair right at the junction of life, in my last year at primary school.

I'm definitely not gorgeous but I've already learned there's a charming side to my goofy-toothed-ness that people warm to. The dimples and the fact I look about six help too. When I smile, I look happy. But, apparently, I am a complicated character with at least one chip on each shoulder. I was told that by Mrs Atkinson, an elderly teacher of everything, including geography, maths, art and probably PE, at West Southwick School. She might have only been a homely 40 to be fair, but she seemed elderly to me. I'm still eight years away from the first time someone calls me 'mister'.

West Southwick is a strange school in a strange building with strange teachers and strange kids. I was transferred there, along with the rest of my too-young-to-care classmates, when High Southwick Infant School was closed to make way for a community and sports centre. I had to walk to school on my own and I couldn't go any other way than up through Beaumont Street – I thought I was likely to get killed there every day for the rest of my life.

Beaumont Street runs parallel to Shakespeare Street and separates the two halves of the estate. It is where the shops are: a newsagent's, a fish and chip shop, a grocer's that sells everything. It has a brick corner-wall, where everyone goes to sit and hang around after school. There are usually lads with bikes like BMXs, Grifters and older lads with cans of beer.

Beaumont Street turns into The Green, which is Southwick's main drag. The biggest building is The Savoy, which was built as a cinema – the Savoy Electric Theatre – but which hadn't shown a film since 1959 when Gregory Peck appeared in *The Man in the Gray Flannel Suit*. It was turned into a bingo hall.

The buses ran up Beaumont Street before turning into Ridley Street. It was here, a couple of summers ago, after Brixton and Toxteth had gone up in flames, that a group of lads hijacked a bus. There'd been days of tension which broke when they put burning bins across the road, forced their way on to the bus and stole the driver's money. Then windows began to be smashed.

High Southwick was across the road from St Hilda's, a much smaller Catholic school. They wore short trousers and all had short hair. Their mams all had nice coats and came to pick them up after school. Some of them had cars. Most of them lived on the bottom, softer side of Southwick. They were, I thought, rich, cocky bastards.

When I say 'rich', I mean Southwick rich. They didn't have to buy yellow-label products from Fine Fare or go for the really cheap option of Winners on The Green, opposite The Savoy, where the 135 bus sets off up Beaumont Street.

When my teacher Mrs Atkinson wasn't angry, she had a lovely rosy-cheeked, smiling face and she usually had on a mustard or plum turtleneck sweater underneath a cardigan that she always wore loose. She rolled the sleeves up to expose a gold bracelet adorned with charms that she kept playing with.

She had kind of woolly, light-ginger, curly hair – not tight woolly, but wiry woolly – and I don't think she liked it. She was always touching it. I always thought if she was happier with her hair, she'd be less angry. I also thought: *If you're so bloody warm that you need to roll your sleeves up, why not just take the cardigan off?*

I never told her that to her face.

She would shout at me for anything. I think she taught my sister, Joanne, at the old school and didn't like her either. That happened a lot actually – at school we were always 'one of the Bromfields'.

We genuinely tried to be nice. At Harvest Festival, we were all asked to take in some food that the teachers would give to underprivileged kids in Sunderland.

I took in a tin of corned beef and another of plum peeled tomatoes. Once I took them, it meant we only had a tin of Irish stew between us for Sunday's dinner. Mam had bought the corned beef because she was going to make us corned beef and tattie hash.

'Mam, can I have this for school?'

I couldn't be the only kid who didn't take food in.

At Monday's school assembly, we all queued up, waiting our turn to put food on the stage. I was so tempted to try to hide the corned beef down my trousers, so that we didn't have to give it away, but Mrs Willis, older and more kindly than Mrs Atkinson, had already twigged me.

'Morning, sunshine. Eeeh, well, that's really nice of you, Craig. We know it's not easy for yer mam and we weren't expecting you to bring anything in. It's really nice that you'd think of the other kids worse off than you.'

'That's just the way Mam brought us up, miss.'

Anyway, we are *the underprivileged kids. We'll probably be getting it back next week.*

My crush was the dinner lady, Mrs Evans, who had black curly hair and lovely brown eyes. Weirdly she also worked part-time in the lottery booth at Fine Fare on The Green.

It was only a short walk to the shop from school if you cut through the churchyard. I used to run like the clappers as soon as the school bell went to try to get there before her, so I could wait for her with a flower I had taken from the cemetery on the way through. Not once in two years did I crack it. Mrs Evans was always sat down, smiling and ready to serve whenever I showed up, no matter how fast I ran. I never arrived before her, no matter how hard I tried. Either she had a double or I wasn't going to be the next 'Yifter the Shifter' after all.

I couldn't even buy a lottery ticket. She told me with the warmest smile I've ever seen that even though I definitely looked 16, she knew I couldn't be 16 yet – if I were, she'd have to stop giving me extra-big portions because I would be too old to be at *that* school.

Quite how Mrs Atkinson came to the chip-on-the-shoulder conclusion, I'll never know. It wasn't my fault I'd handed in an essay where I'd attempted to solve all the world's economic problems in two pages. She gave me 18 out of 20, but said it was cocky, then went bright red when I said, 'It's not cocky and it's not even the best essay I've written this year.'

'Aye,' she said. 'It's too bloody good for your age.'

She was shocked at the very thought of anything to do with 'price elasticity of demand' that I'd heard from our Dazzy the night before. I was told to cut out trying to be a smart-arse and just be normal. She kept saying, 'The homework was supposed to be about your day out at Southwick Village Farm.' She kind of sang the 'South-wick vill-age faaaarm' bit in case I didn't hear it properly. 'You know, animals, smells? What you did?'

She was fuming and she had a Geordie temper that turned her face purple, so off I trotted, mumbling under my breath. I wanted to ask her, 'What can I write about, if not that?'

The farm wasn't much to write home about. There was a goat that smelt really bad, a couple of ponies, some cows and some chickens, and the day I was there it was cold, so I got talking to the woman who ran it. She told me they were going to have to shut it down because they couldn't afford to feed the animals. Everyone got in for free, she told me, and the only money they got was from selling the eggs or a postcard.

I couldn't imagine *anyone* wanting to admit they'd been to visit Southwick by sending a postcard and I'd already seen Wayne Litster had nicked three eggs and put them in the hood of his parka so they wouldn't be selling many of those today either.

When I got back to school the next day, I'd written two pages suggesting the council could charge every resident of Southwick a penny for an open ticket to the farm. I figured the price was low enough that loads of people would pay it, then, unless the farm bought a giraffe or something cool like that, most of them wouldn't show up anyway because it was so boring, but the animals would be fed, *et voilà*, I've just cracked price elasticity of demand.

I didn't know if I had *really* or what it meant *really*, but I didn't care *really* either. Either way, Mrs Atkinson wasn't a fan: 'It won't work and the council wouldn't have time to read two pages anyway,' she told me. 'And by the way, your writing is too big. You could have fitted it on a page and a half if it was neater. I'll give you a penny a week for an open ticket,' she sneered – I don't think she meant it as an offer.

All I know is that if our bloody Dazzy had written it everyone would have taken notice. Dazzy was my first idol; a smart, intelligent and very witty young lad. He is four years, one week and one day older than me. When we were in care, the social services file on Darren recorded: 'his intelligence can never be underestimated'.

He passed the 11-plus easily and should have gone to Bryan Ferry's old school, Washington Grammar, but Mam and Dad wanted Dazzy close to home so he went to the nearest comprehensive, Hylton Red House, where he became incredibly popular.

He was well liked by the teachers and he acted in the school plays. He was brilliant at computers and at chess and at pool and at 'posts', the football game he invented using the bus stop pole – and at making stuff up. While we were out walking to wherever it was we needed to get to, he would entertain us for hours – he played a huge role in my upbringing.

Southwick was a weird split of streets and squares. The squares are more like oblongs actually. Some of them have an escape route at the bottom, but others don't. Escape routes were important because there were always lads, sometimes older, sometimes just bigger, who would happily give you a kicking. Faber Road, Ellis Square and Dyer Square had escape routes – cut throughs to the Bowling Alley, a vast expanse of grass which was never used for bowling, but where we did play football. The other squares were traps, dead-ends, where you could either fight your way out or run through somebody's garden and climb a fence.

Shakespeare Street – 'Shakey Street' to its residents – was split into five mini sections from The Green upwards. It definitely stopped being any kind of posh at Cobham Square, if not just before. Cobham was three squares up from Bhajies, the Asian convenience store, and the home of the legendary 'Yoss' (Steven Home). He was one of the nicest, funniest lads you could ever wish to meet. Usually very positive, he was always funny, looking for an opportunity to make a quid or two. More often than not, he'd be stuffing a finger roll filled with cream and jam called a Devonshire Split sideways into his mouth. He nearly always smeared cream on his glasses that were National Health although he swore they weren't.

Yoss didn't go to the same schools as us – he went to Monkey House, or Monkwearmouth Comprehensive. It was where *all* the really good-looking girls went. Unfortunately, at that time he hadn't developed either the looks or the chat to take advantage. He was always surrounded by girls, but he got scared and shy if ever they tried to go near him.

Yoss turned into a very decent footballer. The first time I saw him play he fell over and everyone was laughing and calling him Penfold, after the hamster in *Danger Mouse* who wore thick black glasses, so he ran off crying. The second time he scored a hat-trick and nicked the ball.

I couldn't play football to save my life, but I could run all day. Whenever I could, I used to race the bus as fast as my little legs would carry me. I'd be at Hetherington's, an ironmonger's that sold just about everything, waiting for it to turn up past the bingo hall at the bottom of Beaumont Street. It would only be about 400 yards from home but at the age of 10 it seemed like a mile.

I'd run with my arms out like Zola Budd, who had come over from South Africa to compete for Britain in the Los Angeles Olympics. On a really good day I didn't stop till I got home. I used to run thinking I was a cert for the 800 and 1500 double at the Olympics. Running home from anywhere and everywhere gave me the chance to practise my 'kick'. I did it, as well, because Dad told me to do everything properly.

No point doing something unless you could be the best. So there I was, practising my kick and getting closer and closer to beating the bus home. Who the hell did I think I was kidding, practising a kick?

My dad taught me a fair bit about sport. As I got more interested, he'd tell me, 'Watch how Ovett or Crammy do it – save a little bit of yourself, so that when it gets close to the end and you're still not tired you can run faster and harder.'

Dad didn't know I loved Seb Coe and although he was from up the road in Jarrow, I hated how smug Steve Cram was. For a young lad with such stupid curly hair and sticky-out arms, he didn't half fancy himself.

Dad told me I was already pretty fast and the only way to get better was to work harder so we made a deal: I used to run to get his paper around half three in the afternoon. He liked to get it as early as he could and we agreed if I could get back before he counted to 100, he'd pay me 5p extra for going.

I wanted to prove myself to him, so I'd volunteer to run any kind of message (errand) and he knew I'd run till I got there, turn round and run till I got back. Most times he'd send me to the Chinese, which when you ran all the way down Shakespeare Street and turned on to The Green was the first shop you came to. He knew his chips would come back hot. That was when I started racing the bus, on Chinese or paper-shop runs. I used to set off at a steady but sharpish pace, saving as much as I could until I reached The New Jade, where I'd get Dad's gravy and chips or mixed grill.

Standing at the counter, not really able to see over the top, I'd be asking the Chinese woman every 30 seconds how long it was going to take: 'Please, missus …' I knew the bus time-table off the top of my head and I didn't want to miss the bus run. If the food came before the bus, I'd always nick some – I'd eat as few or as many chips as it took for the 135 to arrive.

Today, half three on the dot – paper run time: 'Craigy, will you go and get me an *Echo*, son?' Then he starts counting: 'One, two, three – you'd better get going or you'll never make it – four, five, si …'

I'm long gone, running like the wind. I run past Bhajies so fast, my big hair was flying everywhere. On the way down, even though it's a straight road, I'm hurdling fences, running through bushes, dodging discarded bottles.

I get to the shop. There was no way I'd been this fast before. It was so fast, I decide I wouldn't even wait to race the bus before starting out on the way back.

I worry I might have dipped a bit too early, but it's definitely my fastest time yet. As I hurdle the wall and run past the front window, the grin turns to a grimace, the rush turns to horror.

I can hear him counting loudly: 'Ninety-eight, 99 …'

I burst through the front door and by the time I made it to the kitchen table where he was working, I heard, 'A-hundred-and-one, 102 … ooohhh, unlucky, son! You got really close though.'

Gutted wasn't the word.

I just *had* to find some way of getting that 5p bonus. That night, I went to bed and slept for less than a second – I was thinking of possible shortcuts for the next day's run.

I couldn't wait. All day at school, all I was thinking about was the *Echo* run. I was really nervous, but I had a plan. It meant lots of hurdling, but it might just do the trick.

Already I'd started thinking that I needed to smash the four-minute mile. I'd heard at school that if there were a nuclear attack on Sunderland, there would be a four-minute warning. If it went off when I was at school, I wanted to be with Mam when it happened. And if I couldn't even get to the paper shop and back in 100 seconds, at that rate I'd be lucky to make it as far as the top of Ridley Street before the world ended.

When I came back from school, Dad was waiting in the kitchen, making one of his matchstick pool tables.

Of course, I had to go and get his paper again and this time I was definitely going to make him pay up. I'd decided on a change of tactics and planned to go to the shop on Beaumont Street instead of the one on The Green. It was riskier, but if I could avoid the kickings from any of the rough lads lurking on the corner, I should make it back easily in time.

Even before he's started counting, I'm off already, jumping over the puddle down the side of the house. I turned left, sprinting like mad, not even thinking about saving a bit for later. Then, out of the corner of my eye, I caught Kenny Ellison, the paper lad, about to turn up Faber Road. It was a risk, because if I went to talk to him there was no way I'd get back in time.

I see Kenny and have a mischievous little thought: *Hmmm, I wonder …*

'Got any spares, Kenny?'

He said he didn't, but then he sold me an *Echo* anyway because I promised him 5p instead of the 4p the paper cost. I thought it was a penny worth paying as I'd still be left with 4p off Dad.

Kenny would just have to say he made a mistake putting the paper through the wrong door. He reckoned he was allowed two mistakes a week and I could be one of them. He had his 4p for the price of the paper and he was happy.

I always liked people called Kenny.

The whole deal took about 15 seconds, plus another 15 or so each way, there and back, so about 45 in total. There was no way I could suddenly knock 55 seconds off my personal best, so I had a bit of time to spare. I climbed over my neighbour's fence and waited at the side of the house.

I listened.

Not once did the bastard count. I even heard him singing that Chris de Burgh song that I hated, 'Patricia The Stripper': 'Aaand with a swing of her hips – ba bum! – she started to strip, to tremendous applause she took off her drawers …'

I went in through the back door, as out of breath as I could pretend to be. It was 73 seconds, 74 max, and the cheating bugger looked round nervously and shouted, 'A-hundred-and-one … ooohhh, ever so close!'

I told him I really thought I'd done it this time and asked was he sure he'd got it right as I'd even climbed over the neighbour's fence to be faster. Then I said I didn't hear him counting when I snuck up the side. He said he was on the toilet, but had a watch on so could see – it was really close though. So now I owed Kenny Ellison a penny *and* Dad didn't give me the bonus for making it back quicker.

Dad's passion for coaching his family ran to organising 'house tournaments', competitions he invariably won. When it came to cricket, he didn't accept the concept of 'walking' when you knew you were out – or even the concept of being out at all.

He had taught me to bowl overarm: 'If you're going to do something, do it properly,' he said.

I did it properly. The ball was as fast as a rocket and didn't really need the lucky bounce off the edge of the drain to fool him. He swung the bat as if he were going to smash it a million miles, he looped it right and high up in the air. If I didn't catch it, he would have had a six-and-out anyway, because it was going over the fence. I only went and caught it, diving full length from the clothes-line pole, even scratching my chin on the fence to complete the catch.

'HHHOOOWWWZZZAAATTTTTT!!!'

But he was having none of it: 'I'm not out, because Tippy walked in front of the crease.'

Tippy's one of our two dogs. She's whoring herself about because she's on heat again. There wasn't a dog in Southwick who didn't try it on with our Tippy. Kim's the only puppy of hers that we've ever kept. We told everyone they were miniature Alsatians, but by God, they were the biggest mongrels in the world.

'You know the rules, son,' he said, tapping his bat on the crease and kicking the Presto plastic bag out of his way.

'Ah, haway, Dad man, that's not fair! You're fucking out – you know it, I know it, so fuck off out!' I think I must have mumbled it, I didn't tell him that to his face.

He went on to score a very respectable 84 not out, before retiring to watch the news.

3.

The Pool Match

20 October 1983

Now is probably the right time to mention that my dad is also an occasional drug dealer and a thief. I might not have mentioned it yet – we live with a black, drug-dealing, muscle-bound, tough guy, conman, creative genius, thief of a dad who would beat our mam. It would be for the smallest of reasons, like bones in his salmon or soggy egg-and-tomato sandwiches, or an inability to sell enough brass off the wall to our various neighbours, so that he could have a decent night out at The Transport, The Wheatsheaf or The Terminus.

The fact he was black and Aaron had brown skin was the chief reason we were pursued through the squares and alleys of Southwick.

He had a great way of doing things and of getting us to do things. He'd put four bars of chocolate on the mantelpiece and two piles of folded pieces of paper, 'Tasks' and 'Forfeits'. Like everything else, it was Dazzy, the eldest, to choose first, then Joanne, then our Azzy and finally me. So many times I got left with the Curly Wurly or the Fudge while everyone else took anything that came in twos or more – Twixes, Twirls and

KitKats never survived for long, but none of us liked Marathons because the nuts made it too salty.

We'd choose our chocolate bar, then open up the 'Task' paper. On it was usually something like 'tidy the bathroom' or 'go to the shop'. The forfeit could be as harmless as putting an elastic band around your forehead and letting go until it pushes your hair up into an Afro (try it, it works well) or it might be something pretty freaky like 'run to the top of the street and back, backwards'.

It was a real double blow today. All three tasks before mine were easy and all the forfeits were about getting ready for the house tournaments. He'd never have all four nice. My task was to brush all the downstairs carpets, including the passage and stairs. We didn't have a Hoover. The forfeit was 10 seconds with the pincers. Thank God he couldn't find them – instead we settled on the pliers. Character building ...

He could be lovely; he could be funny. He was brilliant at pool. Not only did he play rugby for Seaham Harbour, he had been on *It's a Knockout* (well, the regional heats, which were on the radio not the telly).

He was also a total poser. He used to put olive oil on his curly hair and on his muscles so that he shined a lot. Sometimes, when he was attempting a difficult black on the pool table, the oil would drip into his eyes and he would miss.

He was a great player though. He very much thought of himself as the black Alex Higgins, with the occasional bit of Jimmy 'The Whirlwind' White thrown in for good measure. Alex, I could understand, but Jimmy? Jimmy looked about 15 and he had goofy teeth, just like the bloke from Queen that Dad also liked.

He played pool for the Transport Club First Team, Division One but hated playing doubles. He'd tell me he liked playing on his own, because the rest of the team were old duffers: 'There's no room for safety, son. Not in pool or snooker. If you can't pot, don't play.'

That was his attitude to everything actually: 'Play properly, play fair, don't ever bottle taking on something you think you can't do.'

You could have paid me my 5p – that would have been playing fair.

I didn't say it out loud.

Mam is back home and tonight he was playing in the Sunderland and Durham district pool semi-final singles. If he won, the final was to be played tonight as well. He took us along to watch, because he hadn't seen us as much as he should have lately, as long as we sat there quiet and didn't bother the locals.

He pulled off some outrageous shots and took great pleasure in knowing his angles. You could see his face light up when he got out of a tough snooker: 'Take that, you boring bastard! My lad over there would be embarrassed to play a shot like that' – pointing over at Dazzy – 'and he's only 15.'

Cruelly, even after all the bravado, Dad finished joint third. He was knocked out by some boring twat from Fence Houses, who just kept playing safe. I could see Dad's face and he was losing his cool. He kept snarling and tutting; he kept getting snookered, then getting out of it and potting one, then getting snookered again. In the decider he came off at least 14 cushions to pot the black superbly, but the cue ball went in-off horribly, so he got beat. The old bugger he was playing didn't even take his roly out of his mouth to shake Dad's hand.

We sat waiting for Dad's third-place medal for more than an hour. He had been told by the committee man that if he didn't wait for it tonight, he'd have to go back later and get it. According to Dad, he didn't ever want to see this shithole of a pub again.

Around the pool halls, Dad (who outside of the pool halls went by the name of Gerald George John Paul Bromfield) was known as 'JC', so, while the medal was being engraved, he was telling us his 'JC' nickname came from the initials for Gerald 'Jerry' Collins. It was his real family name from Jamaica, or the name of the people who adopted him in Newcastle – it depended how drunk he was and which version he was telling. I still have no idea at all where Bromfield came from.

I had to go and tell the man doing the engraving what Dad's name was.

'It's Gerald George John Paul … ahh, you know what, mister, it's JC.'

'How do you spell that, son?'

'It's just JC, mister. J – C. That's all.'

I was proud of him when he got the medal. Third was still great and he'd played the right way. He'd potted some fantastic shots but lost to a boring, chain-smoking grandad. The medal was bronze-coloured in a red velvet box. It looked really cool. Then Azzy snatched it out of my hands and asked, 'Why have they called you "Jaycee", Dad?'

'Because they mustn't know how to spell "Bromfield", son. Show me. Where? Ah fer fuck's sakes, Craig, can you not even get that right?'

Whenever we were talking about running, he always used to ask me who finished second in the Olympics. Then, when I couldn't answer, he'd remind me that no one ever remembers the runner-up. While we were waiting for the taxi, I remember thinking, *If no one remembers second, then you're really buggered, because you were third.*

I didn't tell him that.

I wasn't convinced this was going to be an easy night for Mam. He was going home early, getting knocked out in the semis of a tournament he'd expected to win. I hoped she'd got some chips and gravy for him.

I knew it from the second we walked in the house and he threw his jacket at Mam. She'd got him mixed grill and he only wanted chips and gravy. Mam had his jacket hung up and supper on his chair when he came back from the toilet.

'Where the fuck are we getting money from to pay for mixed grill, you stupid bitch?'

Oh God, please not again. Not tonight. I was so proud of you two hours ago, I forgot about this. Don't make us do this again.

'Dazzy, pleeaasssee try something?' I whispered to my brother.

'Ssh, Craigy, it might be okay. He's just drunk. He'll eat and it will be alright. Stop crying or that'll make it worse.'

It got worse anyway.

'All that fucking money wasted and you can't even serve it warm!'

Then the food is all over the wall, the liver is sliding down the wood panels. Mam's crying, trying to wipe it up, and he throws a pan at her head.

'Please stop, Dad. Please stop.'

I don't think I said it loud enough.

The smashing had already started. A lot of the time he smashed things we would have been able to sell, then he'd hit her some more because we had nothing to sell. Tonight, I couldn't understand why. He had money, he had beer, he had food – nothing was wrong.

He went to the kitchen and slammed the door.

We ran out, all four of us kids. We had crouched behind whatever we could hide behind when it got started. It was still only just after 10 p.m.

Mam was crying and already she had a bruised cheek. 'Go on, sweethearts, you get yourselves outside for a while. I'll be okay. He's calmed down. It'll be alright now. Go on, out for an hour while me and your dad talk.'

We all went out knowing there was more chance of it starting again than there was of stopping it. We went out anyway. We left Mam crying and with a cut lip.

How could we just walk out like that? How could we leave her?

We talked about what we would do. We talked about running away forever and we talked about how we all had to stick together and look after Mam and make sure he never did anything to hurt any of us.

We sat there at the back of Hahnemann Court, a great, grey block of 1960s housing, shivering and talking and singing, with me rattling 'Silent Night' with my teeth. Azzy would nearly always pipe up with a punk rocker outburst while playing the air guitar and shaking his wavy hair. He usually did it while we three little angels were singing 'Where Is Love?' from *Oliver!* in perfect harmony.

We loved singing. We sang on buses on the way to Nana's and people used to give us money. I think we made so much money on those bus rides that it kept us in food for days. If we had to stand, Joanne would get talking about how we were going to visit our nana and we got sat down, we got sweets and sometimes we even got money – just for being polite.

We eventually went back home around midnight and only then because we thought we'd get shouted at if we went back later. The house was dark but you could see the downstairs window was broken.

We'll have to have cardboard on the window again.

All of the lights were out and it was quiet. We hadn't run out of electricity, so it might have meant they were asleep.

I was so skinny that my arm could fit through letterboxes. I only ever used this talent for nice stuff – people used to come to the house when they were locked out and pay me 5p, 10p, once even 20p, to get them back in. I'd twist my arm, turn the latch and the door would open. I needed soap or oil to get the arm back out, but at least everyone loved me.

I got my hand through the letterbox and of course Tippy and Kim started barking. I'm whisper-shouting, trying to be as quiet as I can, worried my arm is going to get pulled off by the letterbox when I try to get it back out.

'Haway, Tippy man! Shut up, please. I can't open the door till you two bugger off. Dazzy, help – the dogs won't shut up …'

'Hurry up and get in, Craigy … and shut up.'

When we turned the front room light on, Mam was asleep on the couch with a coat over her. He was upstairs. We had woken him up. He came roaring down, slapped Mam again and dragged her by the hair out onto the streets. She was only wearing her nightie.

He was not letting go of her hair and snarling: 'I told you to get out! Who the fuck let you back in?'

Fucking bastard. If only I hadn't been so loud.

Mam went upstairs to try to put some clothes on and he followed her. We were on the front wall when the upstairs window opened and he was trying to push her out. He'd got her halfway out, so her legs were dangling, nearly touching the top of the downstairs window, and he had hold of her by the neck.

I couldn't stop screaming. Mam was hanging out the window and Dazzy was waiting underneath in case she fell. We were pleading with him to stop. So he did, eventually. He let go, cool as you like, and Mam hit the paving stones with a thud and then fell backwards into the front garden.

But he didn't care. He went back in, put some clothes on and came downstairs to say he was going for a walk.

None of the watching neighbours said or did anything. None of them.

On his way past Mam and us, who were sitting on the wall across the road, we got 'I told you to fuck off. So, fuck off. Fuck right off.' Then, 'You'd all better be out when I get back.'

Mam was telling us we were staying: 'He's not kicking us out of our own house again, kids. I'm not having it. If anyone's leaving, it's him.'

Dazzy said: 'Let's just go out for a couple of hours. We'll have a walk and come back tomorrow when he's cooled down. You know what he'll do if we stay, Mam. We've got to go, we've got no choice. C'mon, it'll be alright.'

Everyone was crying apart from Dazzy. Our Dazzy never panicked.

One hour later, we decided as a family we were out again. A couple of carrier bags packed, Mam's purse totally emptied (because she wasn't 'leaving with a penny of his fucking money'), then we had to walk. We had to walk to wherever, usually first to The Green, but sometimes the police station there wasn't manned. If not to The Green, then to The Wheatsheaf. If not there, then to Sunderland's main police station, Gill Bridge, where Mam had a friend who was a detective who had arrested Dad and her before – he knew what Dad was like and sometimes he'd help us get a nicer place to stay.

The police station at Southwick Green was unmanned, The Wheatsheaf was shut, which meant we had to walk to Gill Bridge, which meant crossing the river.

We walked through Thompson Park with its football pitches, well-kept bowling greens and graffiti-covered bandstand, turned right just past Newcastle Road Baths, down past the indoor bowling place, past The Wheatsheaf pub, past the shuttered police station and the Nash, what we called the social security offices.

Three or four doors down from the Nash was the Transport Club. It was Dad's favourite pub, because they had a 'Blue Movie Sunday' and he played pool for them, which was always handy because it meant as soon as we had the money from the Nash we could drop it off for him a few doors down.

We didn't want to walk along the main road unless we had to and that meant we took the long way round. We walked past the Railway Museum. All the way, we were looking for 'dumpers', discarded, half-smoked cigarettes that we could put in our pockets and maybe sell to someone later.

We walked over the Wearmouth Bridge, kicking a can between us until Aaron booted it and it fell through the railings into the river. We turned right and went past the place where we got our school uniforms from, Caslaw, Hayter & Tate. I hated that shop, especially now as my shoes were so tight that the athlete's foot was cracking and I could feel water leaking around my toes.

I'd really had enough by then. I was freezing, we had nowhere to go and I wanted to go to bed. We walked another half an hour with Mam telling me every 10 seconds, 'We're nearly there, son. We'll be alright.'

My feet were bloody killing me.

At about half two in the morning, I eventually walked, freezing cold, tired out and sniffling, into the biggest police station I'd ever seen in my life. Strangely, even at 11, I'd seen a few. Gill Bridge was a great concrete slab of a police station, four storeys high.

'Hello, mister. Mam told me I had to ask the man on the desk if Mr Naisby was in tonight?'

'You mean Detective Naisby, don't you, son?'

'I honestly don't know, mister. I only know he's a copper.'

'He's in, but you need to wait to see him because he's busy. Come with me, you can wait in here.'

'I'll just go and get Mam and the rest of us, mister. I'll be back in a second.'

When we got let through the gate, we had to walk past some of the cells to get to the canteen bit. It was closed when we got there anyway. We got sat down and we got our hair ruffled. We were asked if we were alright and if we wanted anything to read. We got a cup of tea between us and Detective Naisby bought us a packet of fruit and nut biscuits from the vending machine. We got half a fruit shortbread each. We only had to wait two hours to find a place to stay and they would even give us tickets so we could get the first bus.

Naisby reminded me a lot of Sherlock Holmes – he smoked a pipe and had a jacket on. He was sorry that he couldn't take us himself, but something had come up.

While Mam was talking to Naisby, a social worker came over to us kids and started asking us questions. Our Dazzy had already told us not to say too much.

'Did he hit yer? Does he ever hit yer? Does yer Mam hit yer?'

Mam seemed to be pretty pleased when she came back with a piece of paper. She wouldn't have been if she knew what the social worker was asking us.

'Ah, that place is nice,' said the social worker woman. 'It's in Peterlee and it's full of women who have been battered before, so they'll know what you're going through. There's some nice kids there like you lot and you'll really enjoy it. It's the best we could do at short notice.'

Mam perked up.

'Come on, kids, let's go. They know we're coming and they've got the kettle ready ... It'll give us time to settle down while we find a more permanent place ... Ah, come on, you lot. Smile a bit, it's not that bad. You can have a couple of days off school as well, because they can't find you a place yet ... We're going to Peterlee, kids. We'll be alright ... It'll be an adventure ...'

She got some money, probably no more than a couple of quid from the policeman. She made an appointment with the emergency Nash office, who I think were even going to come out to see us in Peterlee, a new town built for mining families in the East Durham coalfield. We'd been pushed right to the top of the waiting list for a place to stay full-time.

It was awful though, as we still had to wait for a bus. It was still dark with no sign of dawn. We walked past the leisure centre and T Y McGurk's, past the cinema on the corner, into the newsagent's, where we bought tabs and two ounces of pineapple chunks to share between us, before getting to Park Lane bus station.

There was a tiny little waiting room at the top of the station, across the road from the inspectors' room, but they were all in there having a cup of tea when we arrived and they didn't like us because we kept getting on the bus with no money.

We had to wait two more freezing hours for the first bus to leave. We didn't have enough money for tickets and food, so the police had given us a little slip of paper that we had to show the bus driver. It was horrible getting on a bus with no money for a ticket. They had to let you on, it was the law, but they didn't half make you feel like shit.

When we got on the bus, I sat on the seats with the wheels underneath because they always got warmer. I couldn't sleep – I never could sleep when I was nervous or excited. I never stopped looking out the bus window all the way until we got off and had to start walking again.

We got to the house in Peterlee, which was two houses put together. It had a decent-sized bit of grass in front of it and there were some shops across the road, but it had bags and bags of rubbish outside. It stank and there were some old nappies on the path. I hoped this wasn't the place.

Mam was giving our Joanne a front-way piggy-back, because she was tired and her shoes hurt. Dazzy and Azzy were carrying the bags, so Dazzy delegated the door-knocking to me.

'Are you sure it's the right place, Dazzy? What if it's not?'

'What choice have we got, Craigy-boy?'

He knew I hated 'Craigy-boy'. It was Mam's cute pet name for me, that and 'Craigy-baby'.

I knocked and this woman came to the door, wrapped in a blanket and yawning. I told her the social had sent us. She said she knew nothing about us and was I sure I'd got the right place?

Are you funning? How many families were you expecting at half six on a Friday morning?

I asked her if this is the place that takes in families who have been thrown out by their dads.

'Aye, that's us. You better come in.'

Suddenly the kitchen was full of women. They'd all heard the door go and come to see who it was.

We got sat down on cold plastic chairs in a kitchen with a cold floor and no carpets. The sink was full, the wallpaper peeling off the wall and there was a real smell of baby wee. We got listening to all the 'oohs' and the 'aahs' and the 'oh, you poor little buggers'.

Mam borrowed some bread from one of the women, the one who had got up to let us in. We'd give it her back when the shop opened and we got money from the Nash. The woman was nice actually and said we could keep it. We could have a slice and half of toast before going to bed. The smell of margarine made me sick, so I couldn't eat mine. The woman was trying to be nice, putting loads of margarine on it. I'd have liked her a lot more if she'd left it dry – I was starving.

We went to bed for a couple of hours and when we woke up, Mam had already been to get some food. There were some other kids there, but most of them were from Newcastle, not Sunderland, and they all talked funny. You could see straight away that they were trying to pick fights with us as well, calling our Azzy 'chocolate drop'.

What do you mean 'chocolate drop'? His name is Aaron. Fuck off!

After we'd had a bit of breakfast, our Azzy went to his other mam's in Penshaw, a village on the outskirts of Sunderland, because she said he could stay there for a week. Our Dazzy and Joanne went to Nana's in Houghton, but me and Mam stayed in Peterlee to tidy the place up a bit. Mam got really angry, just because I wasn't doing the washing-up properly, and she sent me to my room. She told me as well that there was no way we were staying there long and we just needed to wait for Dad to calm down and ask us to go back.

Fucking hells bells! We're going back? Already? I'm not going anywhere, I just want to go to sleep.

I went up to my new room and sat there crying again for about 30 minutes. When it's like that, there's no worse feeling, but even at 11 years old, you know that crying is for girls.

I started looking around my room, at the *Shoot* football pictures all over the wall, and wondered what type of lad had been here before. He'd left some toys, some Lego blocks and some comics, in a box under the bed. Out of the corner of my eye I could see a trainer that had been put under a leg of the bed. At first, I thought there was only one, but then I found the second shoe on the window sill. They weren't brand new, but they were definitely in better condition than the ones I had on. They were much too small for me as well, but my God, they were Nikes! I'd never been close to a Nike shoe of my own. I put them on, actually squeezed them on, and stood for five minutes thinking how cool I looked. Then I went out, told Mam I was going to the shops and just started running and running. The shoes were incredible, really soft, and made me spring so much better than anything else I'd had until then.

This is it! This is all I need to win the Olympics.

I ran for hours and when I got back, Dazzy and Joanne were already home with some sweets and some money from Grandad, who would always give us money. The difference was that when he emptied his pockets, Joanne would get the silver – 'the snow' as Grandad called it. I would have to make do with the copper.

When I told them that Mam had said we were going back to Dad, we had an emergency family meeting, where our Dazzy told Mam that if she went back, we'd all run away and she'd never see us again.

We stayed in Peterlee for three days before he came to visit us. He promised he would change; he was sorry and couldn't live without us. It had been a horrible few days but at least I got some cool shoes.

4.

There Must Be an Angel

Friday, 19 October 1984

I've always been really lucky in life – Mam had told me that loads of times. Apparently if I fell into a pile of shite, I would come out smelling of roses. She was convinced there was an angel looking out for me.

Maybe she was right, maybe there was – just I hadn't met him yet.

Tonight, I'm 11, nearly 12. A few years ago, Dazzy had come up with the idea of Guying to earn some money when it got too dark to do people's gardens or wash their cars. We'd make our Guy by stuffing newspaper into old clothes, which was sometimes bloody hard because we didn't have many clothes to spare. Then we'd go round knocking on people's doors and asking them straight, 'Penny for the Guy?' same as we did asking money for our Hallowe'en lantern or carol sing-ing.

It didn't make us much money, but we did alright and usually earned enough to buy Mam a Christmas present. Each year, we'd try to find different places and we'd walk for ages, looking for posh houses with lights on – our Dazzy thought they were more likely to give us money than anyone we knew in Shakey Street. They were also less likely to try and kick our heads in.

We usually started about two weeks before Fireworks Night, which gave us 14 days and, at an average of 10 quid a day, that would give us enough to buy Mam that carpet she wanted or she could use it for Christmas shopping. No matter how much we struggled all year, we would always eat like kings for a few days.

We soon realised that if we had a Guy each, we could split up and make more money, so we'd all go out into town with a Guy on our shoulders. We put some effort into these Guys and usually on the first night they were cleaner than we were. That wouldn't last though. The second we stepped foot into one of the squares the other kids would all be out, laughing at us, spitting and trying to pull the legs off – ours as well as the Guy's. The pillowcase heads would be pulled off and we'd be chasing them, trying to get them back. I can't remember ever making it through first night without having to put the Guy's head back on.

We did okay, going around knocking on doors, but nothing like what happened when our Azzy discovered the Seaburn Hotel. Seaburn was on the coast, it was fairly posh. We could get money off the rich folks staying at the hotel and the drunks going up and down the seafront. Azzy suggested we go down there for a couple of hours on Friday because it was pay-day.

I owe everything to our Azzy.

We had just the one Guy between us, with my old brown cords with the scuffed knee, an old blue and yellow school jumper and a stolen pillowcase for his head as usual. We tied all the ends up with string and filled him up with newspaper. Our Joanne drew his face on, but we didn't have a felt-tip so she used Mam's lipstick and our Azzy was going mental: 'I'm not carrying a puff [poof] Guy!'

We called him Gus. He looked great and I was proud to be carrying him. I was going to do my best to make sure he stayed fully stuffed at least for tonight so, to avoid trouble, we cut through some back roads to the Seaburn. We got him to the hotel fine and started badgering the passers-by for money.

We weren't doing great, though. It was a bad idea not to make two Guys. We wanted to cover both the entrance to the hotel and the Indian restaurant on the seafront. I was stood on the seafront with Gus for the first hour and Azzy was round at the hotel door. I told him to ask people for a 'penny for the Guy' even though he didn't have one. If anyone pointed out this fact, he should send them round to me so they could see it for themselves. I knew it wasn't going great when I didn't get a visitor from him at all – not one person came past and said, 'Your brother sent me.'

I had made just over a quid but 75p of that had come from two blokes wearing red tracksuits who talked funny. It got worse before it got better. When we were out with our Guys, every now and then we'd have some bother with a group of kids or a drunk, but tonight, it was a skinhead. A big, broad lad with a green bomber jacket and Doc Martens. He must have been about 18, but right now, he looked like an adult: a big, menacing adult.

I saw him coming a mile away and probably should have picked up Gus and run like the clappers, but, by the time I'd made up my mind to run, he was already too close. As he got closer, I was whistling like mad, trying to sound confident. This yob had been around a few times last year and it was always the same result.

When he started talking to me, it was much nicer than usual.

'You on your own tonight?'

'No, the others are here as well. They're just coming now,' I said, in case he was thinking about starting a scrap with me on my own.

'Ah good. Well, good luck tonight,' said the skinhead. Then he added, 'Oh, by the way, where's that black bastard who usually comes with you?'

'So what that he's black?' I snapped. 'That's my brother and he's not a bastard! He's got a dad!'

'What did you fuckin' say?'

Boot, first of all my leg, then my stomach, then Gus's head, then his body, then his trousers. The skinhead's booting it all over the path and I'm crying, not because he hurt me or anything, just because I was running around trying to pick up the paper balls, but, as fast as I picked them up, he was booting a different part of Gus about. It reminded me of the Scarecrow in *The Wizard of Oz*.

I was also worried he'd take the money I'd made so far, but a bloke came out of the Indian and shouted at him to pick on someone his own size. The skinhead ran away. He yelled he'd be back for me later on.

I got Gus back together as best I could. The two blokes in tracksuits were walking back past – I wasn't even going to ask them, but they came over to me.

'Are you okay, son?' said one of them. 'You look upset.'

'Do you make much standing here like that?' said the other.

'Not really, mister,' I said, 'but it helps us buy Mam a nicer Christmas present, so it's alright.'

'Is that your mate round the other side of the hotel?'

'No, mister, that's my brother, but you don't need to give him any money because you've paid me already and we share it. Thanks.'

'This is for you, son,' said the man, giving me some more change. 'Don't stay out too late – it's cold and the place is full of drunks.'

His mate chucked me some more money as well – another £1.50 between them!

Five minutes later, our Azzy came round from the back of the hotel – he had made a measly 13p.

'No one wants to give me money when I haven't got a Guy. I'm having him for a while and you can stay here.'

Then I told him about the skinhead and we both decided it would be better if we stayed round the other side of the hotel together just in case he came back. We weren't missing much here as the seafront was really quiet.

'Did you see the men with the same tracksuits on?' said Azzy. 'They must be a team because there's loads of them. They all went out for a walk together.'

'Aye,' I said. 'I only saw two, but they gave us a few quid!

Their top's got some kind of a flower on it. I think it might be Sunderland basketball team or something like that.'

'Why don't you ask them?'

There were three more of them coming round the corner.

'Hello, mister – penny for the Guy?'

'Sorry, son, I've left my money upstairs,' said one of them. He was handsome with light brown hair.

I decided to use one of Dazzy's tricks: 'That's okay, mister – we take MasterCard or American Express as well!'

He chuckled. 'My wallet's upstairs, honest,' he said, patting his pockets. I couldn't hear any change, so I had to believe him.

'Do you mind me asking, mister?' I said. 'We saw you all with the same tracksuits. My brother thinks you play basketball?'

'No, son, it's football we play.'

'Who do you all play for?'

'We play for a team called Nottingham Forest. We're playing Newcastle tomorrow.'

'Ah. He's a Newcastle fan,' I said, pointing to Azzy, 'and so is my dad, but I hate them – Newcastle, I mean, not my brother and dad – so I hope you win!'

'Thanks, son,' said the brown-haired man. 'We'll try.'

Then I had an idea.

'Do you mind if I ask for your autographs, mister?'

'Of course not, son, just give me a minute and I'll get some of the other lads to sign theirs as well. Can you wait five minutes? I'll be back out. My name's Kenny, by the way.'

He went back into the hotel and as soon as he was out of sight, our Azzy pinched my arm.

49

'What did you tell him it was me who thought it was the Sunderland basketball team for?'

'Haway, Azzy man, at least I talked to him and we're gonna get their autographs. That's brilliant, Azzy man!'

'I'd rather get 20 pence,' he said.

The effing ungrateful bugger.

There was one man who kept coming past year after year. Every time he walked past, we'd ask him and every time he said he'd see us on the way back. On the way back, he never gave us money either, so, 20 minutes later, I was thinking 'Kenny' had lied to us and just said that stuff so that he could get away without paying up.

Then he popped his head around the door again.

'Hey, lads, come inside for a minute while I wait for one more.'

'We can't, mister,' I said. 'The man in the hotel always chases us. He won't let us in.'

'Well, at least come and stand in the door. I'll wait with you. It's freezing outside. Come on in.'

Some other player came past with two pieces of cream paper, thick cream paper with nice brown writing on it: 'Swallow Seaburn Hotel' and 'with compliments'.

Kenny told us he was sorry, but he hadn't been able to get all the autographs as some of the lads had already gone to bed, but he promised us that if we went back in the morning, around 10, he would get the rest for us.

He also gave us a five-pound note. In four years of Guying, I never once got a five-pound note. If I'm honest, I spent more time looking at that than I did looking at autographs.

While he was talking to us, another couple of footballers came past.

'Hey, Dav, these are the lads Gunny was telling you about. They're doing a penny for the Guy for their mam for Christmas. You ever heard anything like that? Have you got some change?'

By the time we'd left the reception area, we had 12 quid just from the team and we had two sheets of paper, each with some names on it that we couldn't read at all. Kenny told us he needed to get some rest but he'd see us in the morning.

'Don't stay out too long, lads, and be careful on your way home.'

We stayed outside another hour after that and topped up the money with another three or four quid. We left with £17.54. What started out as a horrible and quiet night had just turned around.

Me and Azzy ran all the way home to tell Dazzy and Joanne about what had happened. They would be gutted they missed it. We talked about whether we should keep some of the money for ourselves, but decided we'd let our Dazzy choose. Dazzy used to 'save' some of the money just for us, so we could have afternoons out in Newcastle, but the rule was that only Dazzy could take money from the Guy pot.

When we got back, Mam was round a friend's having a snakebite and a talk. Before we told Joanne and Dazzy anything, we asked them to guess how much we'd made. They were miles out. When we told them we thought it was close to a record first night, neither believed us. I told our Azzy to empty his pockets and let them count up. Azzy only had about four quid and I had hidden the rest in my shoes – the fiver was in my sock.

Dazzy counted Azzy's part of the money: 'Record, my arse!'

When we pulled out the fiver, that's when we *had* to explain the rest of the story. No one normal would ever give a fiver for the Guy. Dazzy made us agree to tell Mam that we'd made £7.54 and the tenner we would keep for emergencies. If Mam and Dad knew we had nearly 18 quid from the first night, they would already be asking to borrow from it.

I then spent ages looking at the autographs and thinking about tomorrow.

Should we go back? Is there any point really? It's a long way to go just to get someone to sign some paper. Kenny was nice though and he had said 'see you tomorrow', so I don't want him to think we only wanted the money.

We'd agreed to meet Kenny at about half ten, after breakfast. I went to bed that night comparing the autographs to my Panini '84 sticker album, because it was really hard to read the players' writing on the paper. The only Kenny in the team was Kenny Swain. I couldn't be sure, because I didn't have any Forest player stickers, only the badge – 'It must be him,' I told our Azzy. 'It must be.'

We went to bed that night with Mam telling us how lucky we were to have met them and that of course we should go back tomorrow. Dazzy wanted us to take the Guy again, just to see if there was any point in going on weekend days.

I didn't sleep a wink. That was partly because I couldn't stop thinking about what had happened, but also because Dad wasn't home from the pub yet and I wasn't sure what kind of mood he was coming back in.

Yesterday, he and Mam had an argument, but didn't fight. Tonight, I slept awake in my clothes, in case we needed to make a quick escape. He eventually came home at 2 a.m., totally shitfaced. He came upstairs, said goodnight and told me he was proud of us both. Fucking hell! I loved making him proud.

We got back down to the Seaburn about half eight on a cold, bright morning the next day. It's funny seeing as we lived so near but I hadn't really been at the beach like that too often. It wasn't warm at all, but the sun was shining. We decided that, while we were waiting, we'd go and have a splodge in the sea.

Saturday, 20 October 1984 will likely not be noted in Sunderland's hottest-day-of-the-year records. After running for what seemed like miles on the sand, we eventually got to the water, close to the pier. Less than 10 seconds later, Azzy was in. He'd already had his top off while he was running, banging his chest and making Tarzan noises.

'Aaar y y aaar araarara!'

Trousers and socks off and he was in.

I hated water. I couldn't swim anyway and I regretted taking my socks off within about three seconds of the cold, salty water touching my athlete's foot toes. They got so cold and stingy, I thought they were going to snap.

While Azzy swam-splashed, I jogged along the sand, thinking I was like the men in *Chariots of Fire*, telling myself it was good practice for the Olympics. By the time I got back, Azzy was out, dressed and waiting at the top of the steps, shivering like an idiot. He was waving and bouncing and smiling and telling me to hurry up. I got there thinking he'd found something.

'Look over there.'

'What? Where?'

'Over there at them men, man.'

'What about them?'

'That's Brian Clough, that is. He's a football manager. He's been on telly before and I know it's him. He's supposed to be a bit angry though, so *you* go and ask him where Kenny is.'

So I did, almost without thinking. Brian Clough, the most famous football manager in the world, told us to follow him.

'I really hope you win against Newcastle today, Mr Clough. I don't like them.'

'I hope we win as well, son,' he said. 'I know how much you don't like Newcastle, I'm from round these parts myself. It was very nice of you to call me "Mr Clough", son. Did your mam teach you that?'

'Yes, Mr Clough. Until we get to know you, we should always call you "mister".'

He started laughing.

'Have you two rag-tags had any breakfast yet? And where are your coats? You'll catch your bloody death!'

We followed him up to the hotel door, then stopped.

'Come on, lads, get in here. We'll have some breakfast. You'll get your autographs and everyone will be happy.'

'We can't go in there, Mr Clough.' I explained about the hotel man chasing us with our Guy.

'You're with me, son, and as long as you behave, he doesn't need to like you, he just needs to let you in. Now come on, hurry up before I change my mind.'

He's through the doors with me following and Azzy right behind. I get into the reception part with no fuss, but our Azzy keeps on going through the revolving doors, running faster and faster, round and round with a huge smile on his face: 'Weeeeeeeeeeeee!'

Then the man who usually chases us starts coming down the main stairs.

'Hey, you two! Get out! What have I told you before? Get out of my hotel and stop messing around with the door. Sorry, Mr Clough, I'll have them out in a minute. Go on, get out of here!'

'It's okay, young man,' said Mr Clough. 'They're just kids, having a bit of fun. They're coming upstairs with us and we're having some breakfast. They'll be staying about an hour, then they'll be off home, alright? Come on, lads, get in 'ere and you stop that bloody messing around.'

You should have seen the look on Kenny Swain's face when we walked into the breakfast room with Mr Clough asking if there was space for two more.

'Hello, lads,' he said. 'Nice to see you both again. Is it half ten already? How did you get in here? Sorry, Gaffer, they're kind of with me. Is it okay?'

I heard Mr Clough again: 'Lads, there's tea, toast and all that type of thing over there. Help yourselves and grab a seat.'

We went and sat with Kenny. It was only just after 9.30 a.m.

Questions every two seconds: 'Who? How? What do you do with it all? You're brothers? How old are you both? Really?'

I just answered honestly to everything. Azzy interrupted a couple of times, to add little bits that I had missed or forgotten about, and everyone was laughing. It was lovely. The tea was lovely too. I had marmalade on brown toast with melted butter and *that* was lovely.

Kenny told us where Nottingham was, somewhere in the middle of England, in the Midlands. Azzy asked him if the beach was as nice as Seaburn. They all laughed.

They all played for Nottingham Forest, but they weren't all from Nottingham. They all had different accents and kept asking me if I would 'climb a moontan fer a canny bag a chewdah' and squeaking 'why-aye man' in my ear.

Kenny had a funny accent as well. He said it was because he was from a place that sounded like 'Baconhead', near Liverpool. Apparently, it was the posh bit, though. Then he asked us if we wanted to go to the game with them. The 'Gaffer' had said it was okay if he invited us. They would take us to the game on the team bus and get us tickets so we could watch. We'd have to come home by ourselves, but we could go and watch the game if we would like to.

'Would we *like* to?! On the *bus*? It would be great! Thanks!'

'We'll just have to give your mum and dad a quick call,' said Kenny, 'to make sure it's okay with them.'

'Oh, sugar!' I said, 'we haven't got a phone. We live really close though – can we go and ask?'

They were leaving the hotel after some lunch. It was agreed that, if we could get home and back before then, we could go.

We finished our tea and toast, said thanks and we told them we'd be back.

We ran all the way home. It was always harder on the way back because it was mostly uphill, but this time I don't think we cared. Azzy was faster than me, much faster, but he kept stopping to get his breath back and I just kept running and running and running.

For the first time ever, I got back before he did. I burst through the back door, shouting to Mam and Dad that we had to go.

'Maaa-aaam, quuiiiiiiccckkkkk!'

Dad was in the kitchen, gluing tiny red Trillion sweets to the snooker table he'd built from matchsticks. He'd made a mini triangle out of lolly sticks and stained it dark brown so that it matched the table.

'Ma-am, it's us, we're back! It was great! We got the autographs, we even had some breakfast and watched some telly, but we've got to go. I'll tell you the rest later. Can we get 10 pence each, please? We've got to go.'

'Woah, slow down there, son,' said Dad, 'what do you mean, you've got to go? What's going on?'

'They've invited us to the game, Dad. Kenny is getting us tickets and we're going with them on the team bus to watch the game. Can we go, Dad? *Can* we?'

We'd already agreed yesterday that we were going to go and try to sell some of his matchstick wishing wells that afternoon and now he thought we were just trying to get out of it.

'You're taking the piss, son. You're trying to tell me that a football team you only met yesterday is taking you to a game on their bus? What do they want? Why would they invite you two? Where's Azzy?'

'They said we were funny, Dad. The Gaffer said we kept them relaxed, so he wanted to take us to the game. Maybe he thinks we're lucky?'

'What do you need the 20 pence for? I hope you're not just ganna buy some sweets and piss off out for the afternoon?'

Our Azzy came through the door, out of breath, knackered, smiling.

'Can we go, Dad? Mam, can we go? Go on, *please.*'

Mam made a deal. She'd let us go, but we'd have to give her some of the Guy money, so Dad could go out. We would usually get him money from selling something and if we weren't going to sell anything, he still needed money. Also, they didn't think we needed 20 pence, so they gave us 10 pence between us.

I went to see Dazzy upstairs. After last night, he would definitely let us have the other 10 pence we needed, but the bastard had gone to the chess club. He'd hidden the Guy box and none of us ever knew where he kept it.

We would have to run to the hotel and use what money we had to get a bus ticket back from Newcastle. The last thing Mr Clough had said to us was: 'Make sure you bring your coats.' I had one coat – a green parka – but all the white feather lining had gone from it so it was just a shell. Azzy didn't have a coat at all so he borrowed Dad's Crombie jacket. It was so big, he kept tripping on the edges.

It's a couple of miles from Shakespeare Street to the Seaburn Hotel. The bus would have to be at St James' Park an hour and a half before kick-off, which meant it would have to leave at half twelve. Time was getting away. We had no other options. We ran.

And we kept running. Down Sea Road, through Fulwell with its big Edwardian houses set back from the road. Past the park. We were going downhill now towards the seafront, past a white little souvenir shop where the man behind the counter would sometimes give us sweets. Then a sharp left into the car park of the Seaburn Hotel. In front of us was a bus, its engine running.

The driver was in his seat and the kit bins were being loaded in. Some players were already on board, a few were still milling around.

We made to get on the bus. 'Blow me, are they your coats?' were the first words Brian Clough said to us. Everyone began looking us up and down, taking in the coats. Muted laughter ran through the bus.

Brian was at the front – 'Bugger off, you're not sitting next to me! Get up to the back of the bus. Keep your heads down and don't disturb the lads. There's chocolate down the back, fill your boots.'

At the back of the bus were boxes crammed with chocolate bars, crisps and cans of soft drink. We took half a dozen bars and packets of crisps and stuffed them in our pockets.

We crossed the Tyne Bridge. The bus nosed its way up Gallowgate and into St James' Park and we all piled out. Forest's club secretary, a balding man called Ken Smales, handed us two tickets: 'Put them in your pockets and don't wave them around.' Kenny Swain gave us a hug and a fiver to get something to eat in the ground. Mr Clough gave us a 'See you later'.

St James' was busy but not full. High up in the Main Stand the wind was rattling the girders and, to keep warm, Aaron and I ran the length of the seats, shouting 'You Reds!' We were stared at.

Events down below on the pitch didn't keep us captivated – we were kids. The one thing that stayed in our memory was how much they could charge for a packet of crisps at half-time. We shared some crisps and a Bovril and kept the rest to give Dad. If he had enough cash on a Saturday night, things were usually alright and if you were the one who came back with money, you could be the hero for the evening.

It finished as a 1–1 draw but we didn't stay for the end. It was freezing cold and Aaron wanted to go. I told him we had to stay until the end, wait for the players and say 'See you later'. But he wasn't having it. He started walking out of the ground and the only choice I had was to follow him to Newcastle station.

No sooner had we returned to Shakespeare Street than we were back out Guying. By a quarter to seven, we were on the seafront again. Out there, we had the most profitable night of our lives. We must have taken 25 quid. Aaron and I were just bouncing about grinning to ourselves. This had been a day beyond the very reaches of our imagination.

When I woke up, the one thing that nagged at me amid the memories of this perfect day was that we hadn't said goodbye. I sat down and wrote a letter.

I addressed it to:

Brian Clough
The Manager,
c/o Nottingham Forest
Nottingham.

We got a reply.

5.

The Stars Align

The letter came in a thick white envelope with the red crest of Nottingham Forest. I had been waiting for a letter, not in a thick, white envelope with a drawing of a tree but a thin brown one with the words 'Department of Health and Social Security' on the front.

We were expecting a giro and I'd been kept off school to make sure it had arrived. This one was addressed to me: Craig Bromfield, 91 Shakespeare Street, Sunderland, and it dropped with a thud.

Inside, was a letter from Brian Clough. It was typed. He was glad we had enjoyed our day at Newcastle. He said he hoped to see us soon. With the letter were pen portraits of the Nottingham Forest players. He had signed it: 'Be Good, Love Brian'.

There were two reasons for Nottingham Forest to come to the North-East: Sunderland and Newcastle. If they were in the same division they would go there once a season. But this time they would make four trips to the North-East. They drew Sunderland in the League Cup and Newcastle in the FA Cup. All our stars were aligning.

When we heard they were coming to Roker Park for the League Cup, the day after Bonfire Night, excitement crackled through our house. It was like electricity. It was everywhere. In the kitchen. In the lounge. But most of all, it was in our bedroom.

'Are you going?' Mam asked.

'Of course we're going. He's invited us. He said in the letter: "I hope to see you soon". This is soon.'

They would be playing on a Wednesday night. We didn't go to school that day. Azzy and me just waited for the time to crawl by and then, around lunchtime, we walked down to the Seaburn Hotel as if we had been given a written invitation.

We arrived long before the team. We waited a couple of hours outside, listening for the sound of any engine that might be a bus. Then, at about two o'clock with the light just starting to fade, they were here. In the car park. Brian, who always sat closest to the front door, was first out. If he was surprised to see us, it didn't show. He strode over and wrapped us in a hug.

'You two! Come and eat with us, you look like you could do with a good meal.'

Without waiting for Kenny Swain – and it was Kenny we had really come to see – we were swept into the hotel and upstairs to the restaurant.

The team wasn't staying the night at the Seaburn. They'd left Nottingham that morning and would be going straight home after the game. They were just resting in the rooms for a couple of hours after the pre-match meal.

As we sat down, Brian flourished the menu and opened it like a book: 'Go on, lads, order anything you want.'

'Can we have chips, please?'

Jim McInally, the club's Scottish defender, leaned over: 'You really can have anything. Don't worry, the club's paying.'

'We'd just like chips, thank you.'

We sat in the lounge while Brian talked to Ronnie Fenton, his number two. Glasses of Fanta kept appearing for us. When it was dark, they got up and we got up with them. They got on the bus and we got on with them, waved towards the back, towards the chocolate. Then the engines growled into life and we set off on the five-minute drive towards the lights of Roker Park.

As we got off the bus, Kenny Swain pressed two tickets into our hands and we went round the other side of the ground to the Clock Stand. Sunderland, who would reach the League Cup final that season, won, 1–0, and after the game we went back to the team bus to sit with Kenny for 10 minutes and say goodbye properly.

We didn't speak to Brian. He was something we had never seen before: angry, agitated, distracted. We told Kenny we would see them again when they came back on 23 December.

At Christmastime, decorations hung from every lamppost that ran the length of the seafront until they mingled with the lights of the amusement arcades. The tinselly colours danced in the mixture of fret and sleet that came off the North Sea in midwinter. Sunderland looked something it so seldom was: glamorous.

Through the glass revolving doors of the Seaburn Hotel was another world. If we had never gone on the Nottingham Forest team bus or met Brian Clough or Kenny Swain, what was inside the Seaburn Hotel would have been magic enough. The big wide carpet, the armchairs that folded into you, the dark polished wood. In a corner was the sort of Christmas tree you only saw on television, draped with decorations that stretched to the ceiling.

The team had brought presents when they came back on the 23rd. Azzy and me were given padded Nottingham Forest jackets. 'Now you've no excuse for not bringing your coats,' said Brian. Kenny presented us with an orange adidas ball, signed by the team. We varnished it so the signatures wouldn't fade. We could have walked to Roker Park; it was half a mile away but they asked if we'd like to arrive in style. With the team.

We were wearing the jackets when we got off the bus by the main entrance to Roker Park. I looked across. Four lads staring at me – lads I ran from.

'What are you staring at?' Brian asked me.

'It's them. Those boys bully me the most.'

Brian went back into the bus, rummaged around and pulled out four complimentary tickets. He strode over to them: 'Lads, here's four tickets. I don't care what you do with them. You can sell them or you can go to the game, although I'd prefer it if you watched us play. But let me just say one thing,' he said pointing at me, 'if you ever touch this young man again, I know who you are and I know where you all live and I'll come round to yer mams'. Now bugger off!'

That day, 23 December 1984, was the day I stopped being bullied. It was the day I stopped sprinting down Beaumont Street. It was the day I stopped being the Running Boy.

* * *

In May of 1985, Sunderland did something stupid: they got themselves relegated. There was now only one reason for Nottingham Forest to come to the North-East: Newcastle United.

Forest were due to play at St James' Park in October 1985. I couldn't sleep the night before. I'd read in *Shoot* magazine that Kenny Swain had been transferred to Portsmouth and we had no idea if Brian would still like us, or even remember us.

I was at secondary school then, Hylton Red House. We still needed money to get to Newcastle.

This time we knew we needed 20p each so we asked for 50p between us. Mam agreed, but there was a condition: 'I'll give you 50p, if you go to the post office for me tomorrow before you leave. If you get up early enough, you'll be back here for half nine.'

When Mam came down at eight o'clock, she was already dressed. I wasn't going to the post office on The Green, we would be going to Washington.

We got a lift off one of Dad's mates in an Audi that had electric windows, but the steering wheel was on the wrong side. On the way, Mam promised to give me a quid instead of 50p – 'You can keep the extra 50p for yourself, son. You deserve it.'

You could, apparently, cash two weeks' worth of books at the same time by signing someone else to collect your money. Mam wanted me to take a stolen pension book into a strange post office and sign a false name, pretending my auntie had sent me.

It was a decent enough plan. A kid with big hair and a shy smile would not come across as your usual fraudster. All I had to do was act natural, smile and tell them I was picking up my auntie's money for her because she was sick. If they asked why I'd gone to Washington with a Sunderland book, I had to tell them she was staying with my nana, who lived nearby.

Easy, really.

We got to the post office in time for it opening at nine. As I opened the door, the bell rang. It scared me. I walked to the counter and the woman behind it scared me. I gave her the books and didn't say a word, I just looked down. I was nearly wetting myself, waiting for the woman to wrestle me to the floor until the police arrived. The pen was chained to the desk.

They must know that everyone who comes in here is a criminal.

She stamped the stubs and looked at me. She stamped the other half of the book and looked at me. She was wearing a pair of glasses that sat on the edge of her nose. It took me a couple of seconds to realise, but even they were chained to her.

What is this place?

She tore both books twice each. Four weeks in total. She looked at me. She took ages to count the money and she looked at me. I started whistling. I always whistled when I got nervous, but the not-looking-like-a-criminal bit worked: I came back with £94.20 and eight milk tokens.

When I got back into the Audi, Mam began kissing my head, telling me how brave I was – I'd been so long, they thought I'd got caught. I noticed they hadn't got out of the car to check if I was alright. They didn't even give me the spare 20p – I just got the pound. The driver was given £13. I was thinking: *He did nowt flash for that 13 quid.*

When we returned, Azzy decided we would save some money and have a brisk walk down to Seaburn instead of catching the 107. After that morning, I was loaded. We didn't need to walk. I argued my point, got a clip and off we went.

We had walked it at least a hundred times before. This time we reached the Seaburn at about eleven o'clock. I was going mental, sweating from the pace, and because I thought we might have missed them. We definitely weren't in time for breakfast; we had done all that to save five pence each.

Azzy then wanted to go home because, as he said, we hadn't been invited. But I was having none of it. We waited for ages – me at the front entrance, Azzy at the back, watching the car park. Every time we heard an engine, we'd be off to check if it was the team bus.

A freezing hour passed before Azzy gently persuaded me to go in and ask the receptionist what time the team were coming.

I walked sheepishly into the hotel. They knew who I was.

'Excuse me, mister …'

'Hey, sunshine,' the greeting did not sound as nice as it looks. He was scary enough. 'You're going to have a long wait if you're waiting for the team bus. They're not staying here this time. They've decided they want a change of scenery. Staying somewhere in Washington instead.'

'Eh? How? Why? Come on, mister, you're joking …'

I went to tell Azzy. Then I had an idea. I went back inside, walking carefully, almost sideways, ready to run out again.

'Excuse me, mister. Me again.'

'Go on. What do you want now? I've told you, they're not coming here.'

'Yeah, but you said they were staying in Washington, right?'

'Aye, at some posh hotel. Don't know why this place suddenly isn't good enough.'

'I need to ask you to do me a favour and I don't want you to say no, pleeeaaasssse. You know that he always invites us to the games, because you've seen us in here with him. You know we're nice lads really, even if you don't like us for the Guying. Honest, mister, he must have tried this time, but our home phone got cut off and maybe he couldn't get through. He wants us to be at the game. Ah, go on, mister. Please!'

I was genuinely upset as well and I think he could see it meant a lot.

'Son,' he said, 'I don't know what you're talking about. Anyway, I always thought you both just snuck in and Cloughie was too nice to kick you out. Now, what is it you want me to do?'

'Could you ring the other hotel and ask them to tell Brian we're coming to the game?'

'I'll tell you what, son – for you, I will. I'll do it if you'll say "good luck" from me to Brian for tonight, if you get to see him. The name's Peter. Tell him it's Pete from the Seaburn. He'll know who it is and he knows I hate Newcastle. Now, good luck, son. Out you go!'

'Thanks, mister! I'll tell him good luck from you.'

I didn't see him do it but in my heart I knew Pete kept his promise.

I ran out of the hotel with the revolving doors still spinning away.

'Azzy, Azzy … get in! You'll never believe this but we're going, we're going to the game! You know the guy in the hotel who chases us, Pete? Well, he's rung the hotel where the team's staying and it will be alright if we go to the game. Haway, Azzy man. It'll be like an adventure.'

I could see Azzy wanted to go, he just didn't want to admit it so I clipped his ear and set off like Alan Wells, fist pumping, mouth blowing and everything. We were going to sprint all the way to the train station. Actually, I made it a hundred yards before choking on the last bit of a Cola Cube, the chewy bit you usually had to pick out of your teeth.

Azzy didn't belt me when he caught up. I took that as a sign he was 'in'. We ran all the way along the seafront, past the big houses on the right, turning left along the green girders of the Wearmouth Bridge, close to the big, concrete police station where we'd been before.

Sunderland had a drab railway station built into a shopping centre, which meant the platforms were underground. We waited there to jump the train. If we were stopped, we had money and we would say we didn't have time to buy a ticket.

Azzy was such a massive Newcastle fan that he didn't actually know where St James' Park was and had less of a clue how to get there. Our Azzy supported Newcastle after our dad. Dad was a Newcastle fan living in Sunderland. It wasn't enough for us to be the kids of a dreadlocked, drunken, dark-skinned drug dealer, he had to go one step further.

As the train reached Seaburn Colliery, I was chewing on my jumper sleeve. I can't explain why, I just liked the taste. I was also trying not to look at the Newcastle supporters on the train – the Mags. Then I wondered if the lovely girl with the short hair and the blue blouse could see I was looking at her through her reflection in the window.

By the time the train had reached East Boldon and begun its turn towards the Tyne, the only thing I could think of was what would happen if Brian blanked us:

What will I say to Azzy? I made him come and told him Brian already knew we were coming.

We crossed the rail bridge over the Tyne, which was a long, dark oblong encased in grey steel girders. I was terrified of it. I have a memory of the train going dark as it entered the bridge but it might have been me squeezing my eyes tight shut.

Once off the train, we were swept along in a black and white river of Newcastle fans. The ground is at the top of a slope called Gallowgate, where they used to hang witches. There was a big slanty car park, then some bloody big steps that led to a door underneath a sign that said: 'Welcome to St James' Park'. It seemed welcoming enough.

I had agreed to do the talking. There was this friendly look-ing old bloke on the door, wearing a cap and a big, long coat.

'Hello, mister. Can you tell us if the Forest team bus has turned up yet, please?'

'Piss off, you scruffy little twat!'

'Mister, I don't want to be rude, but that's not fair. Me and me brother are waiting for Mr Clough and the Forest team. We're meeting him here, because we're his friends from Sunderland. He doesn't like swearing and he doesn't like people who shout at kids.'

'Eeeh, you cheeky little sod! Piss off and take the little darkie with you. Brothers ... meeting Mr Clough ... my arse! Now bugger off, ah tell you, before I get the polis.'

He may have looked 73, but I was ready to launch into him when there was a sudden booing. People were crushing us and every time we tried to get near the rope they were putting up, we were pushed away. No matter how many times we said we were with the Nottingham Forest team it didn't seem to help:

'Fuck off, ya Forest-supporting, scruffy, gap-toothed little Mackem* twat, if you expect me to let you through.'

Then I saw the Nottingham Forest coach rolling up the hill. I could see Albert, the driver, had a tab on and a big, cheesy grin. He waved, but I don't know if he waved at us or he was cleverly flicking the Vs – he said he sometimes did that to the nastier fans and could get away with it because it looked like he was giving them the royal wave.

The coach parked up and over came one of the lads. Albert had seen us and pointed us out to Brian. When we clambered on board the bus, we were greeted with: 'How did you two get here? What have I told you about wrapping up? You'll catch your death!' It could have been said in a softer tone.

'Hello, Mr Clough.'

'Hello, son. Nice to see you. Now what are you doing here? Does your mam know you've come out dressed like that? You do know Kenny has gone, don't you?'

---

* Before the 1980s, everyone from the North-East was routinely described as 'Geordie'. In recent decades, the term 'Mackem' came to be used to describe those from Sunderland. It was said to be a play on how the words 'make them' were pronounced on Wearside.

'Yes, Mr Clough, but we still thought we would come and say hello to everyone else as well. Didn't Pete from the Seaburn tell you?'

'Pete from the Seaburn? I'll bloody Pete-from-the-Seaburn you! No, he didn't bloody tell me, we didn't stay there. Now get down the back of the bus, get a cup of soup and then get back up here quick! I've got work to do. And I've told you before, you can call me Brian, lads.'

I caught a thick, gooey bit of soup in my first mouthful and burnt my lip and the top of my mouth. When I told Brian about the man on the door, he asked me to point him out.

Once off the bus, the players began getting booed. There was a different reaction to Brian:

'Howay man, Cloughie!'

'Brian, sign this!'

You get what you deserve if you don't say 'please' and, if you don't call him Mr Clough, you get bugger all.

'Are you sure you weren't rude to him, son?' he said to me as we were coming down the coach steps. 'You're not lying to me? You just asked him as nicely as that?'

'Yes, Brian, I asked him nicely.'

He jogged into the ground and it was all I could do to keep up with him. I pointed at the doorman loudly: 'Him. It was him. That one there, Brian.'

As we ran towards him, I waited for Brian to say something. I was ready to back him up if needed. Not a peep. Just a 'Good afternoon, sir, these two are with me.'

Doors opened and in we went.

He's not as scary as they make him out to be, this fella. If that was my mam, she'd have had his hat off and her finger down the old git's gob by now.

We were inside. We were juggled along the corridor, not knowing where or when Brian would say: 'Wait here.' He didn't say it. After a minute or two, we were in the dressing room.

Most of the lads picked up a programme, a cup of tea and packet of Wrigley's, then went down the tunnel to look at the pitch.

'Hey, you two,' said Brian, 'get out there with them lot. I've got work to do. When you get out there, make sure you breathe in and fill yer lungs. Put a couple of them jackets on and bugger off for 15 minutes.'

We were down the players' tunnel. There were 'keep off the grass' signs everywhere and the stewards tried to stop us getting on the pitch.

Ian Bowyer, Forest's midfield ginger bomber, was having none of it: 'They're with us and they're coming with us. We're having a walk. Come on, lads.'

We were on the pitch, feeling a hundred feet tall, wearing jackets that were too big for us and neither of us had stopped smiling. How could we ever top a feeling like this? I wasn't brave enough to look anywhere other than in front of my nose but I could feel that every single person in the ground was wanting to be doing what we were.

'I told you, Azzy. I told you it would be an adventure.'

We waited for a couple of the lads to go back and sidled up alongside them until we were sitting on the edge of the dress-ing-room bench, trying to be as inconspicuous as possible.

'Hey, you two!' barked Brian. 'One rule and one rule only when you're in here: say nowt, keep yer big heads down and get stuck in if something needs doing. Any of the lads want anything – tea, orange juice, anything – go fetch it. Pick up the shirts and the socks after and put them in that basket. Do that and you'll be alright. Now, do any of the lads need anything?'

'Dunno,' said Aaron, shrugging his shoulders, hands in his pockets.

I was already off with the teapot and plastic cups, quietly making sure everyone had a drink.

That was at least five rules and I definitely didn't catch the last one. I'm not going to ask him to say it again.

Brian didn't really say much. It was calm, a few jokes flew around, with everyone breathing deeply every now and then. Someone on a table was having his legs bent backwards way too much by another fella. There was a queue of three more waiting. It hurt my legs just watching.

The dressing room smelt sensational. The scent of the Deep Heat hit you and almost took out your eyes. The language was small, electric sentences.

'Hey, skipper, get hold of the ball.'

'Get on the front foot, lads.'

'This lot'll be going nuts for the first 15 minutes. Give 'em nowt.'

'Give them nothing. *Nothing.*'

'No daft fouls, son, stay on your feet.'

'Give it and go, son, give and go.'

'Get hold of the ball, son.'

'Get it and knock it past him.'

'I'm telling you, their right-back is older than me. He's shot it. I'd have you over him any day of the week, son. Any day of the week.'

It didn't sound like much but everyone in that dressing room was nodding and a few of them were tapping their heads as if to say: 'Think about it.' A bell went off and they started shouting:

'Come on, boys!'

'This is ours!'

Metal studs banging on the floor.

I couldn't move. It was incredible. The hairs on my arms were standing up and I just wanted to start shouting, 'Go on, lads! Fucking go on!' I didn't say a word.

Then we were out with them, running into the dug-out, into the noise, the freezing cold and a really nasty Geordie crowd. Azzy was spat at and told to fuck off home. He couldn't have looked more than 10 and I don't think he could have been mistaken for Forest's secret midfield destroyer.

It was horrible but amazing to be walking past thousands of mental Geordies. Doing it alongside Brian Clough meant you knew you were safe. I banged my head on the roof of the dug-out and couldn't even cheer when Forest scored their first goal.

The game went by in a heartbeat. I can't remember any specific moment, although the records show Nottingham Forest won, 3–0. All I remember was sitting back in the changing room after the game, looking around and feeling pleased I had got stuck in.

All the shorts were away, the socks straightened out and the tape that kept the socks up was put in the bin. I heard Ronnie Fenton asking if we had our bus fare home and our Azzy answering, 'Yes.' Then Brian said, 'They can't be going home on their own tonight and I'm not going to bloody South-of-whatever-it-is to drop them off. I want to get home, I've shot it.'

Southwick, Brian, we live in Southwick.

'Hey, lads, have you got school Monday?'

Quick as a flash: 'No.'

'Then how about you come down to ours for a few days? We'll get you some fresh air and get you fed up. You look like you haven't had a decent meal in weeks. You can stay with Ron – can't they, Ron?'

I wasn't the best of judges but I got more than a slight feeling Ronnie Fenton didn't fancy the idea as much as Brian had hoped.

Just then the dressing room door opened.

'Hello, Mr Clough. Can I come in? I've come to say sorry to the two boys of yours.'

It was the old bugger from the entrance!

'Lads,' he said, 'I'm sorry if I shouted at ya and ah never meant to swear, like – that was wrong as well. I just didn't believe ya story, like. Ahm sorry. Eh, no hard feelings, ah hope?'

I was about to tell him to piss off. He'd really offended me and no amount of grovelling, just because Brian had asked him to do it, was going to soften my mood.

'Hey, thanks a lot for that, young man,' said Brian, 'it means a lot that you came in here. Now you take care and see you next season.'

Finished off with a kiss on the cheek.

How could you not love that? He totally blew me away with how he handled things.

'Now then, son,' he said, turning to me, 'when you talk to anyone, you make sure you're always polite and nice, but if someone is nasty to you, you have a right to speak out, okay? Now, if you're not at school, how do you fancy a little holiday?'

'I, err … we'd love it, Mr Clou— I mean, we'd love it, Brian, thanks.'

'Hey, Scotsman,' he called to one of the players, 'get their mam on the phone. Tell her, if it's okay with her, they're coming down to my house for a couple of days. Tell her not to worry, we'll look after them and make sure they get home safe. By the looks of them, she'll be pleased to get rid. And hey, son, tell her it's Brian Clough who's asking.'

He turned his back to us. 'Now, you two, bugger off with him! The nice gentleman on the door will show you where the phone is.'

Jim McInally made the call. He was from Glasgow, played right-back and had signed from Celtic. When, soon after he signed, Brian discovered Jim was having Christmas alone in the Balmoral Hotel in Nottingham, he invited him to spend it with the Cloughs. Brian was concerned Jim didn't eat enough vegetables and presented him with a plate of Brussels sprouts – he served him the roast later.

Of course, we didn't have a phone so we gave Jim the Pennocks' number. The Pennocks, Kenny and Betty, were our neighbours and were part of the glue that held Southwick together. When we ran out of food, they would hand us bowls of soup over the garden fence. When we had no hot water, they would heave over kettles of boiled water. After 12 or 13 refills, we would have enough for a bath.

Because they had a phone, our neighbours also took messages for us. I was as nervous as hell they wouldn't answer.

Jim was saying to us: 'Surely, your ma can't agree to this? She has no clue where you're going. The Gaffer is daft for asking me to do this. What the fuck do I say? Sorry for swearing. Shit – I mean *sugar* – what's yer ma's name? Quick, it's ringing!'

Thirty-five seconds later, Jim is saying, 'Sure, I'll tell them. Thanks a lot, bye.' He hangs up. 'Hey, lads, your ma says she'll miss you, but have a good time.'

Mam agreed at once. She would have been excited for us. Me and Azzy were running around the corridors of St James' Park punching each other in the arm and leaping around in celebration. We were going away with Brian Clough and we felt like princes.

We walked out with the team. The Newcastle fans who had stayed for autographs were looking at us as if we were traitors. We got on the bus. *We got on the bus!* The doors closed and Albert the driver waved nicely as we left.

'Right, lads,' said Brian, 'get down the back, help yourself to chocolate and crisps. Stay out of the lads' way and if you can, get your heads down for a few minutes. I'm down here and if I hear any noise coming out of the pair of yer, I'll get Albert to drop you off on the motorway.'

Then he turned to the driver: 'Scotch Corner, Albert,' he said. 'That's where we're stopping, right?'

'Yes, boss, Scotch Corner.'
'And how far is that from South-wherever, Albert?'
'It's a long way, boss.'
'I'm only kidding, lads. Now get out of my sight!'

6.

Those First Impressions

The house was huge. There were front lights on it, flowers growing up the sides, wisteria leaves over the windows. There were three cars on the drive. It looked like something you would see on *Dallas*.

At 14 and nearly 13 years old, the two of us had knocked on a lot of strange people's doors. This time we both knew it was really different.

'I'll knock, you talk.'

That was the deal I'd struck with our Azzy on the way up the drive. He wasn't the brightest lad in the world and I'd already twigged the hardest part would be explaining just why we were knocking.

Brian had already briefed us on the drive from where the bus had dropped us off. He had the gift to make you do anything you didn't want to; an ability to make you feel six feet tall with one comment, sometimes even with one look. I would do anything he wanted.

'Now then, rag-tags,' he said as we pulled up not far from his ... I was going to say 'house', but it was much bigger than that. 'It's a nice night. Come on, we'll walk the rest of the way.' He turned to his agent, Mike Keeling, who had picked us up from the bus in Brian's gold Mercedes. 'Mike, you drive up behind us and park the car up. I want to set some things clear with these two busy bollocks.'

We got out of the car. It wasn't cold but it was wet. Brian was wearing the same clothes he had on when we first saw him on the beach at Seaburn: jacket and training gear that had seen better days.

He opened the boot of the Mercedes and threw me and Azzy a jacket each; not aggressively but definitely hard enough to make us have to catch it. Mine was huge – it was an Umbro. Azzy, lucky bugger, got an adidas.

I became lost in the sleeves of my jacket and then nearly had Azzy's eye out, playing windmill. How was I to know those sleeves had press studs in the end?

My pockets had half a packet of Halls Eucalyptus and a bottle of smelling salts, which Brian made me try within three seconds of my asking: 'What's this?' It nearly took my head off.

There was also a hairbrush, one of those spiky, circular hand brushes that you put your fingers through the strap to sweep your hair right back. There was an absolute bloody fortune in coins in the right-hand pocket – a good few hours' Guying money.

Brian must have caught me counting it in my head. 'Having a good feel around in those pockets, son?' he said, catching eye contact and making me feel three inches tall.

'Don't worry, I'm only kidding. Help yourself to mints and put the coins in the ashtray when we get in.'

I creaked out a nervous smile.

He went on: 'Okay, lads. Now, the rules. Will you remember them all?'

'While you're here, you can call me anything you want, alright? "Brian", "Big Head", "Shithouse" … I don't mind. As for the kids, Simon is Simon, Nigel is Nigel. Elizabeth likes to be called Lib, sometimes Libby, but only if she likes you and you'll have to work that out for yourselves.'

'Okay, Brian,' I responded, hiding the nerves. Our Azzy just beamed a smile and nodded. Azzy had a very nice smile.

'But one rule, as long as you are under my roof,' he said, wagging his finger up to the house, 'Mrs Clough is *always* Mrs Clough. And hey, lads, I'm not kidding. If I hear anything else out of those mouths, I'll knock yer daft bonces together. Now, get on up that drive.'

Brian's voice had a habit of getting louder with every word and ever so occasionally he had a way of snarling at you without you ever feeling really threatened. Shit scared, yes, but never threatened because you just knew that you were going to do what he asked.

We were pretty disorientated, having just spent four hours on a bus with 15 grown men. Some we'd met twice before, others we'd met for the first time. They kept giving us chocolate, Coke, Fanta and crisps and occasionally asking what the fuck we were doing on their bus. Jim McInally and Ian Bowyer, who were a bit older than the rest, told them off for swearing. I liked those two straight away.

On the inside, I was nervous and just wanted to curl up and go to sleep. On the outside, I was smiling, trying to joke and show I wasn't scared. For the first time in ages, I felt special, but I was worried they would discover just how scared I was. I'd drunk too much pop and didn't dare go to the toilet on the bus. You had to move three crates of Coca-Cola to get to it, squeeze past that big, bald Dutchman, Johnny Metgod, the one with the deep voice, and then cram yourself into a tiny space and wee standing up on a moving bus. I remember thinking, *I can hold it.*

I got Nigel and Simon confused the first few times we met so, when I saw either of them, I just nodded hello. One of them had followed us back from the hotel where the bus had dropped us off in another car. That must have been Nigel because he had been on the bus with the rest of the lads. Nobody on that bus had mentioned he was the manager's son. He was 19, but tipped for greatness.

The third time I got them mixed up caused Azzy to snap at me: 'You'd have thought the tash would've given it away by now.' Sometimes, Azzy could make a very valid point: Simon had the tash, Nigel didn't.

There were other differences. They were both born in Sunderland but Simon was the older of the two. He was very good-looking and spoke slowly with a deep voice. He could sing beautifully with it, often in the car. His standard dress was a shirt and a tank-top, which was partly why he looked older than he was. His nickname was 'Victor Mature'. To me he looked like Paco Diaz, who played centre-half for Melchester Rovers in *Roy of the Rovers*.

Simon had been a very good centre-half until, like his father, a knee injury forced a change of career. Now, he managed AC

Hunters in the Derbyshire Sunday League. They would play in the Nottingham Forest kit, which took some courage in Derbyshire and which once led to Nigel, who would sometimes turn out for the team, having a cup of hot coffee thrown over him in the dressing room.

Because of Nigel's education in top-flight professional football, the family deferred to him on financial and property matters. Curiously, it was Simon whose views on football Brian sought out. Brian very rarely talked football at home. However, when Simon came round for Sunday lunch, they would have deep discussions about the game.

With *Mrs Clough, Mrs Clough, Mrs Clough* repeating through my brain, we were halfway up the drive when we heard a loud whispering: 'Oi, rag-tags – get back here a minute.'

It was Brian. He had a plan. He huddled us together and was giggling and snorting with laughter at the same time. 'It'll be great,' said Mike, 'Really good idea.'

Mike was wearing a suit jacket in the rain, squinting through the drizzle, belly laughing and pulling up his trousers at the same time. I didn't like Mike and I'm not sure he ever liked me. 'Take their jackets off, though Bri. Otherwise, she'll know they've been with you.'

'Hey, Dad,' said Nigel. 'I'm not sure Mum will take it as well as you think. Let's just all go in together. It's been a long day, I want to get some sleep. This just sounds too daft to be true.'

Brian was still laughing. He had a way of putting the whole of his hand across his face when he laughed or smiled.

It was a warm laugh. His head would be thrown back and sometimes he would laugh himself to tears. It was contagious. Then he'd end it all just as quickly with a 'weeeaa, give over!'

He bounded over: 'Lads, I want you to go to the front door, alright? That's the one on the right-hand side of those bushes.' Mike began hawking the jackets off our backs. Once he took the jacket back, I felt gutted I hadn't taken at least 20p out of the pocket – they would never have missed it.

Brian had managed to steady his laughter but his face was still bright red. 'I want you both to ring the doorbell and when it's answered, you should ask the lady if she is Mrs Clough. When she says "yes", I want you to tell her that you are my kids from Middlesbrough. Tell her that your mam has sent you to get some money from me and that you're not moving from the doorstep until you can talk to me. Alright? Now off you go.'

He turns around and starts jogging gently back down the drive, scuffing his feet as he runs, laughing: 'Mike, turn that bloody engine off and them lights n'all. She's not bloody deaf, you know.'

It seemed an age to walk the hundred yards from the gate to the front door. The lights of the Mercedes were off, we were surrounded by huge trees. It was bloody dark and freakily silent.

I am not scared of this.

I ring the bell.

The light goes on.

The door opens.

This lovely woman with curly hair and, as Brian would put it, 'a smile as wide as Stockton High Street', greets us with, 'Hello, pets, what can I do for you two?'

Azzy smiles and stammers.

I did the talking. I always did the talking.

The more I talked, the more Mrs Clough's friendly beam turned to a look of confusion and then horror.

Within two minutes and 30 seconds, we were in the lounge, shoes and socks off, something I'm pretty sure Mrs Clough regretted as soon as she realised I had my stinky feet playing curly-wurly with the loveliest, fluffiest green carpet ever.

The fire was put on. We were given a cup of tea and a couple of biscuits with a thickness of chocolate I'd not seen before, not even at Nana's. Then Mrs Clough came back with a glass of milk and a promise of cheese-and-tomato sandwiches.

I didn't have the heart to say I'd just stuffed my face on Twixes and Fanta on the bus, thinking I might never get another chance. Mixed in with all that loveliness were phrases like: 'He should be home in a short while', 'You poor lads. How *did* you get here?'

Brian must have waited a good five minutes before sneaking into the lounge and winking: 'Has she twigged us yet, lads?' before going off to hide in his study. He tripped over a box of Milk Tray and promptly got caught. Then we had 10 minutes of proper introductions. There was a little confusion when we said we were brothers because of the colours of our skin. We had to explain that Azzy's dad was my stepdad and my mam was his stepmam.

'I know it's complicated,' I blurted out. 'Sometimes, I'm confused as well.'

They started laughing.

In the same way he insisted on calling Jim McInally 'Scotsman', Brian had now decided to refer to me as 'Sunderland'. He announced: 'Sunderland, tell Mrs Clough what you told me when I asked you why you weren't eating at the Seaburn.'

'I'm not that quiet, Brian. I just needed a few minutes before I could eat. I'm always nervous when I first meet famous people. I definitely wasn't telling you off though.'

She laughed – they all laughed – they all 'aaaahh'ed.

What had I said?

Our Azzy didn't say a bloody word, he just sat there smiling.

It took a good while for things to calm down. Eventually, we were packed off to bed. Two single beds in a huge room with a fluffy, light-blue carpet and very heavy blankets. It was perfect tucking-in material – I didn't ever want to wake up.

The talking downstairs went on for an age and then they all came up to say: 'Goodnight, lads, sleep well.'

We woke up for the first time in the village of Quarndon. We both opened our eyes at the same time, not quite knowing what to do; we only had the clothes on our backs.

The bedroom window had a view to the front garden. The whole of the front of the house was covered with climbing leaves.

Boredom claimed us. Temptation became too much. Azzy was the first to open one of the massive wardrobes. It was full of Brian's suits. Then, I slid open a wardrobe. I had never seen so many cool things in one place. T-shirts, adidas and Umbro. Tracksuits, jackets, jerseys, shorts, socks, underpants. There were even the legendary green jumpers Brian wore on the touchline.

The moment I picked up a T-shirt, there was a quick knock, a pause and the door opened. The pause was not enough to be able to put down the T-shirt. The door opened and in walked Nigel. With a stern but confused look, he said, 'Breakfast is on the table downstairs, lads. The faster you get down, the hotter it will be.' We dropped the T-shirts.

Brian loved being in the kitchen and had just made bacon sandwiches. The bread was wholemeal, heated, not toasted. The butter was thick and the bacon had just the right amount of tomato sauce melting over it. Then there was cereal – Kellogg's Start – with milk that didn't have water in it. There was something I had never seen before, called a honeydew melon – it was bloody lovely. There were two cups of tea and an orange Club biscuit to finish.

Brian said: 'Nigel tells me you were looking in some of my T-shirt cupboards. Get upstairs and choose any two things each that fit you. But, remember, it's my stuff and I worked bloody hard to get it. If it doesn't fit, don't take it. Go on, bugger off out of my sight! Fifteen minutes to get ready.'

He stopped me: 'Hey, son, on your way up, ask Mrs Clough if she wants anything from Park Farm. Tell her we're going shopping for you two rag-tags.'

That's how I met Elizabeth. I walked to the foot of the stairs, looked up and saw Libby and Mrs Clough chatting, probably about what the hell had been going on these last 12 hours. She was 19, tall, grown-up, cool. I was 13, fluffy hair, yellow teeth and there may have been a yellow patch on my canvas trousers where I hadn't been able to hold in the wee on the bus. There was no way I was talking to her. I mumbled something about 'shopping' to Mrs Clough, dashed downstairs and sat in the car.

Park Farm was a shopping centre in Allestree, a few miles away. It had a small sports shop that should have been shut at half 10 on a Sunday morning but the man who ran it was doing some stocktaking. We knocked on his window and began trying on all kinds of shoes. Brian chose and paid for one pair of Nike Division for Aaron and I chose adidas Samba. The guy behind the counter said our accents reminded him of Middlesbrough, his home town, and offered us an extra pair because Brian was a 'special customer'.

We went to Quarndon Stores and brought pâté, bread, cheese and fresh ham. Then it was to the flower shop to buy some freesias – Mrs Clough loved freesias.

We drove past Brian's old house on Ferrers Way, the one he lived in before he got the pay-off from Leeds in 1974. He did his rounds like a politician in his constituency.

We met Percy Yeomans. Even if you didn't know he was a former army officer, you could have a pretty good guess. He always wore an immaculate suit with a pressed handkerchief in the top pocket and his hair was perfectly white. He had lived diagonally opposite Brian in Ferrers Way. Brian kept a strong bond with those who had been good to him when he first came to Quarndon to manage Derby County.

Mr and Mrs Jeeson, who seemed even older than Percy, had been the first couple to welcome Brian into the village and helped with the children when they were younger. We gave them the freesias, the pâté, the ham, the cheese and the bread. There may even have been some chocolates and a magazine in there as well. If Mrs Clough had been anything like my mam, she would have gone crazy knowing Brian had wasted all that money on the Jeesons.

As we walked away, Brian saw a telegraph pole with a sticker saying: 'Vote Conservative'. He growled: 'Not if I've got owt to do with it you won't' and, after failing to bring it down with a stick, he ordered Aaron to shin up the pole and untie it.

All morning, Brian had been saying he'd be taking us to Kedleston Hall because we needed to roll in the cow shit in the fields. It would make us grow up bigger and stronger. Apparently.

I was nearly crying with fear and apprehension when we got there. I only stopped when he said he wasn't going to rub my nose in it: 'It's okay, son, I'm only kidding. Weeeaaaahh ... You smell bad enough without rolling in it. Just smell that fresh air. We're going to meet Brian Moore, the man who does the commentaries on the telly.'

We were shown into the restaurant, where the tablecloths were as white and deep as blankets and the wine glasses sparkled. Brian Moore was sitting with his producer, a young, fresh-faced man called Trevor East, who kept us entertained through lunch when the two Brians went off to 'discuss business'.

This was to be a documentary, *Cloughie, The Brian Clough Story* – in which Brian would agree to open up about his life outside football.

Brian liked Brian Moore, partly because the other Brian thought Nigel was going to be a very good player and partly because they had known each other a very long time. He thought Brian Moore was the best commentator in the business, while Brian Moore thought the 'Old Big Head' stance was a bit of a front, that Brian could be shyer than he let on.

When Johan Cruyff joined him on the ITV panel for the 1978 World Cup, Brian seemed in awe of the Dutchman and asked if he could always be sat next to him 'so some of the magic can rub off'. Brian had just won the league title with Nottingham Forest.

They were very close. When Brian suffered his worst defeat in football, losing 8–2 at home to Bristol Rovers when he was manager of Brighton, he had agreed to be interviewed by Brian Moore the very next day. He wouldn't have done it for anyone else. Nigel had sat on his lap and Brian Moore had asked what he thought of the game – Nigel said Brighton had done alright.

In the documentary, Brian would talk about socialism and parenthood: 'I have taught my children to be generous, not with money but with their time and with their smiles.' He would describe his three years at Sunderland as 'the happiest of my life'. Sunderland people, he said, 'were beautiful people'.

What really impressed me was that he was managing to talk and eat at the same time, a trick I've yet to manage – 'Look, Brian, you know we haven't been up to the levels I'd like, but that bloody new stand is nearly paid for and there's some good young players coming through. I'm telling you, in a couple of years, we'll be right up there. Challenging like we used to.'

I'm not talking or eating, I'm just staring at my plate. When we were in care, in Thorney Close, we were given a posh lunch on Sundays. Roast beef, Yorkshire pudding and Brussels sprouts. We had never seen a Brussels sprout before. Dazzy put one in his mouth and was sick. Some of the sick went on his plate and Aunty Audrey told him to finish the meal.

Now the potatoes have something green on them, something that looks like grass. Brian turns away from his conversation and says, 'That, son, is called parsley. Eat it up, it's good for yer.'

But I can't, I just can't. While Brian is talking to Brian, I am throwing the parsley and the bits of potato with parsley on it under the table. Finally, when Brian Moore gets up to go, his beautiful black leather shoes are covered in bits of potato and parsley. He looked at them, laughed and presented us with £20 each.

When we got back to Brian's house, I wasn't sure what else he expected. Knackered after all the walking, the smelling and the name remembering, I slumped in his reclining chair and watched *The Abbott and Costello Show*, eating a Terry's chocolate orange and a Yorkie that I'd 'found' in the study.

Brian walked into the living room. 'Aye up, smiley,' he said to Aaron, who was walking behind him, holding a glass of milk. 'Look at Rigor Mortis over there. Hey, son, hey, Rigor! Do you need a crane to get you up? Are you tired already? Get some milk down you, instead of eating that garbage. Look at him,' he said, nodding towards Azzy, 'he drinks gallons of the stuff. Come on, we've work to do.'

I had no clue who Rigor Mortis was or what he did, but soon it was the name everyone started calling me.

I could sense the start of a growing rivalry between me and Aaron when it came to impressing Brian. Aaron had just finished circling six trees with a lawnmower before taking out some weeds with a pair of secateurs while I'd been watching *Abbott and Costello*.

When we did get out into the garden, I began playing wall tennis while Aaron was stung by two wasps as he was tipping out the grass. Nobody had ever seen wasps this late in October and now Azzy had discovered a nest of the buggers.

We finished the day by sweeping the drive. By now, Percy Yeomans had come round and busied himself showing me why my way of holding the brush was not as efficient as Aaron's.

A pretty girl came out with a plate of biscuits for us while we swept the drive. Her name was Margaret. To me, she seemed to carry herself like a princess. She told me to take no notice of Percy, I was doing a great job.

Percy retaliated by telling me off for taking two biscuits when the plate came to me. 'You only need take one at a time, young man. They won't run away.'

He'd obviously never been round our house.

Margaret and Nigel took Margaret's spaniel, Snoopy, for a walk while we went to watch a training session with AC Hunters, the team Simon managed. There was the biggest bag of footballs I'd seen in my life. They were all pumped up so hard, they nearly broke my big toe when I kicked any of them.

We were invited to take part in some of the training routines and, horribly, I couldn't keep the ball up for more than three goes while Aaron seemed to break the world record for keepy-uppies and speed running simultaneously.

He was carried off in triumph by his new mates. All I got was: 'Start off with one on your knee, it's easier ... oh for fuck's sakes!'

For supper we had fish, chips and mushy peas from Mr Mo's in Allestree. We went with Tash to collect them. He introduced us as his 'friends from the North'. He drove bloody quickly. He kept looking at himself in the mirror, flicked his hair far too often and sang into an imaginary microphone on his gearstick.

After supper we played that dice-popping game, Frustration, where Simon kept threatening to 'spew in my goulash' if I threw a five. I began learning how to lose tactically. Afterwards, I was upstairs. I had found an old programme: England v Sweden, Wembley Stadium, 28 October 1959. England with Jimmy Greaves, Bobby Charlton and Brian Clough facing the team that, a year before, had played Brazil in the World Cup final.

Then, the man whose second and last appearance for England that would be popped his head round the door and looked hard at what I had in my hand: 'Now then, put that back in its box and get downstairs. You've got two minutes to get that lot cleaned up and put back where it came from.'

If Brian Clough told you to do something in two minutes, you did it in one and a half – and that's if you were being cheeky.

Downstairs, there was more Frustration, this time with Nigel. Then it was Horlicks and cheese on toast before Brian's final announcement of the day: 'Now, lads, get yourselves upstairs, brush your teeth and get some sleep. Early start tomorrow, we're off to work.'

7.

Shopping

We were woken up at horrible o'clock. I finished breakfast first and went exploring. It still wasn't half seven when I opened the door to Brian's study.

Brian was in the lounge, reading a newspaper over his glasses, not watching a football match that was playing on the telly with the sound turned down. The study was dominated by a large desk in the middle, some framed photographs of some really famous people and a big 'Manager of the Year' picture provided by Bell's Whisky. Everywhere you looked, there were cups and bottles full of coins – I'd never seen so many full piggy banks in my life. And then there were shelves and shelves full of video tapes – movies, serials and, my favourite section, football matches. Someone had spent an age organising the tapes, first by the type of video and then into alphabetical order. The first three movies I watched, I didn't put back or rewind.

Nigel said to us: 'Lads, if you borrow something that isn't yours, make sure you put it back where you got it from. You should respect other people's stuff.' He didn't raise his voice, it was an attempt to teach us.

We were inside Brian's gold Mercedes just before eight. He said he ran a 'cold car' and it was bloody freezing inside. I had the big Umbro jacket on again but I still rattled my teeth to 'Me And My Shadow' that was playing on the car stereo. Brian had brought us both a cup of tea to keep our hands warm.

We turned right past the church, past Kedleston Park and eventually hit the A52. We passed the place where we had got off the team bus the other day. We went through Bramcote, past the post office where Brian said his brother, 'our Gerald', worked. We passed the studios of Central Television and Aaron started doing the 'ar-er' noises made by Mr Babbage whenever someone got a question wrong on *Family Fortunes*.

All the while there was music playing and a man singing about flying to the moon. Brian knew the words to all the songs and was always two or three seconds ahead of whoever was singing. Every now and then he would add a little 'oh yeah' or repeat a line. Or he would start talking to the singer: 'Mmm, Frank. Fly me to the moon.'

It was amazing how many people stared at the car. I counted at least 20 times that Brian put his thumb up to say hello. He would smile at the person while gritting his teeth, saying: 'Aye, shithouse – it's me, it really is … I've said hello, now bugger off!' He waved and smiled as he said it.

As one couple went past, pointing with mouths wide open, I did a variation of the Pope joke: 'Look, who's that bloke dressed in white, waving next to our Johnny?' I told Brian they were waving at us and asking who was in the car with Craig and Aaron. Brian laughed at that for about 10 minutes: 'Weeeaaaahhh!'

Brian told us that we'd be staying in Nottingham for a few days. He'd sorted a nice place for us so we could be closer to the lads in training. I dug our Azzy in the ribs: 'It's 'cos he caught you trying to nick his T-shirts. Now, we'll never go back to the house again.'

After about half an hour, we turned on to the Victoria Embankment. Brian pulled over, told us to get out of the car and said, 'Look out for the seats and breathe in when you see them.' The first time I saw the ground with 'FOREST' written in white letters on the red seats, I got goose bumps – it took my breath away.

He said this was a magic view and this was a magic road. It was beautiful; tree-lined with football pitches on the left-hand side. On the other side ran the River Trent.

When we saw the City Ground and the Trent Bridge cricket ground, Azzy and me kept nudging each other, saying, 'Look at that!'

We got out of the car in front of a sign that said 'Nottingham Forest Football Club' in red letters across a white background. I'd seen that sign in a picture in his study. There, he had been shaking hands with a man with white hair. He told me that man was the chairman, Jim Willmer, and it had been taken on Brian's first day of work here in January 1975.

Walking through the main doors, there were three separate entrances. On the left was where his secretary, Carole, and the rest of the admin staff worked. The one directly in front led to the dressing rooms, the directors' box and the Jubilee Club.

The club shop was situated at the bottom of Brian's offices, on the right-hand side as you walked through the foyer. Brian's door was first, then Ronnie Fenton's and the coaching staff, where the television was. Then there was the club secretary's office, where Ken Smales worked. The next office on the right belonged to the chairman, Maurice Roworth, although he was seldom there. His office had a drinks fridge and could be used when guests arrived. Usually, it was empty – the room, not the fridge.

The first person we saw was Brian's secretary: 'Morning, Carole. Get me that shithouse, Ron Atkinson, on the phone,' he said. Brian never liked anyone who was manager of Manchester United. 'Oh, and do me a favour and get these rag-tags a plate of sandwiches made up, would you?'

The next person we saw was Archie Gemmill, who had won the league with Brian and was now first-team coach. 'You two still here?' he said in a hard, Scottish drawl.

I nodded and smiled.

'When are we getting rid of you?'

It wasn't a question that invited an answer. Was he having a go? I went red. Archie had a really dry sense of humour but he could also be a nasty bugger and that morning, I wasn't sure which side of him I was facing.

A man popped his head around the door. 'Morning, boss.' This was Dave Pullen, the commercial manager.

'Hey, Dave, just the man actually. Get yer big bonce back in here for a minute. These two are young pals of mine from Sunderland. They'll be staying with us for a few days and I want to get them shown around. I've got some work to do, so can you get them in the shop for half an hour and get them kitted out? Anything they want, it's on me.'

'Sure, boss,' said Dave. 'Just give me five minutes and I'll come and get them. Hello, lads, I'm Dave. Wait here for me and I'll be back in a bit.'

Brian left, picking up his squash racket. He said he would be a couple of hours. 'Try not to nick owt,' he said with a wink.

His office was a simple affair. On his side of the desk was a chair he was always sitting back in – he forever looked as if he were going to fall backwards. In front of the desk were three uncomfortable, connected flat leather chairs and three more to the right-hand side. Above his desk, a tiny window ran full-length along the back wall. There was a small drinks cabinet that would only ever be stocked with fruit juice and on the walls were little signs, calendars and a couple of posters. There was a coat rack and usually a walking stick or a squash racket balanced against the wall – you could always find a tennis ball there.

Dave returned with another, slightly taller Carole. We walked down the corridor, through a back door that had coded access and arrived in a wonderland: the club shop.

Bigger Carole looked us up and down, then started to throw us little see-through bags. We each got a home shirt with 'Skol' on the front. We got shorts and socks to go with it. We got grey sweatshirts with Forest badges and red and blue diamonds at the bottom. We got a grey Skol padded jacket that made me feel like toast inside. We got a Skol body warmer with removable sleeves. We got T-shirts. We got cotton trackie bottoms that I hated because my legs looked like chickens' in them.

We got a proper Forest tracksuit each, with red top, black bottoms. We got scarves, mugs, badges, pictures, programmes.

We got our hair ruffled a million times by everyone who walked in and we had to tell the story of how we'd met Brian to everyone who asked.

If he was ever listening to us telling it, Brian would always jump in with 'Wait till I get hold of that Kenny bloody Swain – I'll brain him.'

'Have they got one of everything?' Dave asked Carole.

We had. I loved it. Everyone loved us.

After about half an hour people were queuing up to see us. 'What did you get, lads?' and 'Do you like it?' were the first two questions everyone asked us. I didn't have the words to describe how I felt – I never had anything cool in my life and now there was two bin bags full of stuff.

Dave took us and the swag back to the office, where Brian and Ronnie Fenton were waiting. I didn't see Dave give Brian a bill.

Ronnie told us someone was going to take pictures of us on the pitch: 'Get your new kit on and follow me.' We went through another set of doors. We popped our heads into the boardroom. Brian disliked the place and the people who sat around that polished table. His mentor had been Harry Storer, who had played cricket for Derbyshire and managed Derby County. Brian described him as 'a wise old owl of a man' who advised him: 'Don't ever forget; directors never say thank-you.' He had fallen out with the chairmen of Hartlepools* and Derby, who thought they were as responsible for the club's success as Brian Clough. What he liked

* Hartlepool United were known as 'Hartlepools' until 1968.

about the men who ran Nottingham Forest was how weak they were.

Then it was up some steps and into the directors' box; the inside of the ground was bloody huge.

'That's where you want to be,' he said, pointing to the pitch. 'Let's get going.' It took me 15 seconds longer than Azzy to hurdle the rows of seats and reach the pitch. I'd made the mistake of keeping my new Nikes on – Brian spotted it.

'Hey, Sunderland, get those bloody new shoes off! I didn't buy them so you can kick the toes out of them. Go and get changed and get back here sharpish.'

I mumbled under my breath, 'I got these ones for free, Brian. You bought me the adidas.' But I don't think he heard me.

When I got back, I had my Nicks on again. Aaron was running the full length of the pitch, taking himself on with a running commentary. He was knocking the ball about 20 yards in front of him, then haring after it. All I could hear was, 'Azzy, still Azzy, *still Azzy* … he shoooooots!'

He managed to scuff one in from about 30 yards. There was a cameraman there from a show on Tyne Tees Television called *Extra Time*, who filmed it. He told us he was going to make a video that he could send to our mam. If he knew we didn't have a video recorder at home, he might not have bothered.

I was on the right-hand side of Brian, Aaron on the left. We were playing little half-metre balls to each other and we looked like Charlies doing it that way. The television reporter, a bald man with a moustache called Roger Tames, was watching by the edge of the pitch.

I'd had enough: 'Hang on a minute, mister. This doesn't look very good and I want my mates to know I can play a bit as well. Can we spread out a bit?'

Brian laughed. The man from the telly told me not to worry as they could do magic with the video and make us look really good. *Fair enough*, I thought as Brian lashed one into the top corner from what seemed like 80 yards.

'Still got it, lads, still got it! Ooh bugger, me knee …'

Then some man from the local paper came to talk to us and we had some pictures taken of us in the dug-out. He asked how we had met Mr Clough and whether we were having a good time. Brian went off for a jog around the touchline and all I could hear in the background was 'that Kenny bloody Swain'.

Two days later, we were on the telly and, sure enough, Aaron and Brian's launchers were both there for all to see. Then there was me with goofy teeth, Zola Budd arms and skinny legs nearly falling over a two-yard pass. It was not exactly the magic I'd been expecting.

We were in the *Nottingham Evening Post*, the *Daily Star*, the *Sunderland Echo* and the *Newcastle Chronicle*. Most of the articles had little quotes, usually from Aaron as he was older.

'Aaron, 14, from Sunderland, said he was "having a great time and the nicest part was driving around in Mr Clough's beautiful Mercedes". Younger brother Craig [12 or 13, it varied] agrees.'

Why didn't they ask me? And if he thinks that was the nicest part, our Aaron is dafter than I thought.

This was about the time I started to suspect you shouldn't

trust everything you read in a newspaper. Azzy had only spoken to one man for about 15 seconds and all four of those stories had him saying something different.

After we finished, we were told we could watch the players train – we might catch the last 15 minutes. We went for a tour of the dressing rooms, saw the boot room and the laundry room and worked out how to get through the boiler room and out to the back of the Trent End.

When we arrived at the training ground, Brian was still watching. There were two moments that ensured we would be invited back, even just for comedy value.

There was our first Forest training session. Azzy took the ball and started taunting me with it on an empty training pitch. I was already angry about the disaster at AC Hunters: *I'm a much better player than him and he knows it – he's just bigger, faster and stronger than me.* So I launched myself at him but missed. He poked it past me, ran after the ball and slotted it into an empty net: 'Yes, one–nil.'

I took the ball to the centre circle, tried to take him on, lost it. He launched it 60 yards with a toe-poke. Two–nil. It was three, four and five before I got one back. Six and seven were scored in the same way before I got a strop on. If he wasn't even going to try to play properly …

It was then that Brian Rice, the ginger winger – though he might argue strawberry blond – who had been signed from Hibernian in the summer came over.

'What yer doing?'

We explained we were playing a game and it just turned into a one-a-side on a full-length pitch with full-sized goals.

'One of you might want to play in skins so you don't get confused,' he said.

Aaron promptly took his top off.

It finished 19–4 before I caught Azzy on his ankle. One little ankle tap. He was all pace and no heart, our Azzy.

We set off back to the ground and were given the referee's room to ourselves. We got two towels each, some Radox (oh my God!) and as much water as we could fit into the baths. Nobody had to boil a kettle and we didn't have to get out sharpish so our Dazzy could have a warm bath, too.

At home I always volunteered to go in first so I would have the cleanest water. This was my first 'belly button bath' – where the water came over your tummy – outside of Nana's house.

After we'd changed, Simon came into the ref's room. I remembered him saying he worked close to the ground. We were going with him to his shop and he'd drop us back at the ground so his dad could take us home.

'Forty-five minutes, lads. I'll be back for you. By the way, wash the bath. Someone's got to get in that after you two scruffy buggers.'

It was the way he said it that surprised me: he did it without raising his voice. In Sunderland, if people wanted us to do something, they shouted.

Soon we were back with Carole in Brian's office with sandwiches and a couple of bottles of orange juice each. Then a man called Irving Korn came in. He said he was on the board and he ran a company that made sweaters – 'Hang on a minute and I'll bring you a couple to have a look at, see if they fit.'

He brought 12 sweaters in see-through bags. There was black and cream with stripes, blue and black, cream and red with segments and squares. There were round necks, there were V-necks. The price tags were still on them. They were £19.99. Each.

'Have a look through them, lads. Let me know if they fit. You can have a present from Irving as well. I'll be back in 10 minutes.'

'Thanks very much, Mr Korn,' said Aaron.

'Please call me Uncle Irving, I'll be back in a while.'

There were 12 sweaters. We divvied them up between us and stuffed them in our bags.

The chairman was next to come in. 'Hello, lads. Here's 20 quid each.'

Mam had always taught us to turn down money – 'It's important to be polite,' she would say.

'No, thank you, Mr Roworth,' I said. 'We shouldn't take your money, thanks anyway.'

'Come on, lads, look, it's only 40 quid and I'll make it back like that.' He clicked his fingers. 'Buy your mum something nice when you get back home.'

Now Mam had always taught us *never* to turn down money twice – 'Don't be bloody idiots. If they offer twice, snap their hands off.'

There was a queue of people, popping in for what seemed like 15 seconds, giving us something and then buggering off.

Simon arrived, running late: 'Come on, lads. Let's get going.'

We passed Uncle Irving in the car park. He waved but in a weak, open-mouthed, rather shocked way. I found out later we were only supposed to have chosen one sweater each – we had taken the lot!

We were driving quickly through West Bridgford towards Central Avenue. Simon's still singing. He gets very loud to 'Gold' by Spandau Ballet and then there's some song about a young man taking his time by a lad called Junior.

'Brian said we were staying somewhere else tonight,' Azzy piped up, interrupting the singing. Rib-dig from me.

'No, you'll be staying with us for a few more nights. Maybe next time you can stay here, close to the ground.'

It made me smile to hear it.

Simon ran a newsagent's called Central News and there we met Stuart Dryden, the man who had been chairman of the club before Mr Roworth. Stuart was a man with a very posh accent and a very chiselled nose. He ran a post office in Ruddington, near Nottingham, but had to stop being chairman of Forest when it was discovered he had been cashing in dead people's pension books. If only he'd asked, I could have shown him how to do it properly.

We ripped up some boxes, filled a shelf up with crisps and put some cans in the fridge. I had a game of one-touch footie with Simon in the stockroom. He kept fouling me, then taking two touches and screaming, 'Play on!' I'm not surprised he won.

Nigel came in to pick up some ice lollies and magazines. He stayed for 20 minutes, spinning Simon out in a game of cricket before casually lobbing the ball into the bin from 10 yards with his right foot and leaving with his arms aloft. Then Brian came to take us home.

We went to Allestree to pick up a Chinese in Nigel's little Peugeot 209. The SportExtraPlusTurbo version. Whatever car it was, it was bloody fast! Nigel's music was different to Simon's. He played Bob Dylan and drove with his knees while playing air guitar. There was less mirror-checking, hair-flicking coolness.

'Fancy a game of table tennis, lads?' Nigel said when we got home.

Upstairs, up another level from the bedrooms, was the real jewel in the crown: the games room. There was table tennis, darts, pool, Subbuteo – with every imaginable accessory – and a multi-gym. It was also the treasure house of Brian's football career. On display was every pennant from the big European games, including the two European Cup finals.

It was full of programmes and pictures. There was a photograph of Bob Stokoe, wearing a trilby and a mac over a tracksuit. He was manager of Sunderland then and they had just beaten Leeds to win the 1973 FA Cup. He was 42 when the picture was taken but he looked ancient, his mouth open in a toothless grin.

When Elizabeth was younger, Brian would give her a choice if she'd been naughty: she could either eat soup with a fork or 'go upstairs and look at the picture of Bob'. It was a strange photograph for Brian to have in his house because he hated Bob. When he was lying on the pitch at Roker Park, covered in straw and snow, when he tore his knee ligaments, Stokoe had stood over him and told him to get up and stop cheating.

That was Boxing Day, 1962.

The thing with the Clough family was that they would open their arms to you, but if you offended them you would never be let back in. Not even if you won the FA Cup with Sunderland. Not even if you beat Leeds United, managed by Don Revie, in the final.

Nigel and Simon challenged us to a game of pool. I squinted a lot but still won. They were both impressed by the fact I could stun the white. Well done, Dad!

Next up was darts. Nigel was pretty handy and did round-the-board doubles faster than Azzy and me could do singles. All the while, the table tennis table was being cleared for the 'proper tournament'.

In the first game, Simon whitewashed me 11–0. According to him, it was 'the drubbing you know you deserve.' Nigel won the next game, against Aaron, 11–1. He wasn't even trying and Azzy's point came from a fluke that hit the edge of the table.

Everything was set up for the final between the brothers. I was sitting on the multi-gym with our Azzy throwing table tennis balls in the air for me to head. I was practising power heading while Simon won the table tennis tournament 26–24 after an astonishingly competitive match, which saw them taking shots from the back walls and the window sills.

Simon and Nigel had left. Azzy and I were about to go downstairs when I picked up the cue ball from the pool table with a mischievous *Hmmm, I wonder.*

'Azzy, get up, son!' I shout and loft the white cue ball into the air. In Nottingham, they still talk of a Don Masson header for Notts County that hit the bar with such force it swayed and rattled for what seemed like minutes afterwards – Azzy's header was in that league.

It took a second longer than I expected for him to realise and that gave me the head start I needed. I was off down the stairs like a rabbit, with Azzy screaming all kinds of blue murder.

One rugby tackle later and I'm pinned to the orange upstairs carpet. Mrs Clough, Brian, Simon, Nigel, Nigel's girlfriend Margaret and even Snoopy the dog were there to hear Aaron tell them what happened when they finally dragged him off me. They creased up with laughter. That was the second incident that guaranteed our comedy value and ensured we would be invited back.

'Right, lads,' said Brian after he had recovered. 'A cup of Horlicks and some toast, then off to bed and brush yer teeth. We've got Arsenal tomorrow and you've also got to pack to go home.'

Even though we knew that eventually we had to go back home, we went to bed on Friday night surrounded by lots of laughter, covered in lots of bruises and folding lots of new clothes into two new bags. Tomorrow was our first live game at the City Ground, the home of Brian Clough, the best bacon sandwich-maker England never had.

8.

'Brian Clough, We Want Something'

Brian woke us up on Saturday morning with a cup of tea and a promise of those bacon sandwiches. He told us to relax, take our time and put back all the T-shirts we'd nicked before coming down for breakfast. He'd be starting the sandwiches in 15 minutes.

I was a mess of emotions. I didn't know about Azzy but I'd become a convert to Nottingham Forest. I couldn't quite believe I'd be going to see them play Arsenal. We'd have to leave right on full time because our train was due to leave just before half five. Yet, I was also heartbroken we would be leaving a side of life I had not known existed.

We had seen more of it than we should have done. We were due to leave on Thursday but Mike Keeling, Brian's agent, had decided to buy us an open, white saver ticket. It was more expensive than a normal ticket but we could use it on any train going home and the return was valid for another three months.

'You never know, lads,' said Mike when he handed them over, 'maybe Brian will invite you down again or maybe he will let you stay a couple more days. It's been nice having you around.'

It was Mike who suggested we stay and watch the Arsenal game and winked at me and Azzy as he said it.

'Good idea, Mike. You can take them to the train station after the game and make sure the little buggers get on it,' said Brian. 'I'm starting to think we'll never get rid of them. Their mam must've thought she's won the pools.'

The delay meant I got not one but two pairs of glasses. Since we'd come down to Quarndon, Brian and Mrs Clough had noticed how I squinted at everything and how when I watched telly, I sat right in front of the screen – and I mean *right in front*.

When I began borrowing Brian's glasses, he told Ian 'Bomber' Bowyer, the club captain, to take me to an optician not far from the ground on Bridgford Road. He told Bomber to keep the bill and he would square up with him when we got back.

I tried on a couple of pairs of glasses but couldn't decide which ones I looked better in, so Ian bought me both – he reckoned I looked older in the gold ones but cleverer in the silver ones.

My eyes were so bad, they would have to use special, thicker lenses. Because the lenses were so expensive and I should look after them, he bought me two special cleaning cloths impregnated with a fluid that protected the glass. All in all, the two pairs of glasses cost £124.80.

Brian did his nut: 'I said get him some bins, Bomber, not buy the bloody shop! Blow me!'

We'd be leaving to go to the ground at half nine. We could either finish watching the *Abbott and Costello* film or have an hour in the cricket field. I was settling down with the remote and a Caramac when our Azzy came in, padded up, tapping a bat on the floor. We spent the next half hour in the nets at Quarndon Cricket Club with our Azzy bowling like Malcolm bloody Marshall.

It was the first time I'd picked up a proper cricket bat and not one made out of a fence or some other random bit of wood. Bloody hell, it was heavy! By the time I'd lifted it off the floor, our Azzy had knocked the metal stumps over. The ball struck me on the foot a couple of times.

I'd wanted to play with the tennis ball but Azzy was having none of it. He went all Bodyline on me, getting his revenge for the cue ball incident.

Brian came out to walk with us for a few minutes and told us that, if we worked hard and kept doing as our mam had told us, we'd grow up to be lovely lads.

Hmmmm ...

Mrs Clough had made up a packed lunch: sandwiches, yoghurts, fruit, crisps, pop, pork pies, chocolate biscuits. She was worried we might not eat at the game and didn't want us going the whole day without food.

Brian came with a couple of pound-and-a-half boxes of Milk Tray and some magazines for Mam: *Elle, House & Garden, Vogue* and *Marie Claire*. Although she would devour Catherine Cookson novels, Mam had never read a magazine in her life. They were also bloody heavy and the pages were a bit too smooth and shiny to use as toilet paper.

Brian had also put two £20 notes in an envelope, sealed it and told us it was for Mam to treat herself to something nice – 'She must be bloody exhausted having to look after you two shithouses all the time. And lads, I'll be ringing her to make sure she got it.'

Simon and Nigel had packed a bag of their old stuff for us too. Most of it was way too big for either of us, but Simon told us not to worry: 'You'll grow into them by the time you come back. If you keep training hard, next time you'll be as big as me and I'll be borrowing your stuff.'

You can have my chinos with pleasure, they just need a quick wash.

Everyone was cuddling us, telling us it had been lovely to see us and they hoped we'd stay in touch. Mrs Clough zipped up our Forest jackets. There was a little peck on the cheek, followed by a squeeze.

'Make sure you write us a letter and tell your mam she can be really proud – you've been little angels. It's been a real pleasure to have you, eeh, it really has. Take care and see you soon, pets.'

Already lip-wobbling before she spoke, I didn't want to leave. Brian then threatened not to take me anywhere unless I stopped crying, which only made it worse.

'Come on, son,' he said. 'There's no need to cry. Blow me, we'll see you again in no time at all. Now stop crying and get in the car, we've got work to do.'

We did have work to do: we were playing Arsenal at three o'clock. He had picked the team yesterday but wanted to get to the ground early to watch the young lads who were playing on a pitch just behind the training ground.

We already knew the way: we went through the boiler room, checked in on the laundry room and through the gates at the bottom of the Trent End. Down past the rowing club, underneath the little bridge, then through a gap in the fence and on to the training ground.

The players had started to arrive. We were both sat down in the dressing room with them, reading the programme. Peter Davenport, who had been one of the first in, said: 'Have you been out on to the pitch yet, lads? It's something totally different when the place is full. Come on, come out with us and you'll see.'

We walked out with him, Nigel, Stuart Pearce and Ian Butterworth, who had both been signed from Coventry. At first, I didn't like Stuart, especially when he took over as captain from Ian Bowyer – I loved Bomber to bits.

While we walked around with the players, me and Azzy kicked imaginary balls to each other while the lads waved to the crowd once their name was sung. Nobody knew who we were so they didn't sing our names but I didn't care. I clapped along with the rest of the players, hands above my head, smiling like an idiot in my padded Forest jacket and my new 'bins'.

Carole had promised there would be something on the scoreboard about us. We were told we could sit on the track close to the dug-out – we needed to leave sharpish and it was easier to make a getaway from there than from the stands. Brian also wanted to keep an eye on us to make sure we really did leave for the train.

The atmosphere was brilliant. When one of the Arsenal players handled the ball, the crowd went mad but there was no swearing. If that had been a Sunderland game, the place would have erupted. 'Fuckinhell, hawayman, fuckingrefereeman, that was fuckin' hand ball, yerfuckinbastardman' – all screamed at 100 miles an hour.

Here at the City Ground, there was just a really slow, calm 'Haaaaannnnd baaaaallllll!'

The ref didn't give it. Then came a chant of: 'Who's the bastard in the black?' It went on for a couple of verses before Brian got out of the dug-out and started shaking his fist at the crowd. Straight away, they stopped swearing.

I had read about this in one of the programmes in the games room. The fans had started swearing at games and Brian didn't like it. He had a sign painted with 'Gentlemen, no swearing please! Brian' and had it held up at a couple of home games.

When they stopped, he gave them a quick thumbs up and then sat back down in the dug-out before the whole crowd erupted in a single chant: 'Brian Clough, something, something' – clap, clap, clap, clap – 'Brian Clough, something, something' – clap, clap, clap, clap.

The 'something, something' bit – they sang it really quickly and it wasn't clear at all. I had no bloody idea what they were singing about, but still joined in with the clapping bit.

I asked Azzy what they were singing and he wasn't 100 per cent sure either. I said: 'They're singing "Brian Clough, we are sorry. Brian Clough, we are sorry" 'cos he's heard them swearing and they know he doesn't like it.'

Azzy told me not to be daft. He was fairly sure they were singing, 'Brian Clough, we want something, Brian Clough, we want something' because Forest hadn't won a trophy for ages.

Not since the European Cup in 1980 and that was five years ago.

As we walked off at half-time, I asked Des Walker, who was the substitute, if he knew what they were singing. I told him what we thought and he shook his head, laughed and told us to 'ask the Gaffer' when we got inside.

We arrived in the dressing room just as he was about to launch into his half-time team-talk.

'Brian, I think they're singing "Brian Clough, we are sorry," 'cos they're sorry for swearing, but our Azzy thinks they're singing "Brian Clough, we want something," 'cos you haven't won anything for a while – which one is it?'

'Weeeaaahhhh,' and he's off giggling. 'I'll give you "we want something", you little shithouses!'

The whole dressing room is in fits of laughter.

What? What had I said?

'Weeeaaahhhhh! "We want something"! Now go on, bugger off, get a cup of tea and get out of my sight. Wait outside, I've got work to do. Weeeaaaahhh …'

We returned back outside just in time to see the electronic scoreboard flash up: 'Welcome to the City Ground, Aaron and Craig' with a big Space Invader man bounding up and down.

By the way, Brian's team-talk worked. Forest won, 3–2, with Peter Davenport getting a hat-trick. I was totally hooked: football was all I wanted.

We went back to the dressing room to say our goodbyes. All the players were ruffling our hair, Brian was giving us both a kiss on the cheek, saying he would see us soon and telling Mike Keeling to make sure we caught the train.

'By the way, lads, they were singing "Brian Clough's red and white army". I'll bloody give you "Brian Clough, we want something". Weeeaaaahhh ...' and he's snort-laughing again. 'Lads, it's been lovely having you. Now go on, bugger off. Give yer mam a kiss and hey, lads, be good.'

Mike Keeling took us to Nottingham station in his Mercedes. He put us on the train and gave us another 10 quid each, making us promise we'd take a taxi once we reached Sunderland. Our bags were big and heavy and he didn't want us walking the streets at that time of night.

We ate the packed lunch before we passed Sheffield and most of the chocolate had gone by the time we arrived at Newcastle to change trains for Sunderland.

It was about a quarter to 10 by the time the white taxi pulled up outside 91 Shakespeare Street and we emerged, knackered and smiling. The neighbours' curtains began twitching and the first thing we saw was our dogs, Tippy and Kim, saying hello, tails wagging, eyes smiling. Mam came out to give us a hand with our bags.

'Eeh, lads, it's brilliant to see you both. Look at how much you've grown! Eeh, look at what you're wearing, you both look really handsome. Eeh, come here, I could squeeze you to death!'

We were sat down and emptied the bags to show Mam all our new stuff. Then we emptied our pockets. We gave her the envelope from Brian and the note from Mrs Clough. Mam started crying, she was so happy.

Dad was out. Joanne and Dazzy had gone Guying. We waited up until everyone had come back. We told the stories over and over again. We went to sleep happy. We had money, we had clothes, we had food and some incredible memories. We also had a promise from Brian he would see us both soon.

We had spent time with the most famous football manager in the country, been given the kind of gifts that would have taken many birthdays and Christmases to accumulate even if Mam and Dad could have afforded them. Darren and Joanne, meanwhile, would have existed on thin sandwiches, filled with crisps or jam. And so something else I always took back with me when I returned from Nottingham was a sense of guilt: I had seen another world, a world that Southwick was barely aware of.

When I was in Quarndon, I did ask Brian how much he earned.

'Yer cheeky bugger, I'll not be telling you that.'

Then he turned to me and said it was '£200 a week'. That made me ashamed. I knew Mam and Dad got £94 a week from the Nash. That was half of what Brian Clough earned and our house was not half as nice as his – it was infinitely worse.

I didn't know Brian was kidding. In 1985, his salary was £2,000 a week. You'd need to treble that to see what it would be worth now. That was before he had earned a single bonus payment, written a single newspaper column or made a television appearance.

Sunday was surreal with pretty much the whole of Southwick coming to see us. One or two, who had seen us on Tyne Tees or in the *Sunderland Echo* handed out a few gentle warnings on the lines of 'Don't get above yourselves, bonny lads'.

'You do know Brian Clough's only doing this for the publicity, don't you?' Or, 'It must have been lovely but don't get your hopes up too high that he'll have you back.'

Mostly, however, they were delighted for us. Thrilled.

We weren't going to stay big-headed for long so that night all of us went Guying and made a fortune. For the first time ever, we were better dressed than the Guy.

It was also the last time we ever went anywhere all together again.

9.

The Two Ronnies

Today I am 13, nearly 14. Nearly five-foot-tall and weigh about five stone. I've got a step-and-wedge haircut so my hair doesn't weigh as much as usual.

Thanks to all the training I'm doing when I go down to Brian's I'm fast developing into a bit of an all-round athlete. Running, boxing, football, cricket … it doesn't matter. As far as I'm concerned, I can do the lot.

We went to Quarndon for the Easter holidays, running around the City Ground as if we owned the place. Now we're back in Sunderland. We'd been home less than a week when Dad threw us out again and accidentally broke Mam's fingers by slamming the door on her. She nearly lost one of them and could not use her hand for three months. As always, she would search for reasons why this hadn't been Dad's fault.

We spent a couple of days in the Salvation Army hostel, in Hendon, by the docks. Then, Dad convinced Mam that it had only been the drink talking and so we crossed the river back to Southwick.

I'd made the mistake of telling Dad I liked Bronski Beat and mentioning that their hit 'Smalltown Boy' reminded me of me.

'You do know that's a song about him being a puff, don't you? Aah, that explains why you cry so much. You're a little puff!'

I had no idea. I just liked the fact Jimmy Somerville kept leaving home with everything he owned in a little black case.

After that, every time Bronski Beat or Soft Cell came on the radio, he'd call me a puff until I cried and then he'd call me a puff for crying. I couldn't win.

This time it's worse than usual. Our electricity has been cut off, we've no food and Mam and Dad are arguing about how we can get him some money so he can go out for a couple of beers. Anything we can sell, we do. Even the stuff he promises not to sell, like the Nottingham Forest pennants Brian let us borrow to make our bedroom look nicer.

Every time I come back, there is one less on the wall. One of my Nike T-shirts has gone and Dad's gone out to get drunk.

When we were last at the City Ground, Brian, Simon and Ronnie Fenton were talking to me in Ronnie's office about football. I mentioned I'd started playing for Seaburn United's under-14s at the Sunderland Greyhound Stadium.

I'd just gone along to watch a friend play but on the last game of the season they were short of a sub so the manager, Ronnie Murray, asked me to put a kit on just in case.

We played in the greenest kit imaginable: bright green shirts, shorts and socks. I'm sure it must have been a man's kit because the shorts kept falling down while I was warming up.

I was put on for the last five minutes when we were winning 9–2. Ronnie stuck me on the left wing, where I couldn't do any harm. Despite pretty much standing still with my hands down my balls trying to keep warm, I touched the ball twice in those five minutes; five minutes in which our opponents scored three times.

It was hardly worth getting drenched for, but it was the first time I'd made it on to the pitch in a proper eleven-a-side game so I was proud.

Sitting in his office, I told Clough: 'We won, 9–5, Brian. I did my bit.'

'Weeeaaaahhh!' and he's off laughing again. 'You could talk the bloody hind legs off a donkey, Sunderland! Weeeaaaahhh, I'll 9–5 you!'

Simon's winking and telling me, 'You're getting too good to be playing in stupid colours, son. Anyway, it's about time you started pulling on the Forest shirt. Let me have a think, I'll see if I can sort something out for the start of the season. No promises, mind.'

I asked if they wanted to watch me play. They'd have no bother getting in, they didn't even need tickets. Dad hadn't bothered to watch me once, not even when West Southwick had their cup final. I told Brian that Dad had said I was useless for getting beat and I'd run away, crying, and thrown my runners-up medal into a neighbour's garden.

'Blow me, your dad said that, did he? You should try to find that medal. You might never play in another final in your life and hey, sunshine, don't listen to him. Son, you're a good little player. You just need to remember to pass the ball a bit more often.

'If you're going to be a defender, like the skipper, it's not your job to try to beat everyone. Give the ball to the lad on the wing as soon as you can and let him do his job. Son, do your job first. Anything else is a bonus.

'Your old man has no idea about football, son, none at all. Now, I can't promise to come and watch a game. You know it's bloody miles away and I've got work to do, but I promise to send someone up to watch and maybe get you rag-tags a bit of coaching, if your manager Ronnie won't mind?'

'I'm sure he won't mind, Brian. In fact, I think he'd love some help.'

Then, he's pointing to Ronnie Fenton and telling him he's from that neck of the woods – Ronnie's from South Shields.

'You'll do it, Ronnie, won't you? You can have a couple of days with the family and go and watch Rigor train. It'll do you some good to do some proper coaching for once and you can have a change of scenery! It'll be the Two Ronnies reunited, you'll love it!'

Judging by the look on Ronnie Fenton's face I'm not sure he liked the idea as much as Brian, but that was that. According to Brian, it was settled.

Ronnie was trying his best to get out of it. He was busy and he'd been trying to avoid going back to Sunderland ever since he left the North-East. But he did write down the school where we trained – Monkwearmouth – and said he might just surprise us.

* * *

I loved the training sessions in the indoor sports hall at Monkwearmouth. For a couple of hours, it was just a bunch of lads and a ball. Some were better and some were worse, but in a way, we were all equal.

We were supposed to be there for a quarter to eight and, if we were late, sometimes Ronnie Murray wouldn't let us train. It was his way of letting us know he was the boss and there were rules. After dropping the money off, I had to run like an idiot just to make it for five-to-eight.

As I was walking into the hall, a man jumped out from around a corner.

'Hey, Rigor, come here, son. It's me!'

It was only Ronnie bloody Fenton who'd come from Nottingham to give us rag-tags a bit of coaching. He's in his gear, in one of the green sweaters Brian and the coaching staff always wore. He has a bag of balls and a whistle.

He said he had promised to surprise me – I'd been so surprised, I'd nearly pooed my pants.

'I don't want any fuss, son, so don't tell the kids who I am. I'll just talk to your boss, tell him I'm looking to do some coaching and ask if I can help out. You can introduce me as a pal of yours, but don't tell him where I'm from.'

We go in.

'Hi Ronnie, sorry I'm late. This is my mate, Ronnie. He's from err … South Shields and he's come to help you out, by doing a bit of coaching.'

'What do you mean, Craig? You're late, you're not training anyway, son, and who's he?', before turning to Ronnie Fenton: 'Have you coached before, pal?'

'I've done a little bit, aye. Nice to meet you, I just thought you might want a hand.'

We usually all trained together with the under-15s and under-14s split into four sides with a 'winner stays on' format. Once you won three games in a row, you had to come off so you wouldn't get too tired.

Now, because there were two Ronnies, my gaffer decided that Ronnie Fenton could train the under-15s and he'd take the under-14s.

Ronnie Fenton had to argue my case, so that I could train at all: 'It's my fault he was late, I kept him talking outside. Do you mind if he joins in?'

'Aye, go on then. Just this once, mind you. He knows the rules. If he's late, he's late and if he's late, he doesn't train.'

They pulled a big curtain down the middle of the sports hall and Ronnie Fenton, the assistant manager of double European Cup-winning Nottingham Forest, took the under-15s in a training session that was meant for me. Ronnie Murray, the manager of Seaburn United, took me and the under-14s. Before the session started, he asked Ronnie Fenton if he was sure he knew what he was doing.

Fenton began overseeing proper warm-up drills and stretches with his whistle in his mouth and balls in hand. Murray had us playing five-a-side like normal. It took him 15 minutes to clock that Ronnie Fenton might be a professional coach.

'You've done this before, haven't you?'

Ronnie Fenton finally admitted who he was, where he came from and why he was here. He said he didn't want any fuss but had come to watch me train. He told Ronnie not to tell the rest of the team he was from Nottingham Forest.

I've never tried so hard in a training session in all my life. I was running all over the place. There was no way Ronnie could go back and tell Brian that I couldn't play. I was brilliant, the session was brilliant, and I know that even though I hadn't said a word, the lads somehow found out that this bloke who had turned up had come from Nottingham Forest.

We finished just after 10 o'clock and Ronnie Fenton gave me a lift home. I didn't want him to see where I lived so I got him to drop me off at the semi-posh houses on Coldstream Avenue, a five-minute walk away from my house. I invited him in for a cup of tea, praying he would refuse.

'I can't come in, son. I'd love to, but I'm already late. I've got to drive back to Nottingham tonight. By the way, you were brilliant, son. Well done! I'm really glad I came and I'll tell the Gaffer we should keep an eye on you. If you keep working hard like that, you've half a chance.'

I beamed back at him.

'Oh, and I've got something for you off the Gaffer.'

He gave me an envelope and inside was 20 quid and a couple of return train tickets to Nottingham, valid for three months.

'The Gaffer says he'll see you both in a couple of weeks and there's a bag in the boot. It's from Simon. Something about the kit he promised you for the start of the season, it's that big blue Umbro bag. Do you need a hand carrying it in?'

It was a massive bag and I really could have done with a hand, but of course I wasn't outside my house, so I couldn't say yes.

'Thanks, Ronnie, it's alright, I'll manage. I'll ring Simon to say thanks. It's unbelievable that he remembered and really, thanks for coming, Ronnie. I'll never forget tonight, it was brilliant. See you soon.'

He was off with a wave. I waited until he was out of sight, pretending I was about to go through the gate. Then I picked up the bag and walked home. It took me twice as long and the bag was so heavy, I had strap marks on my shoulder when I got back.

Inside the bag was a brand-new pair of football boots, half a dozen of Nigel's sports T-shirts, layered across the full Nottingham Forest kit. It was the away kit: yellow with the thinnest blue stripes with 'Wrangler' on the front. They were numbered one to 11 and then 12 and 14.

In the bag were a couple of notes. One was from Brian, telling us to 'be good' and that he would see us soon. There was another from Simon, saying it was my kit, but if I wanted, I could lend it to Seaburn United to play in next season.

I put on the number nine shirt, the shorts and a pair of socks and gave Mam the 20 quid on condition there was no way we could sell something as special as this. To make sure they didn't, I told her Simon had only loaned the kit and I'd have to take it back.

That Sunday, I'd agreed to meet a mate at half eight so he could help me carry the kit bag to our match. It was going to be the first time I wore the Forest kit in a proper game and it would be a lovely surprise for Ronnie Murray and the lads, who had no idea I had a new kit for us.

We got to the greyhound stadium early and laid out the kit just like I'd seen them do at Forest on match days. I chose number three because I'd be playing left-back.

When Ronnie the coach came in at a quarter to 10, I told him I was going to lend him the full Forest kit as long as he promised to wash it and bring it back to my house every week. His face lit up, he gave me a cuddle and asked if he needed to give me any money for the loan of the kit. I hadn't thought about money – it would just be brilliant to play in the Nottingham Forest kit and to get rid of the shitty green stuff we'd been using.

It was 10 past 10 by the time all the other lads had shown up. Ronnie locked the dressing room door and made me promise not to tell the lads why. You should have seen the looks on their faces when they walked in and saw the kit hanging on the pegs.

Ronnie said he had an announcement to make, then he would name the team. He told them it had been Ronnie Fenton from Nottingham Forest who had come to do training the previous week and he'd brought a new kit for us all to play in. He said it was Brian Clough's idea and that Ronnie had wanted to do us all a favour because we were so good at training.

He didn't mention me at all, the sneaky Scottish twat.

After the excitement had worn down, he named the team. It took me until he reached number 12 to realise.

'Number 12 is young Craigy Bromfield. Craig, you'll be sub, son. You need to give Spam the number three shirt, he's playing left-back. I'll get you on in a wee while.'

Fucking hell, it's my kit! I've got you all playing in a kit from the twice champions of Europe and I'm not even in the fucking team. Fuck that!

I went into a right sulk, told Ronnie it was really unfair. Even Ronnie Fenton had said I'd been brilliant in training. It should be me who's starting.

He was having none of it: 'Don't worry, son. You'll get a game. I'll get you on in a wee while.'

I stood there for 70 minutes, freezing my balls off while everyone else was having a cracking time. Since I was the only sub, I didn't even have anyone to warm up with. Then, out of the corner of my eye, I saw something I'd never seen in my life: it was Dad coming to watch me play. All week I'd been telling him I'd be playing and I'd love it if he came to watch.

I ran across to Ronnie, begging him to put me on. I told him that was my dad standing on the touchline on the other side of the pitch, he needed to put me on.

Please, Ronnie.

And he did. He was as good as gold; he asked me where I wanted to play. I said left-back and he swapped me straight away for the last 20 minutes. It was plenty of time to show Dad I wasn't the soft shite he thought I was.

All I want to do is make him proud so I remember what Brian Clough told me – Brian Clough, the greatest manager the game has ever seen:

'If you're defending, it's not your job to take everyone on. Give the ball to the winger and let him do his job. Son, do your job. Get it and give it.'

That's exactly what I did. I got the ball and gave it to the winger. Every single time. I didn't lose it once. I did my job, I was brilliant. I kept looking out of the corner of my eye to make sure Dad was watching.

He had moved to the other side of the pitch and was standing next to Ronnie. They were talking and I saw them shake hands. Dad looked pleased.

While I was on the pitch we scored twice and didn't concede to win 5–2. My first proper game in a Forest shirt and I'd won. Dad had bothered to show up and I hadn't let him down. Ronnie gave me a hug and told me the next game I'd be starting for sure.

When I got showered and changed, Dad had already left and by the time I got home he'd gone out to the Transport Club for the afternoon. It was half six when he returned home. I told him he'd made me happy coming to watch and that I hoped he'd seen I could play alright.

'Play alright? You only got on for 20 minutes and every time you got the ball, you weren't even brave enough to do anything with it. Played alright? The little lad on the wing, now he played alright!'

Ten minutes later, there was a knock on the door. It was Ronnie Murray, bringing the kit back. He had told me he'd bring it on Tuesday, not tonight. Dad had told him to come round to discuss whether he could keep using the Forest kit. They agreed it made no sense for Ronnie to keep washing the kit and bringing it back. If he wanted to use it, he'd have to buy it off us.

Dad sold the Forest kit in front of my eyes. He asked for

50 quid for the lot and Ronnie ended up offering a pound for each shirt and a pound for each pair of shorts. He wanted the socks for free. It was an old kit, hardly worth any money really. In fact, Ronnie was doing Dad a favour even giving him 26 quid.

Dad agreed in a heartbeat. He sold the full Nottingham Forest kit, the one I made them promise they would never sell. He even threw in the Umbro bag for free.

I didn't wait to see Ronnie give him the money, I was already crying when I ran away. I stayed out until midnight and got a crack when I went home for making them worry about me. He had no choice, we needed the money for food. Did I want to see us starve?

'It's just a fucking football shirt.'

I will never forgive him for this. Not ever.

The next week, Ronnie kept his promise. I started at left-back for the under-14s. Unfortunately, he'd given the Forest kit to the under-15s and we were back to playing in the green shite.

The only competitive game I'd ever played in the Nottingham Forest kit and I got to wear the number 12. The only time I wore it, I got to be Ian fucking Wallace.

It's a Monday and I'm nearly 14. Azzy is ready to go to the Territorial Army training camp. He leaves tomorrow morning.

Wo-oh-oh, he's in the army now.

I'm on Witherwack Fields, divided into football pitches, just about to go into the community centre to play some pool when a kid called Wayne Litster comes running up like a maniac.

'Howay, Bronda man. *Cloughie's at yours!*'

'Fuck off, Wayne. I don't need it today, I've had enough.'

'Nah, Bronda man, I'm not funning. He's at yours. I just went past and saw his car outside your house. He's got a gold Merc, right? I'm telling ya, he's there! Hurry up and get home ...'

I started running before I had a chance to thank Wayne. I was really excited, remembering Brian had said he couldn't come for tea because it was too far. But he *had* said: 'Maybe one day, you never know.'

He couldn't have been here with the team. There was no chance of them playing Sunderland now. They had already been relegated once and now they were heading for the Third Division under Lawrie McMenemy. He was being paid £200,000 a year, which was more than Brian, more than any manager in the Football League. When the fans found out, his Mercedes was vandalised.

I used to ring Brian from time to time. Whenever he or Mrs Clough answered the phone they would always say the number: 'Hello, 0332 ...' But I hadn't rung him for at least a week and I thought this might be his way of surprising me.

I was running home fast and I was just passing the 104 bus stop a couple of minutes from home when it hit me.

Our house is a shithole. We've no ornaments on the wall any more. The kitchen wallpaper is peeling off. The carpet in the living room has burns from the sea coal and Tippy's just had six puppies, who are living on old sheets of newspaper by the back door.

Dad had sold the two Nottingham Forest jackets when we had run out of meter money and I was sure Brian would ask to see me in one.

What will he think when he sees the house? Why did I even invite him in the first place?

I wanted to see him but I didn't want him to see us. In the end, I decided I had no choice: I had to face him. I turned into our street and saw the car outside.

It was a Mercedes. He must have been doing well because it was brand new, bigger and golder. The seats were a different colour too.

I went in through the back door, rushed into the living room and there was … *not* Brian Clough sitting on our sofa with my mam giving someone else a cup of tea.

'Hello, son,' Mum said. 'You're a bit late. Say hello to Jamal. He's come to talk to your dad.'

The lads in the squares had seen a Mercedes parked outside and no one from Southwick knew anyone with a Mercedes so it had to be Brian Clough. It didn't matter how many times I told them but that day, according to the whole of Southwick, Brian Clough came for tea.

Brian Clough is white, he wears a green sweater and manages Nottingham Forest via Brighton, Leeds, Derby, Hartlepool, Sunderland and Middlesbrough.

Jamal is from Lebanon. He's dark-skinned, smells of too much aftershave and is wearing more jewellery than Big Ron Atkinson.

Luckily for me, when Jamal left our house it was late and already dark outside. He'd waited three hours for Dad but he had decided to go for a pint after work. By the time he returned, Jamal had left.

Apparently, he'd been talking to a mate of his who knew someone who wanted to set up as a dealer. Dad was going to help him. This was Dad's chance to stop being a petty criminal, get himself sorted and start becoming a major one.

10.

Busted

Dad was in and out of prison all his life. In the words spoken to Ronnie Barker before every episode of *Porridge*, he was 'a habitual criminal who accepts arrest as an occupational hazard'.

For Dad, prison was a kind of finishing school. Some of the things they taught him were good, like how to make models from matchsticks. Others, such as how to forge a giro, were not. Every time Dad went to prison, he came back with another money-making scheme, which he assured us was foolproof. In his own mind he was Lex Luthor, a brilliant criminal mind who was only one idea away from being a millionaire.

The latest lesson had been how to turn 10-pence pieces into 50-pence pieces by wrapping the edges in black 'leccy tape'. Then, when they went in a fruit machine or a cigarette vending machine, they would weigh the same as a 50p.

It meant you could get 10 Benson & Hedges for 10 pence instead of 49p. Dad would then send us to stand outside pubs and sell them for a profit.

He'd stack five 10-pence pieces in a column, wrap a little bit of electrician's tape around the stack and then cut and trim them so that the tape didn't overlap any of the edges. Then he'd cut the 10ps out individually. Doing that somehow turned them into 50-pence pieces.

As soon as I came back with the tape, we sat in the kitchen, talking while he worked. As he did with any job, he started by rolling a joint. Within two minutes, he'd be trimming the edges of the 10-pence coins with a Stanley knife.

I told him I was tired of getting my head kicked in every time I went to the shops. He said he would teach me how to box.

Dad had been a semi-professional boxer, when his time wasn't occupied by painting and decorating, sign-writing, rugby or crime. He'd even won a couple of fights but had been harshly forced to retire in his prime for kicking someone in the balls. It wasn't his fault, the other lad had kept hitting him below the belt. The referee hadn't seen it so he had no choice but to take matters into his own hands.

Sometimes, he had to fight for real. There had been a big National Front presence in Southwick and he wouldn't keep his head down about it. Once, when we came back from a day trip to Alnwick Castle in Northumberland, our house had 'Go Home, Nigger' and National Front slogans daubed on the walls. Inside, it had been smashed up. If there was anything of value, it had gone. Otherwise, it had been shredded.

For weeks afterwards, one of the hard lads from Southwick or beyond would turn up on our drive, asking for a fight. They'd get one. Usually they lost. It culminated with a knock on the door. Joanne, who was now 15, opened it and had her leg fractured by a baseball bat. Dad responded by stealing a car and running over the assailant. Dad went to prison, the guy with the baseball bat did not. Dad was very big on being able to defend yourself: 'I'll train you, son,' he told me. 'I'll teach you everything I know and by the time I'm finished, you'll be tough as nails.'

Before he could change his mind, I'm off upstairs. Two minutes later, I'm back, humming the *Rocky* theme, looking like Sugar Ray Leonard in Mam's dressing gown with two towels wrapped around my fists. I'm doing the Ali shuffle on the carpet with Dad laughing his head off.

Because I was a southpaw and led with my left hand, he needed to teach me how to stand properly. He'd teach me how to jab and move. He taught me the uppercut, the left hook, the double jab and how to guard my face. All that took him less than three minutes. I must be a natural.

'Have you got all that, son? Are you ready for a couple of rounds?'

Ding, ding. Round One.

He's hunched on his knees to make it a fair fight. There's about five seconds of dancing and shuffling and then I go for it.

I'm trying the double jab but he keeps moving his head. I jab and move but he keeps catching me with a sly left hook I don't see coming. I'm trying to guard my face and he keeps punching me in the stomach. I guard my stomach and the sneaky bastard hits me in the face.

He catches me once too often with his backhand and that was it. I start blubbing and sit in the corner. I wouldn't be getting ready for round two.

'Fuck this, if all you're going to do is cry every time I hit you, there's no point me teaching you! I'm barely touching you.'

I was crying more because of the shock of seeing one of his shovel hands come towards me like a train with the gold ring dazzling my eyes as I squinted and tried, unsuccessfully, to 'duck and weave'.

It was having the Nottingham Forest kit and the adidas Tango ball, rather than being able to 'duck and weave' that ensured I stopped being bullied. The fact that they had seen me with Brian Clough at the Christmas game at Roker Park also started turning enemies into friends. I was actually popular. For the first time in my life, I felt part of Southwick.

We were playing seven-a-side; Shakey Street versus The Squares. Kick-off 6.30 p.m.

I'd kitted the Shakespeare Street boys out in the Forest shirts. I'd picked the number nine and everyone else could choose their favourite. We needed the shirts back for Sunday because Ronnie had arranged a friendly with Wickham but Mam had promised to wash them. We looked like a proper team.

After two and a half hours of battling, kicking, laughing and the occasional break in play to let a bus through, the teams were level at 19–all. The best two players from each team got together and agreed the next goal would win.

I was in goal because it was my turn. You had to stay in nets until you let one in. If I let one in now, we would lose the game. Suddenly I turned into Jim 'The Cat' Montgomery, hero of the 1973 FA Cup final against Leeds.

Volleys would be tipped full-length round the post. I would dive bravely at the feet of anyone who came onto the footpath – our equivalent of the six-yard box. Crosses would be caught and thrown downfield to launch wave upon wave of counter-attacks.

Shakey Street were on one of those counter-attacking waves when I got a little cocky. I'd just dived full-length to save a 30-yard volley that was flying in off a lamppost.

I quickly bowled the ball overarm to launch a counter-attack and safe in the knowledge it was job done, I turned around to take a suck of my sherbet double lolly that I'd left on the wall behind me. I turned around again to see the ball coming rocket-like straight at my face. It sent the double lolly flying, knocked off my glasses and cut my top lip – I didn't even see who did it.

Both sets of players were laughing while I could feel tears welling and my bottom lip going. Perhaps because of the pain, perhaps because of the embarrassment and perhaps because it was my last friggin' lolly, I ran home crying.

Dad would know what to do.

'Don't come crying to me. Get back out there, find out who did it and fight them. Go on, get out and don't come back until you've hit him back and remember what I taught you: jab and move, jab and move.'

Oh well, here goes ...

The lad whose shot had hit me was Graeme Swalwell. He was the older brother of Peter Swalwell, my mate from school who was much harder than me. Graeme was older and harder than Peter. But, how hard can he be, really? Especially, if I remember to jab and move.

'Come on then, Graeme you bastard, you were laughing at me, were you? Fuck it! Let's go, I've had enough.'

'Don't be daft, Bromfield, man, it was an accident! I didn't mean it and it's just a game of football, son. I don't want to fight you.'

I didn't care whether he wanted to fight or not, I didn't even care that everyone else was telling me not to be stupid and that he'd kill me.

'Fuck you and fuck that, we're fighting, whether you want to or not! Come on, let's go.'

I square up to him, remembering what Dad's told me. I've got a secret weapon, I'm a southpaw. He won't be used to my unorthodox style, so I'm fancying my chances strongly.

I'm commentating on my own fight, in my own mind:

Jab, move. Left hook, duck. Uppercut and yes! He's down, incredible, and it's all over with three punches inside 15 seconds.

Fucking hell! That was much faster and easier than I'd ever imagined.

By the time I'd picked myself off the floor, he had busted my nose, cut my bottom lip and knocked my glasses off again. Once more, I ran home crying but this time it wasn't because of the double lolly, I was in bloody agony. Five minutes later, Graeme knocked at the door to say sorry. He said he hadn't wanted to hit me but I'd gone for him so he had no choice. He'd bought me a double lolly and asked me to come out and finish the game. Apparently, it wasn't the same without me.

I agreed on condition they let me play out. Thirty seconds later, I went on the maziest of mazy dribbles, beating everyone at least twice before slotting the ball into the bottom corner past the despairing dive of Tony Irwin, who definitely didn't let it in on purpose so I could feel better about myself.

I'd earned the respect of everyone except Dad.

'Well, you stupid little bastard! You didn't tell me the lad was twice the size of you. You had no chance, what were you thinking? There's a time for fighting and a time for walking away.'

Joints had always got Dad into trouble. Once, he'd stolen a leg of lamb from Fine Fare on The Green. It meant he had broken his probation and was given six months by the judge, the one he always seemed to get – the one who did not attempt to disguise her contempt for him.

Six months for stealing a joint of meat was something out of Dickens.

Now Dad was starting a business with joints of another variety and once he started selling wacky baccy on a small scale our house was never empty. There were lads from across the river at Pallion and Tunstall Valley, from Hendon and Ford Estate. From down the coast at Seaham Harbour. There were very few from our side of the river because Dad had a rule he wouldn't smoke with anyone from Southwick and would never smoke with anyone who was under 21.

I never saw him check ID when they came through the door but I trusted Dad was an honourable criminal.

Dad's 'friends' would come round, he'd knock one up, they'd smoke it together and then he would shake their hand in a weird way. They would give him £7.50, £14.50 or £28 and he would slyly exchange that for a bit of brown stuff that smelt like shit wrapped in clingfilm. They had to burn and melt it and put it into a cigarette to smoke. It made them laugh a lot and gave them the munchies.

He wasn't a big dealer but some people came for half ounces at £55 and ounces he sold for a hundred quid. Some days we would have six or seven visitors and Dad could never be rude. He had to let them try before they'd buy and it would be impolite not to have a toke himself.

Another rule was that if the customers skinned up before they bought, they skinned up before they left. That meant everyone smoked a minimum of two joints and you could taste and smell the marijuana in the atmosphere pretty much the whole time.

It also meant that, when he wasn't working, Dad would be zonked from half 10 in the morning until he went to bed, although he would pass the day in a pretty relaxed mood. This was partly from the marijuana and partly in the knowledge we had a steady source of income.

There were two little brass bellows hanging on the back wall. We used one to keep the money in and the other for the deals, individually wrapped in little clingfilm pieces.

I used to watch him cutting and weighing and wrapping, making sure all the deals were on the border of being fair. He'd bought from dealers in the past himself and used to get really pissed off if they gave him a dodgy wrap. It got to the stage where I knew as soon as I picked up a deal whether it was right or not – I could weigh it by memory.

Dad had a job working for the Little Sisters of the Poor, the nuns' house off Chester Road. The nuns made their own bread and cakes and every Friday afternoon one of us would come to meet him and he would bring a big bag of teacakes for toasting.

He had also taken some wood from the nuns. They didn't need it apparently and, even if they did, Sister Joan would never know he'd taken it. Sister Joan must have been a better detective than Dad realised because one day, and without warning, he stopped working for the Little Sisters of the Poor.

Dad used the wood to line the walls of the front room. Beautifully sanded, polished and stained, it made it seem like we lived in a log cabin. He had also built a bar in the front room. It had bottles of gin, rum, vodka and whisky, all with proper optics. Called Gilly's Bar, after Mam, he had put a cover of rich cream velvet on it.

He had used different coloured bricks to build a fireplace with the mantelpiece carved from more wood acquired from the Little Sisters of the Poor. There was a gold and brown velvet settee. Mam had a good eye for decorating and had decided on an African theme on the walls. There were pictures of zebras in silhouette. There were masks, a couple of African shields and stacks of brass – on every possible square foot of wall there would be something.

Dad had turned the shoe and junk cupboard into a computer room for our Dazzy, who now spent most of his days writing computer games.

About eight o'clock one Saturday morning, I was off to get Dad's paper. Usually, at eight o'clock on a Saturday, Southwick's pretty empty but this morning, as soon as I stepped outside, I had this weird feeling.

It was almost like things were moving in slow motion. The milkman was on the corner but he had a new float I hadn't seen before. Someone was cutting the neighbours' bushes but it wasn't anyone I knew. The Public Works Department van was parked at the top of the street but the men in it weren't working.

There had never been so many people out so early on a Saturday before: something wasn't right. I ran to the top of the road, as I always did, but I couldn't help thinking these men shouldn't be there.

I doubled back, climbed over the neighbour's fence and ran through our back door. An instinct kicked in. I took the nearly-empty bellows off the wall, picked up the velvet bag with the scales in them and hid them behind the fence at the top of the back garden.

I was going upstairs to tell Mam what I'd seen when three shadows came up the garden path. They smashed the door down with a sledgehammer, shouting as they pushed me through the sitting-room door and ran up the stairs.

'Police! Police! You're busted, Gerry. We know you're here.'

Then there's shouting and screaming, pushing and swearing.

Mam's the first one out of the bedroom, wearing her nightie. As soon as she turns the corner, one of the bizzies has her pinned to the stairs, one hand in her face, the other pushing her arms into her back to put the handcuffs on.

I'm crying at the bottom of the stairs: 'Hey, that's my mam! Leave her alone!'

'Stay out of it, son. It's not your mam we want, it's the black bastard we're after. Where is he?'

Our Azzy came bounding round the corner and did the best thing I definitely didn't see in my life up until now. He might just have cracked the bizzy who was holding Mam so hard, he fell back down the stairs and bust his nose. Nobody saw it. Definitely not me. I was doing just what the policeman had told me. Staying out of it.

Fucking get in, Azzy! Get in, son!

The whole house was going crazy. They were turning things upside down, throwing things out of cupboards on to the floor and asking our Joanne where Dad keeps the drugs.

'I don't know what you're talking about, mister.'

They brought Dad in back through the front door, which was weird because he'd been fast asleep in bed when I'd left to get his paper. He had his vest on but no trousers. He never wore underpants, ever. He was kicking out at them while they were dragging him back into the house with his balls hanging out.

It was interesting how quickly the neighbours came out to look at Dad being carried by four bizzies. They weren't so fucking fast to show themselves when he threw Mam out the window.

Apparently, he'd climbed out of the back-bedroom window when he heard the door cave in. They'd caught him trying to climb over the fence.

If you'd gone the other way, you might have escaped.

I could see Mam and Dad making sly eyes at the wall, looking for the bellows. The police hadn't found any marijuana, just a few crumbs on the floor. They knew he was selling it, they knew he was dealing. So where was his stuff? They didn't think to look at the fence at the back, they hadn't got anything worth finding.

Dad was only arrested for possession. They had scraped enough little pieces from the carpet to make a joint; that was more than enough. Mam was cautioned for resisting arrest. No one had seen too much resisting but it was either that or they took our Azzy to a young offenders' home for assaulting a copper.

None of the other bizzies had seen him do it. Only the one he hit had seen something flying towards him. But he was 99.9 per cent sure it was Azzy so Mam took the blame.

'It was me who punched him and he fell down. What's it like, big man, getting knocked over by a woman?'

'Come on, Gillian. Don't push your luck or you'll be coming with us and the kids will have to find someone else to look after them again.'

They took Dad away. Mam bit her tongue and got ready to go to the solicitors'. Dad was put on bail at £25 – I sold my racing bike to get him out early.

When he came home, he was really proud of me for hiding the empty bellows and I didn't really need the bike anyway.

11.

The Orient Express

One by one, they are leaving. In the summer Darren escaped Southwick to do social studies at the University of Ulster. He got two As and a B at A-level and could have gone to Keele University in Staffordshire.

Northern Ireland wasn't an obvious place to study in 1987. Two policemen and a prison officer, studying psychology, had been killed by the IRA at the university in March. In November, a further 74 would be killed or injured when a Remembrance Day parade was bombed in Enniskillen. It was, however, a long way from home and, to our Dazzy, that was a distinct advantage: Northern Ireland, even in flames, represented a way out of Sunderland.

Dazzy had long stopped speaking to Dad and had even started punching him back when he threatened him. Before he left for Stranraer to catch the ferry to Belfast, the tension in the house was unbearable. We were all praying they would make peace. Then, just as he was about to go, he turned and hugged Dad, who beamed the kind of smile I had hardly ever seen from him. There were tears from us all. He left with £40 in his pocket – £7.50 were from me. Joanne and I had found a bus pass with £15 on a Waltzer at the fair. I gave him my half.

Azzy, too, found a way out of Southwick, the route so many boys from the North-East have taken: the British army.

I feel more alone and more anxious. I never felt safe in my own home; I never knew when everything might explode. The people who were supposed to love you the most were always the ones who caused you the most pain.

I would stay off school to wait for Bob the postman to deliver the giro. I would go out to meet him because our dog, Kim, had a thing for his laces. Then I would go to the post office to cash it and bring the money back.

This time, Bob tapped his cap and said: 'Morning, hinny, nothing for you today.'

I thought about making a mad dash for it but knew in the end I had to tell Mam.

'It's okay, it's okay.' She kept repeating it; fast, slow, loudly, quietly. 'It's fucking okay. In fact, it's wonderful, lovely, absolutely brilliant.'

Phew, thank God for that. For a second, I thought she might be angry.

Then, suddenly Mam's tongue came out. That was never good news for anyone. 'It's your fucking fault. I told you to watch out for him, didn't I?'

Crack.

'Come here!' Crack. 'Don't flinch at me!' Crack. 'Stop fucking crying! I haven't even touched you. Now get up them fucking stairs, get your school uniform on and get out of my fucking sight!'

I was also worried where I stood with the Cloughs. Whenever we went to Quarndon, I always had the impression that Brian and Mrs Clough thought I was okay but they really liked Azzy. He smiled so easily, he did jobs around the house *without being asked*. That was the kind of thing Brian loved. They called me 'Rigor Mortis' because I just sat around.

Now that Azzy was gone, would they really want just me?

I resolved to stay in touch with the Cloughs by calling them from a phone box. Usually, I would reverse the charges. The operator would think I was kidding when I said: 'I want to make a reverse charge call to Brian Clough, please.'

'Yeah, right. You do know we can get the police on to you for this, don't you?'

'Please, missus, I'm not kidding. How would I have his number if I didn't know him?'

I'd hear a loud, exaggerated tut, then I'd hear silence, then Mrs Clough's voice, 'Yes, that's fine, thanks,' and then the operator would connect me.

It's January 1988. I had a 50p from Dad for running a drugs-related errand. It was a forged 50p but it would still work in a cigarette machine or a phone box. I could make the call.

'Hello, Mrs Clough.'

'Hello, pet.' She was shocked I hadn't reversed the charges. 'Don't be spending your money ringing us, pet. I've said before that it's okay to reverse the charges.'

Then some nice chat about school and about how she loved the letter we'd sent and to say hello to Mam and to ask how Aaron is getting on.

'What does he want? I'm paying for this bloody call, you know,' I heard him shouting over Mrs Clough's shoulder.

Aaaahhh, no, you're not, Brian – I'm paying for this one.

'Hello, son! I'm only kidding. When are you coming to see us?'

'Brian's asking when you're coming down next. It'll be lovely to see you again.'

Then he's on the phone.

'Hello, Brian. What do you think about me coming to the Cup game at Orient next week?'

'I think it's a bloody stupid idea, son. Wooaaaah, I think it's too daft to laugh at! You have to come past our place to get there. Why don't you save your coppers and come to a home game in a month or two? You can stay at ours for a couple of days, just make sure it's school holidays.'

A month or two was far too long and there was something really special about the FA Cup. I loved football now and knew he had never won the Cup. I wanted to do my bit. I didn't know how I was getting there but I knew I was going. I also thought that if Leyton Orient was a difficult place to get to, going on my own would prove my loyalty.

We ended up agreeing I shouldn't go, but if I was determined to be there, then yes, of course, I should say hello before the game.

Christmas has just been and Mam told me there was absolutely no chance because she was still paying off Compass, who sold store vouchers on credit, for the presents. The train ticket was really expensive and she was really sorry, but we just didn't have any money.

It's Sunday afternoon, about half five. *Bonanza* has finished and because the telly's on a meter and we want to watch a film tonight, we are all listening to Metro Radio.

I'm sing-shouting along to Elton John, *What've I got to do to make you love me?*

I'm looking at Mam, smiling my head off, trying to give her the sad eyes.

'Bugger off, Craigy. We can't, son, we just can't. Sorry, love.'

Thanks a lot, Elton! Some help you were.

Elton is tailing off. Then I hear a drum.

Bum-bum-bum.

'Non-stop Clipper, here it comes …'

Then an even more dramatic bum-bum-bum-bum-bum. It was like the *Jaws* music, only better.

'Non-stop Clipper, here it comes …'

Then the voice-over: 'From Newcastle to London in five hours, *non-stop*, and with tickets from just £12.50 for adults and £8 for students, children and OAPs, there's never been a better time to treat the whole family to a visit to the capital.'

I stood up, punching the air with both hands.

'I heard, son. I heard! If you can get to London *and* back for 10 pound, then I promise you I'll get you the money, son. I promise.'

I stayed off school on the Monday so I could go to the ticket office. I'd have to go to the office near the leisure centre and then pay £8.50 for a Clipper Tripper – I just needed to make sure I came back on the same day.

The coach left from Jesmond Street in Newcastle at seven in the morning and arrived in London at 12 o'clock. According to the man selling me the ticket, it would give me more than enough time to get to Brisbane Road, where Orient played, even if I had to ask directions every five minutes.

'In that case, the seven o'clock one is perfect, mister. I haven't got any money now, but can I reserve a seat and come back and pay on Friday?'

'Nah, no, noooo, not a prayer.' *Once would have been enough.* 'Not a chance in hell. We sell them on a first come, first served basis, sunshine. No money, no ticket. No ticket, no reserved seat. You'll just have to take your chances.'

'How often do you sell out?'

'There's never been a bus run with an empty seat since we started.'

'Listen, mister, I'm going to meet Brian Clough and Nottingham Forest. I'm going to watch them play in the FA Cup. I've got to get there. Isn't there anything you can do?'

I told him the story right from Guy night. He was fascinated, he even asked me if I wanted a cup of tea while I was talking.

'Nah, no way, you're having me on. How, lads!' he called to his colleagues. 'Come and listen to this little bugger.'

I found out really early that there are times when people will go out of their way to help. Especially when you tell them *the Brian Clough story.* Kenny Swain? Nobody really knew who he was. It was just a nice story until Brian's name pops up, then it gets special.

The man at the ticket office paid for the ticket himself, put my name next to it and told me that, as long as I was back here by 12 on the Friday, he would keep it for me.

By Thursday night, Mam had managed to scrape together £7. We were £3.50 short of being able to get me to Newcastle and then to London and have enough left over for a can of pop and a packet of crisps. She was really sorry but we had run out of people to ask. I was crying because I thought I was going to miss the trip.

Mam got up and put on her jacket. It was half nine. I didn't ask where she was going, I was so angry because she had promised and now she was going to let me down. I couldn't even look at her.

She returned an hour later with another £7.50. She had borrowed the money from the neighbours. She kept £1.49 for four cans of Ace lager, which was cheap because it was brewed up the road in Gateshead. The rest she gave to me.

I had nearly £13. I was loaded and on my way. Mam had dragged herself around the streets of Southwick for the money. She had no tabs, there was no food in the house and she had given me 13 quid to go to a poxy football match.

Non-stop Clipper, here I come!

To get to Newcastle for seven o'clock in the morning, I had to be on the 5 a.m. miners' welfare bus from The Green to town and then on the 20 past five bus from Sunderland to Newcastle. I wanted to make sure I wasn't running around at the last minute so I figured it out backwards. It would take me 10 minutes to get to The Green. Fifteen minutes to wash. Ten minutes to do my hair. Half an hour to get ready – and I wanted to be on The Green 10 minutes before the bus is due so I wouldn't miss it.

Jesus H. Christ! I need to get up about two o'clock in the morning just to be sure. It's already 11 p.m.

'Mam, I'm not going to bed. I'll sleep on the bus on the way down to London instead. I'm too excited to sleep and there's really no point, I've got to be up in a couple of hours anyway.'

'Go to bed, son. I know you're excited, but go to bed and get some sleep. You want to be fresh for the game tomorrow, don't you?'

'I won't be able to sleep, Mam. I'll listen to Metro. Can I stay up, Mam? Please? It's five hours' sleep on the bus, Mam. What else will I do?'

It's about half three. It's pitch black outside and I'm listening to *Alan Robson's Night Owls* on Metro Radio. I'm fresh as a daisy and raring to go. I can leave here at half four, which is an hour away. I'm an hour away from the biggest adventure of my life.

I start sing-humming along to 'Nikita'. I have always loved Elton John and this one was the start of my fascination with foreign girls. It was playing when I met Stephanie, who was in Sunderland on an exchange visit. She was French rather than Russian but she had brown hair, brown eyes and creamy skin. It was enough to make me interrupt my meal and run out of the Wimpy Bar to ask for her phone number.

That was as far as the relationship went. I never dialled the number that began 0033 because we didn't have a phone but I thought about Stephanie a lot and 'Nikita' was our song.

I lean back and relax. As the song plays, I close my eyes and see images of Paris. The Eiffel Tower square on the horizon, the little 2CVs chugging up the Champs-

Elysées, which was probably where Stephanie lived. Me and Stephanie drinking one of those milky, frothy coffees on a terrace:

Oh Nikita you will never know, anything about my
  home ...

What seems like three minutes later, I'm up and stretching my legs, wiping some saliva from the side of my mouth. It's still dark, but suddenly, I feel uneasy.

'Message in a Bottle' by The Police is on the radio. Sting is sending out his SOSs and I've no bloody idea what time it is. I need somebody on the radio to read out the time.

Hurry up with those fucking messages, Sting. You're another one who's from round here. You might be going on the Bryan Ferry list unless you get the fuck off the radio.

I'm singing along, trying to get him to finish faster:

I hope that no one gets your, I hope that no one gets your,
  message in a bottle, yeah.

I thought it had finished three times before it did. Then some overly cheerful bloke: 'Good morning, blah blah blah. It's just coming up to 20 past six and it's gonna be a cold one. Snuggle up, get a cup of tea and some toast. Curl back into bed and listen to ...'

I'm still listening, even though I know he's said it's 20 past six. I did what I usually did in moments like these: I ran upstairs, shouting for Mam.

'Mam, I've slept in! It's 20 past six! I'm supposed to be in Newcastle in 40 minutes. Maaam, *help!*'

'Well, you're a bloody little idiot! There's nothing you can do. It would take a jet to get to Newcastle for seven. Sorry, son, but you've missed the bus. You need to ask them to give you the money back.'

That helped a lot. Thanks, Mam.

I told her I was going to run to London and I'd be back tomorrow. I was only half joking. I jumped down the stairs and headed for the top of Beaumont Street – it must be on the way to London.

I ran round the block, crying when I came to my senses.

The game kicked off at three o'clock. Brisbane Road is in London. The 10 a.m. Clipper gets into London – Vauxhall Bridge Road – at three o'clock. How far away can Leyton Orient possibly be? If I ran all the way, I might miss a bit of the game but at least I would be there.

I went home, told Mam my plan, telling her the Clipper got in at half two rather than three, giving me 30 minutes to get to the ground.

'If you think you can get there on time for the game, son, you go for it. Be careful and have a lovely day. Say hello to Mr Clough from me. Ta-ra, sweetheart. Good luck!'

Apart from a brief stop to get two ounces of sarsaparilla tablets, I ran all the way. Even when I was on the bus to Newcastle, in my mind I was running. I got eight sarsaparilla tablets because I could easily make them last five hours. I'd have one every half hour and it would take seven and a half minutes to suck the flavour off with your tongue. They were the perfect sweet for long trips.

I'd eaten six by the time I got to Newcastle.

I was at Jesmond Street half an hour before the ten o'clock departure.

Nearly-didn't-make-it Clipper, here it comes.

Round the corner and up Jesmond Street, stopping five metres away from my feet. I've no jacket on. I'm wearing my cream chinos and my Gallini sweater. I'm dancing up and down on the spot in Jesmond Street like an idiot, singing quietly, 'Brian Clough's red and white army, tch tch tch tch …' I'm clapping the bus as it gets closer.

It's a double-decker. Lovely blue and yellow with dark, tinted windows and really posh, tall seats with proper head-rests. I'm already up one of the steps and just starting to relax. It's been a strange morning. I've no idea where I'm going once I get to London but at least I'm on my way.

I hand the driver my ticket. Already I'm picking out a seat downstairs, next to the back wheel.

'Hold your horses, sunshine! This ticket is for the seven o'clock bus.'

'Yes, mister, but I overslept and missed it. It's a Tripper ticket I've got, so I can use it on this bus as well, 'cos it's still the same day.'

'Tripper or no Tripper, you've got to book your seat, son. We're sold out. You can't just get on a bus and take someone else's seat. You'll have to wait here. Maybe someone won't show up or they'll be daft and oversleep and miss their bus as well.'

He walked off and started counting the people on the bus and then the empty seats. For 15 minutes, every time he walked past me, he was shaking his head.

It was not looking good. How bloody stupid could I have been?

'How old are you anyway and how come you're going to London on your own? You're not running away, are you?'

'No, mister, I'm 16 this year and I'm going to London to meet Brian Clough. He invites me to games all the time. Nottingham Forest are playing Orient in the FA Cup this afternoon and I'm running really late, 'cos I missed the first bus.

'I slept in like an idiot and I'm really nervous, 'cos the game kicks off at three and the bus doesn't get in until three and now you're telling me I might not even get on it. I'll sit in the toilet, mister, just please let me on.'

I think I've caught asthma for not putting a jacket on because by the time I'd finished shouting all that I was so out of breath, I needed to sit down on the curb by the front wheels. If I didn't get to London, I couldn't blame anyone but myself. I felt sick in the bottom of my stomach.

'Slow down, sunshine, slow down! First off, we'll get you on the bus, so calm yourself. You should have just said, like. Second off, London's a pretty big place, you know. If we get there for three, you've still got to get from our drop-off to the ground. Do you even know where it is?'

'No, mister, but I'll find it. I'll just ask for directions when I get to London. I'll find it.'

'I'm sure you will, son, I'm sure you will. And third of all, I'm the driver. My name's Alan. Now, did you say they're playing Orient? Leyton Orient?'

'Yes, mister.'

'And we need to get you there as quickly as possible?'

'Would be great, mister.'

'Well, in that case, bonny lad, hop aboard the *Orient Express*. I'll see what I can do to get you there before three, but I can't promise anything, mind.'

On the way down, Alan kept pretending he had a bull horn like the American truckers and kept pulling down on it, as if it would make us go faster. I sat in the seat across from him. I had to shout a bit but I promised I'd tell him the rest of the *Kenny & Brian story*.

'Eeh well, you'd never expect a story like that about Cloughie. That's lovely, that is.'

He said it was the nicest thing he'd ever heard and that I was a really lucky lad. All the people on the front three rows agreed with him.

'I know, mister. Mam's told me that for ages.'

Alan drove like a madman to get us to Vauxhall Bridge Road for 20 to three. He was ready to open the doors even before he stopped. We were laughing like idiots because there was a car parked in front of the bus stop. He was shaking his fist like mad at the driver.

'Sorry, son. I did what I could. I hope we're here early enough for you.'

He had just beaten his personal best by 15 minutes and was still disappointed. He kept telling me how he was going to tell his grandkids about the day he captained the *Orient Express*. When I got off, he gave me a pound for some Bovril and said it would be a pleasure to see me back on the midnight bus to Newcastle.

'Good luck, son. It was nice to meet you. Ta-ra!'

I jumped off the bus while it was still moving and ran-wobbled the next few steps. I've gone backwards and the bus has passed me but head down and fists pumping, I run past it. People on the bus are waving, sticking their thumbs up and smiling. I can hear shouts of 'Good luck'. I don't know where I'm running to, but I'm off.

I knew I needed to get on something called 'The Tube' but I didn't know where the Tube station was or where I needed to get off. Compared to Sunderland, London seemed bloody massive, it even smelt different.

No one knew where anywhere was. No one had heard of Leyton Orient, never mind Brisbane Road. One man told me: 'I know how to get to Brentford, is that any good?'

I was running everywhere, getting nowhere. This Brisbane Road might not be as close as I thought.

Come on, son. Get yourself sorted. First, find the Tube station.

I'd turned the wrong way when I got off the bus. If I'd been cleverer, I'd have got to the station at Pimlico 10 minutes before I did, just by asking.

Everyone I stopped either sounded like Stuart Pearce or a Rastafarian. Dad had taught me a bit of Rasta already, but I didn't know what it meant and it could be something really rude. There wasn't a Mackem around.

At Pimlico, there were at least three Tube guards helping and confusing me. First, I needed to get on a northbound train and change for the Central Line at Oxford Circus. Then I could take an eastbound train to Leyton. However, it might be quicker to go one stop to Victoria, take the Circle Line and change at Bank or Liverpool Street. I nodded blankly. All I wanted to do was get there.

'Oh, by the way, it might be even quicker to change on to the overground at Mile End and get a train to Leyton.'

Taking the Tube all the way sounded more exciting. Was it buggery! It was dark most of the way. I hadn't twigged we'd be going through tunnels for mile after mile. Now I know why it was called the London Underground.

I got off at Leyton at about four o'clock. The man had told me to find the High Street and Brisbane Road was right behind it. I was sure that, even if I couldn't see it, I'd be able to find it through the cheering.

There wasn't a bloody sound. I asked one of the locals and even he didn't know. Then, 30 seconds later, there was a roar from round the corner: there had been a goal.

I got to the top of the road and could see the stadium gates. The ground reminded me a bit of Roker Park, only smaller. Like a madman, I ran to one of the turnstiles: it was closed. I ran to the next and then the next – everywhere was closed. In the end, I threw a discarded glass bottle at the metal gate and shouted for help. A steward came to open it and I told him what I wanted.

'Fack orff!'

Here we go again.

'Look, mister, I have the same trouble everywhere I go. I'm sorry I threw the bottle, but you couldn't hear me shouting. Brian invites me all the time. I can see them there in the dug-out. All you've got to do is let me in, walk with me and if I'm not supposed to be here, you can kick me out again.' Then I added, 'Or you can go and ask Brian Clough yourself, but he doesn't like being bothered when he's working.'

He looked me up and down again and then nodded me through. I went into the terrace and began walking towards the bench.

I'd timed it perfectly, just in time to see us score again to go 2–0 up. I hadn't seen the first goal, but it couldn't have been Orient's. They were in the Fourth Division.

I walked up to the dug-out. It was tiny, a couple of chairs at most. I popped my head round the corner.

'Hello, Brian, it's me! Can I sit down? The man didn't want to let me in …'

You should have seen the look on his face.

'I'll bloody sit you down! Get round here and keep quiet, I'm bloody working.'

Graham Lyas, the physio, found me somewhere to sit behind the subs. Phil Starbuck, a forward who'd come up through the youth team, said it was lovely to see me but I was risking it because the Gaffer was in a foul mood.

We were actually drawing, 1–1, but we could easily have been behind. The Forest bus had been delayed and had only got to Brisbane Road half an hour before kick-off. Orient were the better side and it looked like Forest didn't want it enough. In the end, Calvin Plummer scored the second to send us through to the fifth round. I'd not met him yet. He had signed not long back. From a club in Finland.

Back in the dressing room, Brian wasn't happy. I realised he could be angry when we won and really calm when we lost: it depended how we had won or lost.

I was putting the socks away, keeping my head down, making sure everyone had a drink, gathering the tie-ups and turning the discarded shirts the right way round.

'What time's your bus home, Rigor?' Brian said as he turned to me.

There was one at 5.45 p.m. but it was already five o'clock and I didn't think I'd make it back to the drop-off in time. To be honest, I didn't want to try.

'Twelve o'clock, Brian.'

'Twelve o'clock? *Midnight?* I'm telling you, that's a disgrace. To be walking the streets of London at midnight on a Saturday night is a bloody disgrace. You'll have to come with us, son. I *should* bloody brain you, but you can come with us. Now get on the coach, get some chocolate and all that type of thing, and get out of my sight. Try to get your head down, you must be exhausted. And hey, son – thanks for coming today. It's nice to see you again.'

Thumbs up on the way out.

I got myself a can of Coke and some crisps and sat down on the bus. The lads were getting on one by one, some really pleased to see me, others grumpy as fuck.

I introduced myself to Calvin by congratulating him on his goal. To the players, I was either 'Mackem' or 'Geordie', depending on how well they knew the North-East. For the first couple of hours, Calvin thought my name was Malcolm – I didn't have the heart to put him right.

We talked about how I'd got to London; how Sting had made me late; how the bus driver had got me here faster. He asked if I was scared to be out on my own.

'I'm used to it by now, Calvin. I'm nearly 16.'

Calvin's from Nottingham and when Jimmy Hill took an England team to tour South Africa he was the only black player in the squad. He was just 19, but Brian, who hated apartheid, fell out with him. He went to Chesterfield, Derby and Barnsley before ending up in Finland.

Brian decided to give him another chance at Forest and so here he is, peering out the window, muttering to himself, as the bus becomes stuck in traffic getting out of the ground.

I fell asleep for literally three minutes. When I woke up, we were just pulling into the Sandiacre Post House, which was halfway between Derby and Nottingham and where the players were picked up and dropped off for away games. There was dribble running down my chin and I needed to stretch myself from top to toe.

When we reached Quarndon, I got my feet up in his chair and borrowed Brian's glasses to watch the *Victoria Wood* show Libby loved so much. I was given milk and toast and went upstairs to 'my' room. The blankets smelled lovely again.

Brian brought me some Horlicks.

'Eeh, there's no place like home, eh, son? Sleep well and see you tomorrow.'

12.

Auf Wiedersehen, Dad

Southwick was a place where you grew up quickly. I am nearly 16 and worried about what being 16 means. I've got to start growing up faster.

There's no chance of me following our Darren to university.

I haven't been to school for ages and because coursework counts towards the new GCSEs, which have replaced O-levels, I've no chance of passing. I don't know much about politics but I do know those Tory bastards have screwed up my life by bringing in the GCSEs. To get an O-level, I would just have had to pass an exam and I was good at exams. I'd revise like mad, take a 90-minute test, get an A or a B, very rarely a C and I'd be put in the top sets. Then, I'd be kept off for the next 11 weeks out of 13 to run messages or go to Nana's to nick or borrow a fiver, it didn't matter which it was:

'If Nana won't lend it to you, go and see Grandad. And if he won't give it to you either then you know where she keeps her purse. Wait till she falls asleep next to the fire. It's either that or we'll be on the streets again. Don't come back without some money, Dazzy would do it.'

Joanne's looking for a way out. She knows her best bet is to meet someone, someone who might not take her out of Sunderland but who could take her out of Shakespeare Street. Of all of us, Joanne probably suffered the most. Dad didn't want her looking at other blokes and he would go berserk if anyone looked at her.

We were allowed out to run errands, to watch Dad play pool, to play sport. The only reason Joanne was allowed out was to go to school. She had one friend called Karen Porter but Joanne was never allowed round hers. Karen had to come to Shakespeare Street, where Joanne was almost a prisoner.

Now, she's starting to perm her hair, wear make-up and go out. She and Karen went down to Birmingham to appear on the quiz show *Blockbusters*. Because they only answered two questions, they came back with £10, which disgusted Mam and Dad. They were hoping for £250.

Now, before she goes through the front door, Joanne will have to go through a barricade of abuse from Dad. Just as me and Darren were 'puffs', my sister was a 'whore' and a 'slut'.

One day, early in 1988, the abuse stopped because Dad headed south to work on a new housing estate in Cambridge with a few of his mates from Sunderland. One was a brickie, one was a joiner, the other was a carpenter and Dad would do the painting and decorating. It was like a Mackem version of *Auf Wiedersehen, Pet*.

There were closer building sites than Cambridge but, like Dazzy, Dad thought the more miles he could put between himself and Sunderland, the better.

Jamal, the Lebanese with a bigger, golder Mercedes than Brian, had given him £2,000 to set up as a *proper* drug dealer but that money had been frittered away and he really didn't want to see that Mercedes pulling into Shakespeare Street again.

Sometimes, once every few weeks, he would come back to Sunderland with 400 or 500 quid in his pocket. A hundred, maybe more, would be for us. The first thing he'd do was go out to the pub and get shitfaced. He was lying in bed now, his white jeans on the floor, sleeping off the night's drinking. Mam came up to me: 'Get the money from his pockets before he can waste any more of it.'

I crept in, picked his jeans up, began rummaging. There was one 20-pound note and some change. Usually, I would keep the change for myself and there would be a lot more notes than this.

I showed it to Mam.

'Where's the rest, Craigy? You've taken too much and you can put it back.'

'That's all there is, Mam. Honest to God, that's all there is.'

Mam began to tremble and then she lost it completely. She ran upstairs. The first thing Dad saw when he opened one groggy eye was Mam's fist heading straight for his face. She blackened his eye, she grabbed a plastic Fine Fare bag and shoved it over his head. Me and Joanne began screaming at her to take it off. She did, but still shaking with rage, she dragged him downstairs.

This time *she* threw him out.

It was early morning before he returned, holding a hedgehog he'd found in the park. He gave it to Joanne and me to play with before turning to Mam: 'Gillian, you are absolutely mental! Why couldn't you let me explain? Your money's under the bloody mattress. I put it there so I wouldn't spend it in the fucking pub.' When we lifted it up, there was £150.

He didn't come back for several weeks. Usually, he would send us money with a little note saying he was okay. Lately, the envelopes had stopped arriving and Mam was becoming worried. We had enough for two National Express bus tickets so we went for a visit.

When we arrived in Cambridge, it was to the kind of place I could only have imagined. Old buildings in gold stone, green spaces, bikes everywhere. Dad and his mates were, naturally enough, living nowhere near King's College – they were in a terraced house divvied up into bedsits.

Mam knocked. Someone who was not Dad answered.

'He's not here, love. He's been arrested. The supervisor called him a nigger and he beat the crap out of him. Yer need to go to the police station in the city centre.'

Mam turned to go.

'To be honest, Gillian, we're not putting up with it any more. He's always getting into trouble, always making life difficult for himself and for us. When he comes back, we're gonna tell him to bugger off. Sorry, love, but yer knar what he's like.'

To Mam, this ganging up on Dad was hurtful and wrong. If someone had called him a nigger, he had the right to react. He should have been backed up by his mates, not slung out.

We trooped back to the city centre and, once the police had told us we couldn't see Dad for several hours, we went to a big open park called Parker's Piece. Sitting on the grass against a tree was a beautiful Chinese student, reading a book. A drunk came over to her, about 50 years old, wild hair, old tweed jacket, swearing and shouting.

I start to get agitated as I watch the drunk become more and more abusive. The park is packed. People are watching the man but nobody is doing or saying anything: 'Mam, we need to stop this.'

Mam taps me on the knee: 'Don't worry about it, Craig. It's not our business.'

Then he kicks the student in the face. I sprint at him, bring him down. He stinks of booze, sweat and everything else. I lie on top of him until a policeman comes and pulls him to his feet – he seems to know him.

We went back to the grey concrete of the police station, where Dad was on remand, and were taken into a big, white visiting room. As we went through the glass doors, one of the policemen said: 'Are you the lad that jumped on old Benny when he was trying it on with that student?' We were given tea, biscuits and slaps on the back.

When Dad was ushered in, Mam gave him a kiss while I went to the toilets to get the marijuana that Mam had made me hide in my shoe to give to him. In the cubicle I pulled my shoe off. The stuff had stuck to the bottom of my sock, it was caked in it. All I could do was take the sock off and try to scrape it off, using my teeth, wondering when somebody would come looking for me. I came out, gave Dad a hug and pressed the pot into his palm.

I was filled with nerves, telling myself this was the last straw. The second-to-last straw had come when we were told to steal a car a few months back.

There was a cigarette factory in Washington. Dad's big idea had been to steal a car, drive it through the gates, load it with Benson & Hedges and drive out. His mate, Bernie, one of Dad's better marijuana customers, would help him get the car.

We found some posh houses. Bernie had a tool with tungsten on the end that you could pop a car window with. We called it a 'blagger'. Dad told me to put it in my pocket 'because if the police stop us, they won't do anything to you.'

We found a purple Vauxhall Belmont, which not only had a big boot for the cigarettes but the bonus of a black briefcase on the back seat. The raid would have gone off perfectly had Dad not panicked and driven the Belmont the wrong way down a dual carriageway. We saw him being arrested on our drive.

The more I thought about Cambridge police station and the more I thought about the cigarette factory, I knew that if Brian and Mrs Clough ever found out they would drop me like a stone.

When we left the police station, Mam told me Dad was planning to move to London and, if he did, she would go with him. I'd been to London once, that time on the *Orient Express*. I didn't know anyone there and nor did she. It was ridiculous. But that was nothing compared to what happened when Mam went into a phone box to tell our Joanne we were coming home. On the shelf, by the phone, was a wallet: it was big, heavy, leather. Inside was £600. We counted the notes – it was manna from heaven.

Mam picked it up and said we had to go back to the police station and hand it in. I couldn't believe what I was hearing, I had to ask her to repeat it.

'Mam, if you have to do it, just take 100 out. If he's got 600 in the wallet, he's not going to miss 100.'

'Craigy, we have to take it back.'

I don't know why she did it. Perhaps she thought if she handed the wallet in, the police would go easier on Dad. Perhaps she remembered picking up a purse at the checkout at Fine Fare on The Green. She had handed that back too.

It turned out to belong to a shipbuilder's wife and it contained his Christmas wages. It had made her feel she was a good person and perhaps she wanted to feel good again. All I knew is that there were no bloody shipbuilders in Cambridge and while we had a return ticket to Newcastle, we didn't have anything to get us back to Sunderland.

It was horribly late when we arrived at Newcastle bus station. Opposite was a taxi rank. 'Craigy,' said Mam, 'go up to the taxi, knock on his window and ask if he'll take us to Sunderland. Say we haven't got the fare but he can have my family allowance book as security.'

I said no. Absolutely not.

'Your Darren would do it.'

We got a lift as far as East Boldon. We had a four-mile walk past Boldon Colliery, past the greyhound stadium, to home. In the small hours of the morning. As we walked, Mam was kicking out at me, punching me. I kept telling her I was too old to be hit and that she had given away the fare home.

I have to leave. I have to get away from this.

If Dad had Cambridge, Darren had Northern Ireland and Aaron had the army, I still had Quarndon.

* * *

I'm spending more and more time in Quarndon and this after-noon I'm sitting in the lounge, flicking through the television menu. I click on to Ceefax to check the football news for 8 March 1988. And it's staring right back at me in blue letter-ing that looks like it's come out of a typewriter: 'Brian Clough Resigns at Forest'. He can't have done. A few weeks ago, he was threatening to do so because the board wouldn't let him manage Wales on a part-time basis. Now he's done it.

He was furious because he badly wanted to manage an international team. England were beyond him now. Bobby Robson had clung on and had qualified for the European Championship in West Germany by thrashing Turkey 8–0 at Wembley and beating Yugoslavia 4–1 in Belgrade. We are favourites to win it in the summer. There was no chance of his being forced out now.

Wales hadn't qualified just as they hadn't qualified for anything since the 1958 World Cup. They did, however, have the makings of a decent team. Neville Southall and Kevin Ratcliffe played in goal and central defence for Everton, who were league champions. Ian Rush was one of Liverpool's greatest strikers and was now with Juventus. Mark Hughes was playing centre-forward with Bayern Munich. Brian would have fancied doing something with footballers like these.

He had arranged to meet the Welsh FA at the Holiday Inn in Birmingham, which, perhaps not entirely coincidentally, was next to the main studios of Central Television. The Welsh delegation was surprised by how many reporters were at the hotel. Brian probably wasn't surprised – he wanted a wave of public opinion to sweep him into Cardiff Arms Park.

He was serious about the job. He asked for all the passports of the Nottingham Forest squad and went through them, looking for Welsh ancestry. He had persuaded Alan Hill, who once had been Forest's keeper and was now coaching Notts County, to quit his job and be his number two in Cardiff.

When Mrs Clough asked how he planned to communicate with a country he had no connection with, he replied: 'I already know the language, pet, just don't ask me to spell it,' and waltzed from the lounge to the breakfast room saying '*Yaki Da!*' over and over again. He imagined that being able to say 'Cheers!' over and over again in Welsh was the only speech he would need to give.

He did not get the job.

The board of Nottingham Forest did something they almost never did to Brian Clough: they said no.

Brian raged about the nonentities on the board; men who had contributed nothing to the club and some of whom he had loaned money to. They wouldn't last five minutes without him.

Mrs Clough had pleaded with him not to resign. Above all, it would leave Nigel completely in the lurch. He didn't quit.

But now he had? I sprinted through the house: 'Mrs Cloooughh, Mrs Cloooughh! Come quick!'

'There's no reason for it, none at all,' she said, scuttling into the lounge. 'He's not talked about it, he's just done it.' Then she stared at the television and her voice dropped. 'No, son, no. He's not gone, he's just signed a new contract. We talked about it the other day. It says: "Brian Clough Re-Signs at Forest".'

Most days are not like that. Most days carry much less stress. Brian and me start on the Common with a walk around the cricket pitch, warm cups of tea still in our hands. Then, 15 minutes later, we're off through Derby in the blue Ford estate. Brian calls it 'The Dog's Car' because it's the one they use when they take his Labrador, Del Boy – Del makes too much mess for the Mercedes. We're singing and waving at people passing by.

Arriving at the City Ground, we stroll in like we own the place. Brian's got work to do, so I'm running around saying hello to anybody and everybody, knocking on any door I can find to see who's in their office. I'm not sure I should be walking into people's offices but none of them seems to mind and soon I'm away down to the training ground to annoy the fuck out of Archie Gemmill. Then it's back to the gym. Apparently, I'm not going to get legs like the skipper's unless I work at it.

When we returned home to Quarndon, we would watch *Fifteen to One* while Mrs Clough taught me to iron. She excelled at both. She knew virtually every answer on the quiz and every shirt she put on a coat hanger would be starched.

Mainly because they didn't have the big crowds that Liverpool or Manchester United had, Nottingham Forest were very keen on arranging friendlies to keep the tills moving. In Torpedo Moscow, they found a club that took friendlies as seriously as Forest's accountants.

The kick-off wasn't until 7.30 p.m. but the Torpedo Moscow squad arrived to start using the facilities six hours before the start of the game. One of their players came over to me and said: 'Nottingham Forest ... great club, great history. Where do we go to prepare? Where is gym?'

Forest had a little gym, with a couple of exercise bikes, some pull-up bars, mats and a medicine ball.

There are some films which leave a mark on you and mine was *Rocky IV*. I'd seen it a couple of years before. It had starred Dolph Lundgren as a Russian boxer who is determined to prove the superiority of the Soviet system. Naturally, Sylvester Stallone, wrapped in the Stars and Stripes, takes him head-on. I really wanted a haircut like Dolph's – spiky on top, shaved at the sides.

Dad said there was no way we were paying £1.30 for one: 'Especially not when it grows back after two weeks. I can do a Dolph Lundgren easy.' So, he sat me down on a chair in the kitchen, put some newspapers on the floor, took another drag on his joint and went to fetch some scissors. The ones he came back with were normally used to cut wallpaper and stuck together with so much paste, they creaked open. They were so obviously blunt, even Dad relented: 'Don't worry, son, I'll get the thinning comb.' He started dragging it through my hair.

Jesus wept and Moses crept! I'd never felt pain like it. When I walked back into the living room, they all started singing the *Rocky* music from when he was running up the steps in Philadelphia.

Now, a couple of years later, I was watching the Torpedo Moscow team and thinking about Dolph Lundgren and *Rocky IV*.

The only reason these Russians want to use to the gym is so they can pump themselves full of drugs so they can have a victory for Communism. Brian told me to 'keep an eye on them', I've got to stop them doing anything underhanded.

I got on the exercise bike in a pair of jeans and a T-shirt. They're standing around watching me. I needed to impress them, to show them how tough we were at Forest. I need to stay on it long enough so they give up and leave.

I put the bike on to the highest level and began peddling while humming the *Rocky* theme. The fact that the seat fell off didn't deter me. I rode standing up until they left. When I got off the bike, my legs turned to mush and I found myself on the floor, staring up at the ceiling.

I followed them to the Jubilee Club and began playing pool. Another player came over and said: 'Is it possible we can play?'

'Of course, but the rules are that the winner stays on.'

'What is winner stays on?'

'You have to beat me to play your friend and it's a pound for every game.'

They put their pounds on the table. With everything I had learnt from Dad, I beat the players and I beat the officials. I did doubles, I put them in snookers, I hammered home the black. By the finish, I had won £32. My pockets were weighed down with coins. You didn't have to speak Russian to know they were pissed off, but I had proved my point.

When it came to the game, they proved theirs. Torpedo Moscow were brilliant, their technique was superb, they were strong, they were fast. They were far too good for us.

They won, 2–0.

On the way home, I told Brian the story of how I'd beaten the Russians at pool and won 32 one-pound coins.

'That's brilliant, son. You did better than us. Now stick 16 of those coins in the ashtray.'

'Why?'

'Where did you get your pound in the first place?'

'Out of the ashtray.'

'Well, it's like I've made an investment. Put 16 back and at least some good has come out of the day.'

When I'm in Brian's office, I try to be quiet, serving drinks for the guests, smiling and listening until he remembers to introduce me. Each time somebody famous came in, Brian would tell me to be myself. Then we'd tell the story of how we met and we'd get the smiles and someone like Geoffrey Boycott would be asking if I knew how lucky, how special I was.

'Yes, Mr Boycott.'

'You can call me Geoffrey, son. Any friend of Brian's is a friend of mine.'

'Of course. I know, Geoffrey.'

Brian liked and admired Geoffrey and would slip away to Trent Bridge when Boycott was playing there for Yorkshire or England. He had retired now but whenever he came into the room, I would freeze. He would be nice enough but, somehow, he always left me feeling overawed.

Boycott would sometimes come to dinner at Quarndon, as would Lawrie McMenemy, who when Sunderland were about to be relegated to the Third Division had thrown his things into his Mercedes and fled South. Had he stayed, they would have burned his house down.

The day ends with me in the car waiting for Brian to leave. He's got me listening to his Ink Spots tape. I'm practising so we can sing along to the chorus of 'I Don't Want to Set the World on Fire'.

He always tells me there is only proper music in his car: 'None of that garbage our Si has you listening to, son.' It didn't matter who he was with or what he was doing, whenever I checked how long he would be, the answer would always be the same: he would always be 'thirty seconds away' from leaving.

An hour later, he would have his jacket off and his feet on the desk, telling someone the story of how he came to be called Old Big Head. He's going through the routine now as I poke my head round his office door.

His mam's in the kitchen when he gets home from school and he's crying. She's making them dinner, but of course she's worried. He's just finished the bit where he's telling his mam he's getting bullied at school for being big-headed. He's already laughing, halfway through his own story. It'll take him ages yet.

I'm about to sneak away as he's starting the bit where his mam's telling him not to worry at all, that he's really a special lad with a heart as big as a bucket and of course he doesn't really have a big head. Then she asks him to do her a favour and go to the shop for four stone of potatoes. He says he'll go with pleasure and starts looking around for a bag to put them in, but he can't find one.

I love this part, so I hang around for a bit longer while his mam's telling him not to be daft and that he doesn't need a bag, he can carry the potatoes in his cap.

'Weeeaaaahhh! True story, lads! True story!'

The whole room is in stitches and I'm off to the Jubilee Club for a quick go on the fruit machines, thinking he's on a roll with his story-telling and will be there for hours yet. Less than a minute later: 'Hey, Sunderland! I won't tell you again, get off that bloody machine and get in the car, else I'll brain you. You've got 15 seconds. Come on!'

I'd try to tell him I'd waited for nearly an hour and a half and he'd caught me after 45 seconds. It was like he had a bloody sensor that went off as soon as I put the pound in the slot. The conversations after that usually involved balls being cut off and me sodding off back to Sunderland if I was so stupid again. He didn't work this hard all bloody week so I could waste his money in a bloody fruit machine – it was too daft to laugh at.

13.

Broken Hearts

Nigel was 22 now. For the third straight season he had been Nottingham Forest's leading scorer.

Brian was desperately proud of Nigel's ability as a footballer, although he rarely said so to his face. He would sometimes be sent action photos of Nigel, sometimes accompanied by a note saying how similar his goal celebration was to Brian's when he played for Middlesbrough and Sunderland.

He once picked up a photograph he'd been sent of Nigel scoring with a diving header amid a thicket of boots that seemed to be inches from his skull. Brian held it up in his office and announced: 'What's special about this?'

There were a host of unconvincing answers and plenty of shrugs. He showed it to me and I said: 'He's about to get his head kicked in and his eyes are wide open.'

'Spot on, son. Look how brave he is.'

Then Simon came in and Brian held up the photograph. Before he could ask the question, Simon said: 'Eyes wide open.'

He would never show the photograph to Nigel.

Forest had finished third in the league in 1988; Nigel had just bought a new bungalow and had spent most of the summer landscaping the garden and planting trees.

'You're doing bugger-all if you go back to Sunderland, so you might as well hang around here,' Brian said. 'You can help me and our Nige with his garden for a couple of days. It'll do you good to do some proper work and you can get some sun on your back.'

Brian kept coming up with excuses to extend my stay. If he thought I'd not been somewhere or seen something before he wanted to give me the chance to experience it, to broaden my horizons, to breathe in and fill my lungs.

'You've not been to Goodison Park yet, have you, son? Why don't you stay a bit longer? That way you can watch the game and travel back with us. We can drop you off at Scotch Corner.'

The game at Everton would be the third of the 1988/89 season and Steve Hodge's second since his return to Nottingham Forest. Brian had sold Steve – or 'Harry' as every-one at Forest called him – to Aston Villa three years before. He'd not enjoyed it at Villa and, although he played alongside Glenn Hoddle and Chris Waddle in Tottenham's midfield, he'd not enjoyed London either.

Brian had brought Harry back home to Nottingham and told him all week that returning to Forest would see him back in the England squad. He'd played in the World Cup in Mexico two years ago but he'd missed out on this summer's European Championship in West Germany.

The tournament had been a disaster for England – they had lost every game – and Brian had told Harry that Bobby

Robson would have him back in his squad for the friendly against Denmark at Wembley.

The bus had a little elevated treatment couch, which was set right by the back window. It was the quietest place on the bus and Harry loved just to get on the couch and switch off. It wouldn't matter if he had played really well or had a stinker.

I first met Hodgy on our initial encounter with Nottingham Forest at Newcastle in 1984. He had just been part of the England side that had won the European Under-21 Championship but he didn't have a flash bone in his body. He'd taken me under his wing and was one of the first to stick up for me if any of the lads had given me too much stick. I was gutted when we sold him to Aston Villa.

When he came back, the first time I met him was getting on the bus as we were picked up from the Sandiacre Post House for the Friday night trip to Norwich for the first game of the season. I wasn't sure he would remember who I was.

I wasn't in the best of moods. I was looking forward to a big game at a big ground but I knew that getting on that bus meant I was a couple of hours closer to that horrible, sick feeling every time I went back to Southwick.

The feelings would start when I said goodbye to Mrs Clough and left Brian's house, which now had a sign, painted by Dad in beautiful Olde English script on a piece of polished tree trunk, proclaiming it as 'The Elms'. Until then, I'd forgotten about all the crap I had to go back to. The no money, the no food and all the shitty errands Mam would send me on because I was the only one still at home.

'Ay up, Harry.'

'Well, bloody hell!' Then he's got me in a headlock, ruffling my hair. 'You're still around! We've not managed to get shot of you yet, then?'

'Get off me, Harry! You're knocking Brian's glasses off my nose and he'll kill me if I break another pair.'

'Ay up, Macka, son. How you doing? Part of the furniture now? Have you bought your house here yet? It's nice to see you again. How've yer been?'

It was like he'd never been away.

We smashed Everton all over Goodison Park but somehow only managed to draw, 1–1. Hodgy had his lip split and had run his balls off all afternoon.

I'd expected Brian to do his nut at the final whistle but he waltzed into the changing room. He took Harry Hodge's boots off for him and then kissed him on both cheeks.

Brian has his tracksuit bottoms rolled up around his knees, his arms folded and a massive grin on his face: 'Weeeey … Weeeeyyyyyyy … I'm telling you, they couldn't get near us, lads. Ooooohhhhhh, they're the supposed "Big Five" side and they couldn't get bloody near us. We absolutely murdered them, lads, you were fucking brilliant! One of these days, we'll get what we deserve, lads. Keep working, keep playing like that – it'll come.

'Hey, Harry, what did I tell you, son? Get the ball, give it to the centre-forward and then get in the box. That's what I brought you back for, beauty. That's all you ever need to do, son … and hey, Harry, beauty, it's got us a goal today. Ooooohhhhhh, well done, son! Welcome home!'

Brian's first sentence after every game and the way he delivered it set the tone for the after-match chat. It set the mood while the players were getting changed and it set the mood for the coach journey home.

If Brian was angry with the way they'd played, there really would be times when we'd drive for hours with the coach lights out and 16 hurting players not saying a word until it was time to eat. Then the lights would go back off and no one would speak until Sandiacre. Christ, there would be some tense journeys home! Not many, though, because we won more than we lost.

This time, Brian didn't need to say a word, he was pretty much dancing on his toes: 'We're off to Scotland for a couple of days, lads. You've earned it, we've all earned it.'

They were going to Scotland to play some golf at St Andrews and take part in a testimonial at Hearts. Brian saw it as a good way to get the new signings bonded. Brian Laws and Garry Parker had joined the club recently and Brian was hoping to finish off the signing of Lee Chapman, whom he'd been chasing for ages.

Lawsy had learned his football at Wallsend Boys Club on the Tyne, which had produced Peter Beardsley, Steve Bruce and Alan Shearer. Brian wasn't in that class, and in his time at Nottingham Forest he would play above himself at full-back. He tackled as hard as Stuart Pearce and his shot was almost as fierce. I loved him for it.

Garry had been signed from Hull in March but had struggled to hold down a place. Forest had agreed to pay £270,000 but Brian had told Hull's manager, Brian Horton, that the deal would not go through unless Parker had a haircut.

When the time came for Horton to drive Parker down to Nottingham to do the deal, he was horrified to discover the midfielder had had the most miniscule of trims. Fortunately for Hull's finances, Brian was out when they arrived at the City Ground and Ronnie Fenton signed the forms.

At Sheffield Wednesday, Chapman had become one of the most sought after centre-forwards in England.

They would play some golf, stay at Old Course Hotel, where they could have saunas and get some fresh air walking the clifftops. It would give Brian time to relax and clear his big head. I would be going back to Southwick.

We were playing some really good football but Forest hadn't won any of their first three matches of the season. Brian had put a condition on the Scotland trip – if they played poorly at Everton, they wouldn't be going. It was as simple as that. It didn't matter the hotel had been booked. It didn't matter Hearts had sold tickets for the game at Tynecastle, which despite its name was in Edinburgh rather than Newcastle. If Nottingham Forest did not perform at Goodison Park, there was no way they were going to Scotland to be miserable together for three bloody days.

Everyone in the dressing room was buzzing, relaxed. I'm doing the usual – keeping my head down, picking up the socks, slyly high-fiving Des Walker and giving Stuart Pearce the big clenched fist. Brian had told me off many times for getting too excited if we scored so I'd have to find sneaky ways of telling the lads they were brilliant. Bloody hell, there were times I wanted to burst when Pearcey had smashed in another free-kick or wiped out another winger.

Brian caught me getting carried away: 'Hey, son, thanks a lot, but I'll be the one telling the skipper if he played well or not. Now sit down, shurrup and put them socks away, like I asked you.' Then, turning to Pearce, 'Hey, skipper, you were brilliant today, son, brilliant.'

How do I put the socks away while sitting down and shutting up?

The best I could do was a silent mini-Psycho salute while Brian wasn't watching. Pearce knew how much it meant, he could see it in my eyes.

Brian didn't always call players by their first names but, when he really wanted to make a point, he would use the full-length version of it: 'Stephen, beauty, if you can help me play like that every week, I'll die a happy man.'

Then Ronnie Fenton came in and told Brian that Hodgy had been added to the England squad.

'Bloody hell, Harry! I knew I'd get you back in, but I didn't think even I was good enough to do it so quickly. Congratulations, beauty, and really, son, welcome back.'

While everyone else is tucking into a hot meal served by me and Ron Williams, the manager of the Jubilee Club, I'm washing the pots. We're on the team bus on our way from Goodison Park to Scotch Corner.

On the coach, I have taken on the job of Chief Lackey to Nottingham Forest Football Club. It was Stuart Pearce's idea and, apart from Brian, he was the only one allowed to set the rules on the bus. Stuart decided I was an ideal fit for the job when we were on our way back from Norwich a fortnight ago.

I was just getting ready to settle down when I noticed Des Walker was in the kitchen bit of the bus, getting soups and passing them round to the lads. He kept limping past me, wincing and pulling a pretend injured face, then sarcastically asking if I was alright. Was I sitting comfortably? Perhaps there was something he could get me. A pillow maybe? Some slippers? He didn't want me waking up tired tomorrow after I'd had such a tough day. One of the lads who'd just got lumps kicked out of them playing a game of fucking football – which they'd lost – could get me anything I wanted, I should just relax.

'Thanks, Des, that's really nice of you. Is there any mushroom left?'

The whole back of the bus burst out laughing apart from Walker.

'I'll give you facking mushroom soup!'

I don't think he meant it as an offer.

Stuart Pearce got up and went to get it for me instead.

'Hey, Geordie, come and give me a hand with this, would you?' He pulled the curtain closed and put his arm around me. 'You're a good lad, son, and we love having you with us. When you're in the dressing room or on the bus, you're one of us. You know that, don't you? But that means you've got to muck in as well, you've got to do your share. You can't just sit there waiting for the lads to bring you stuff. Every now and again you can get up, you know. You're not glued to the seat, are you?'

I spent the next four hours asking Des if he was alright and getting the lads whatever they wanted. When Stuart Pearce asks you to do something, it gets done.

There's a sign for Knotty Ash. I never knew it was an actual place, I thought Ken Dodd had made it up. There are other signs as Albert takes the Nottingham Forest team coach further up the M62: Warrington, Manchester, Heywood. A white rose tells us we're in Yorkshire. The carriageways divide and there's a farm in between them. How do they sleep in the glare of all those headlights stretching back for miles?

Bradford, Leeds, Wakefield. Then the massive towers of the Ferrybridge power station sweep past my window, pouring white smoke as Albert takes the bus north on to the A1 past Wetherby.

The lads are relaxed. Some are chatting, some are dozing, some are swigging from beer cans. I'm doing none of these things. I'm just staring blankly out of the window. Every sign we pass brings us nearer to Scotch Corner, where I'll get off the bus and one of Brian's relatives, probably his brother, Joe, will take me, and a whole load of presents for his family in the North-East, back to Sunderland.

Back to Southwick. Back to Mam. Back to no money. Back to the fighting, the crime, the hawking round of the few things we still actually own. Every sign we pass makes my stomach lurch and when I see one that says 'Scotch Corner 32 miles', I start to shake in my seat.

Then Alan Clark, one of the youth-team managers, white hair, chubby face framed by round glasses, pops his head round the curtain and says: 'The Gaffer wants a word with you down the front.'

Brian turns round in his seat: 'Are you due back at school?'

'No.'

'Right then, I've had an idea. Why don't you come to Scotland? You can have three days with us up there. We'll drop you off on the way back.'

The relief washed through me. I knew it was only postponing going back but at least it was postponed. I went back down to the players' section of the bus, buzzing. I didn't worry about telling Mam. As far as she was concerned, I was safe with Brian – I turned up when I turned up. If she was worried, she would phone the Cloughs.

Stuart Pearce was now coming down the bus with a bag of cash that Brian had handed him: it was the expenses for the Scotland trip. He laid it down on a table and divided it up. Then he came over to me.

'Look, Geordie, you're one of us now. Here's your expenses.' He gave me 90 quid. Nine £10 notes. There were two apprentices on the bus – Pearcey gave them each £20.

It was gone midnight when the Old Course Hotel, big, stately and bathed in spotlights, appeared in front of us. It made the Seaburn look small. In the lobby, the team paired off with their room-mates.

I was in a room on my own. When I opened the door, there in front was a four-poster bed on which were some chocolates and a note that said: 'With Compliments'. By the chocolates was the softest, fluffiest green dressing-gown with 'St Andrews Hotel and Spa' written on the breast pocket in gold lettering.

Next to the bed was the telephone which had a menu beside it.

I skimmed past the Scottish smoked salmon sandwiches, the Old Course burger and the grilled Scotch fillet steak and focused in on the desserts. Sticky toffee pudding, knicker-bocker glory, chocolate and orange tart, a selection of ice creams. Hot chocolate. All I had to do was press three on the telephone, say what I wanted and, 20 minutes later, someone in a beautiful uniform would carry it in on a silver tray and put it on the table – it was that easy.

When the bill was delivered to the club at the end of the trip, I had the highest charges for extras of anyone in the squad.

After a very comfy night's sleep and a beautiful breakfast, we gathered on the golf course. I would be caddying for Brian Rice, who was Scottish and so was bound to be good at golf. He also had a dry sense of humour, the kind his manager loved.

Nigel had a hand-held computer golf game which he had let me play and I was quite good at judging distances so I had a pretty good idea of what club went with what shot.

The Gaffer didn't play golf but Brian came to watch every-one tee off. Tommy Gaynor, a young Irish forward who had just joined from Doncaster, shanked his drive and nearly hit his manager in the knee.

The knee that had been wrecked at Roker Park. The knee that would always give him trouble.

Brian went back to the hotel to finalise the deal for Lee Chapman.

The course was stunning. A couple of holes hugged the cliffs and, if you mis-hit here, you would see your ball disappear into the North Sea. I could see the beach below and feel the wind on my face. It was exhilarating.

There was nothing much to do once we'd had dinner so we went to the billiards room to play snooker. Playing snooker on a full-sized table was a bit different to playing pool in The Wheatsheaf but, because of Dad, I was still pretty good at it. We played winner stays on – I stayed on quite a bit.

The main point of the trip was to play Hearts in a testimonial for their forward, John Colquhoun, who was something of a hero at the club. A few years later – after failing to score a single league goal for Sunderland – he would return to Scotland and be elected Rector of the University of Edinburgh.

Brian had invited a 14-year-old lad called Levi Stephen, who was said to be the brightest prospect in Scottish football. Already he had taken him down to Nottingham to show him the City Ground. He was blond with a bright smile.

Now Brian asked him to sit with him in the dug-out at Tynecastle to watch Forest beat Hearts, 3–0. I was alongside them and Levi could not shut up. He talked all the way through the game, which was something Brian hated.

When the Hearts keeper was walking around with the ball in his hand, Levi shouted: 'Steps, keeper! How many steps is he allowed?'

Brian turned to him: 'Son, if you're so bothered by it, why don't you go over to the linesman and tell him he's not doing his job.' He told me to go with him.

As we went to the touchline, the ball went out of play and hit one of the advertising hoardings. My first thought was to throw it back but I kicked it. I struck it beautifully and it travelled 20 yards for Brian Laws to control on his chest. When I returned to the dug-out, I heard Brian say: 'Blow me, son, that was a great ball.' I could have burst with pride.

Levi decided not to sign for Nottingham Forest and went to Glasgow Rangers. Brian was angry, convinced Levi had made a mistake.

The morning after the match, I walked through Edinburgh, past the university and into the old town. I had never seen a city quite as old and quite as beautiful. It was like being on the set of one of those historical dramas the BBC would show on a Sunday evening, it felt magical.

The magic evaporated the moment I stepped on the team bus. This time there would be no reprieve. I would be getting off the bus and I would be going back to Sunderland, back to Southwick.

I was so quiet, some of the players asked me if anything was wrong. Usually, I'd come back with a quick quip, which they loved, but this time I sat looking straight ahead.

Lost.

The bus pulled into a service station in Northumberland with signs to Alnwick, Amble and Seahouses. It was just a petrol station with a Little Chef advertising its Olympic Breakfast, the kind you couldn't imagine Steve Cram tucking into before the 1500 metres in Seoul.

I ran into the toilets, sat in a cubicle and waited for them all to get back on the bus and leave. I waited and waited, tears trickling down, until the door was pushed open and Garry Parker stood in front of me.

'What's the matter?'

'I can't … I can't … I can't go back … back to Sunderland.'

'I'm sorry, mate, but you're going to have to tell the Gaffer.'

Garry took me outside and led me back on to the bus. When, shaking and crying, I told him I couldn't go back, that it would break my heart to return to Sunderland, Brian became emotional and angry.

'Alright, I don't know what I'm going to do but, son, let's buy you some time. Come back down with us for a couple of days and we'll have a talk about what we're going to do with you. For now, get yourself down the back of the bus and stay quiet.'

I fell into an exhausted sleep. When I opened my eyes, we were at the Sandiacre Hotel.

When we got back to Quarndon, Simon and Nigel were already there. Brian turned to me: 'Look, why don't you take the dog out for a walk? Take him round the cricket pitch and me and my two lads are going to have a conversation about what to do with you. Be about 45 minutes.'

I went to the back door and put the lead on the dog, Del, the golden retriever that had been bought for Elizabeth but quickly became Brian's dog and as much a part of Nottingham Forest as Stuart Pearce. I was just taking him round the house to the front gate. Suddenly, I heard Brian's voice:

'Rigor, don't bother with the dog. Come on, we've decided. You're gonna go home for a couple of weeks, you're gonna pack your stuff and you're not gonna tell yer mam anything.

When you finish school, you're going to come down here and live with us. We'll decide if you're gonna play football or work with our Simon.'

'I'd like to play football, please, Brian.'

'Weeeaaaahhh! Yer cheeky sod, it's not your decision to make.'

14.

Cheeky Chappy

20 October 1988

I loved Lee Chapman. I never really understood how he managed to do what he did but I didn't care. For a while, Lee Chapman was all I ever wanted to be. Not necessarily because of how he played football.

Brian was supposed to have signed him from Sheffield Wednesday in the summer of 1988 but he went to France to play for Niort. Because they could make more money and enjoy a better lifestyle, quite a few players were going to France. Glenn Hoddle and Mark Hateley went to Monaco. Chris Waddle signed for Marseille. Brian was pissed off. So was Elton John, who had invited Lee to his suite at the Park Lane Hotel and offered him a glass of Cristal champagne and a contract with Watford.

Niort wasn't Marseille, nor was it Monaco. It was a railway town, which Chapman said reminded him of Crewe. It also had less money than he imagined and, when they told him they couldn't pay his wages, Lee became very interested in the deal Nottingham Forest had been offering. Brian had called him from St Andrews: 'We'll get you out of there, hold tight.'

However, Lee also took another call, this time from Robert Maxwell, the chairman of Derby and owner of the *Daily Mirror*. Brian didn't like Maxwell, said he was 'an enemy of football'. In return, Maxwell called Brian a 'big mouth' and promised to 'knock his team into the ground'.

Maxwell offered to pay up Lee's contract with Niort in cash and give his wife, Leslie Ash, a presenting job on a television station he owned. Then he asked Lee to choose a car: he asked for a BMW – red. However, Brian could offer something Maxwell could not: a team that was going places. He's brought Harry Hodge back to the City Ground, he has five players in the England squad, he's on the verge of winning things again. There's a spring in his step. Tonight, is Lee Chapman's home debut.

Forest are playing Liverpool, a team I absolutely hate. In April, we played them in the semi-finals of the FA Cup at Hillsborough. It had been our second trip to Hillsborough in a month. I had taken our Joanne with me to Forest's league game at Sheffield Wednesday. Brian had asked if she would like a couple of days with them. Elizabeth had taken her shopping in Derby and she'd had a wonderful time.

In April, Darren had come back from Northern Ireland for Easter. He said he felt left out. Me, Azzy and our Joanne had all been to see Brian. Everyone except him. I was going back down to Hillsborough for the FA Cup semi-final against Liverpool and Darren insisted he was coming with me.

But I said no. I hadn't told Brian that Darren would be there – it might be awkward and we hadn't got a train ticket. Then I told him we'd go. Without a train ticket.

Dazzy always said that if you were doing something wrong, don't hide. Be really confident. So, we went straight to the buffet car and stayed there all the way to Sheffield, chatting with the guy behind the counter. We could be lovely, charming kids when we needed to be. The conductor walked past us four or five times – we were never asked to show a ticket.

When we arrived at the ground there was an old guy by the gates holding a placard saying 'The End of the World is Nigh, Christ is Your Saviour'. Our Dazzy went over to him and questioned every single thing he said. After 20 minutes of this, the bloke was beginning to doubt himself and put the placard down.

When we met the Forest bus, Brian gave us two tickets for the Main Stand. John Barnes won an early penalty for Liverpool and then crossed for John Aldridge to volley in. However, for most of the match, Nottingham Forest were the better team and, after Nigel had pulled one back, they battered Liverpool without breaking through.

I had half promised Dazzy that Brian would take us back to Quarndon but, as we went down the stairs of the Main Stand, I wasn't so sure. Forest had played really well but they'd lost. Brian had never been to an FA Cup final and everyone at the club knew how much this game had meant to him.

I hadn't gone into the dressing room but when the players came on to the bus they looked drained and upset. Brian walked straight past me. I pushed myself on to the bus and asked if me and Darren could come down for a couple of days.

'Son, I've had enough,' he said. He looked broken, his shoulders slumped in a way that I'd never seen him before. 'I've had your Aaron down, I have had your Joanne down, I've just lost a semi-final in the Cup. Get some chocolate from the back of the bus and bugger off.'

He rummaged around in his tracksuit bottoms for some money but he had no cash on him. I didn't dare tell him we had no money for the rail fare; I got off with two big bars of Dairy Milk and a couple of Twixes.

'You'd better be fucking joking,' said Darren when I told him. 'At least tell me you've got some money for the train.'

Once the bus had gone through Hillsborough's blue main gates, he threw the chocolate at me, kicked me half a dozen times and then walked off. He was striding away several yards ahead and every time I got too close he would pick up a stone or a discarded bottle and throw it at me.

We walked along a dual carriageway past industrial estates and worn-out old factories until we reached the M1. It was dark. We were walking along a great grass bank by the motor-way when a police car stopped us and asked where we were going. They agreed to drop us at the nearest rail station, which was Rotherham. From there we could get a train to York and from York there would be a train to Sunderland. Eventually.

It was two in the morning when we reached York. We had four freezing hours in the empty, cavernous surrounds of the station until someone said there was a Royal Mail train headed for Sunderland and Newcastle. We weren't asked to pay.

To rub it in, a few days later Liverpool thrashed us 5–0 in the league at Anfield. Barnes and Peter Beardsley were untouchable and, of course, that twat Aldridge scored again.

Now, six months later, we were playing Liverpool again. I couldn't sleep so I got up really early and went down to mow the grass at the bottom of the drive. It must have been half six. I'd been at it for half an hour before Brian came down the path with Del. He loved it when he didn't have to tell me to get up off my lazy arse, when I did something without being asked.

'Blow me! Good morning, Rigor. I didn't hear you get up, son. Are you sure you're feeling alright? I bet you don't even remember how lovely this time of the morning is, do you, you lazy little bugger ...'

When I finished, Brian was in the kitchen making bacon sarnies but he had his jacket and flat cap on, ready to go out.

'Brilliant job, son. Thanks for that. Now bugger off to the lounge, get yer feet up and relax for a few minutes. You've earned it. I'm off to work. I might not come back before the game, so I'll see you later this afternoon.'

In the lounge Brian has set up his reclining chair for me. On the little table next to it, he's got me a cup of tea, a glass of milk, a couple of bacon sarnies and the video set up with *Bugsy Malone* ready to watch.

On his way out, he pops his head round the door and starts singing: 'Hey, son ... *You could have been anything that you wanted to be.*'

I'd first met Lee Chapman on Saturday on the bus coming back from Millwall, where we had drawn 2–2. He hadn't scored but he'd done alright and helped set up both of the goals. I asked Lee to sign a photo of himself – I wanted the photo because I wanted to have my hair cut like his. I told him it was for our Joanne.

'That's nice, Mackem. You're the first one to ask. Is it 'cos I used to play for Sunderland? Most of them up there didn't like me, you know.'

They did, however, like his wife. Everyone liked Leslie Ash. I *loved* Leslie Ash. She played a detective in a show called *C.A.T.S. Eyes*, which was on telly on Saturday nights. She was more glamorous than any policewoman I'd seen in Southwick.

When the lads heard Lee Chapman was coming to Nottingham, meeting Leslie Ash was all they could talk about. Even Mrs Clough said: 'You know he's married to Leslie Ash who's in that show, *C.A.T.S. Eyes?*' We all knew.

Usually, I'd go to games in either the first-team trackie top I'd got off the skipper or in one of Nige's sweaters that were just a bit too big for me. Today, I wanted to look really sharp.

On the morning of the game, Elizabeth dropped me, Lee Chapman photo and all, at John Borrington's barber shop. It was the first place Brian got his hair cut when he came to Derby in 1967, a proper, old-fashioned short-back-and-sides sort of place. Simon and Nigel have never gone anywhere else.

You should have seen the look on John's face when I asked him to style my mop like Chappy's. When I told him why, he couldn't stop laughing.

When he finished, I thought it looked pretty much the same as the Dolph Lundgren Dad had given me a couple of years back, but John and his daughter, Joy, who worked with him, managed to convince me I was a dead ringer for Lee Chapman.

I waited outside for Lib to pick me up. She had promised to take me to man2man – 'the most casual smart clothes shop in Derby'. I'd never had hair this short before, my ears were bloody freezing!

Brian had given me 40 quid for doing the lawn and sweeping the drive. I was supposed to have put it in the bank account that he had set up for me at the Nottingham Building Society but this was a special occasion. Tonight, we were playing Liverpool. Lee Chapman was playing his first game for us at the City Ground and Ms Leslie Ash would be in attendance.

I paid 35 frigging pounds for the first pair of smart trousers I tried on. I'd never paid 35 quid for anything in my life! When I told the man in the shop I had only gone in for a T-shirt because I needed to look cool tonight, he asked how much money I had left. He threw in a T-shirt that should have been 25 quid for the spare fiver.

By the time five o'clock came around, I was looking very dapper indeed. I snapped myself out of admiring the haircut when I heard Mrs Clough beep the horn – they were all in the car, waiting for me to come downstairs.

I had spent ages in the bathroom fussing over my hair. I must have nicked at least half a can of Libby's hair mousse. I'd also had a shave, though I didn't really need to, brushed my teeth twice and borrowed some of Brian's really posh Ermenegildo Zegna aftershave that he kept in a special box in the bathroom.

When I got in the car, the girls were giggling. Mrs Clough told me I smelled very nice – 'I'll just wind the windows down for a while though. Did you slip while you put it on, pet? Eeh, mind you look very handsome, son. Is it a special occasion?'

'No, not really.'

When we got to the ground, I spent most of the build-up hiding in the weights room. I'd usually be out on the pitch with the lads but I didn't want to risk dirtying my new gear. The players' wives used to drink in the Jubilee Club or, occasionally, the more formal Trophy Room, where the directors entertained guests.

From the second Leslie Ash waltzed into the Jubilee Club, madness broke out. There were so many people around her, I didn't dare go up and say hello. I was gutted with myself. I'm standing there in my 35 quid trousers and my new swished-back hair, jumping up and down, trying to catch a glimpse. It was as close as I got. Then I went with the apprentices and sat on the track to watch the match.

The electricity flowed from more than the floodlights. The place crackled with 30,000 voices. Liverpool were beaten, 2–1, but I kept thinking that I hadn't got to talk to Leslie Ash or even got close to her and now I was left with this stupid Lee Chapman haircut that would take six weeks to grow out.

I always tried to be first back into Brian's office after the game so I could serve the drinks. The second the final whistle goes, I'm down to the tunnel, up through the changing rooms and into the main office area, quick as a rabbit.

Just as I go through the first set of doors, I see a vision coming towards me: Leslie bloody Ash. She looks as lovely as anything I have ever come close to. I can't think of anything funny or smart to say. She has come down from the directors' box and is looking for the loo. She has to ask me twice if I know where the toilets are.

I simply hold the door open for her, wearing the biggest, stupidest smile I have ever attempted. I probably got too close, trying to smell her as she swept past.

As she disappeared, something struck me: Leslie Ash was a star, she was lovely but she wasn't as beautiful close up, in the flesh, as I'd imagined. I actually thought Simon and Nigel's girlfriends, Sue and Margaret, both of whom had flawless complexions, were prettier.

Forty-five minutes later, Chappy came in to introduce her to Brian: 'Excuse me, Gaffer, but do you mind if Leslie comes to say hello? She's a big fan.'

'Of course not, son. Bring her in. The pleasure's all mine. Weeeaaaahhh, hello beauty, you look even nicer in real life than you do on the telly!'

He had never seen an episode of *C.A.T.S. Eyes* in his life. Whenever he caught me watching it, he told me to: 'Turn that garbage off.' Then, he's kissing her hand as if she's a princess. Say what you want about Brian Clough, but my God, he could be a smooth bugger.

'Hey, beauty, look after him for me, will you? And sweetheart, don't forget – the second he causes you any trouble at all, give me a call and I'll cut his balls off. Any trouble at all. Hey, pet, I'm not joking. Honest. Oooohhh, you're so lovely!'

Still kissing her hand, he's introducing her to everyone in the room.

Lee looks at me. I'm staring *way* too much at his wife.

'Hey, Mack, that's a smart haircut, son. Leslie, come and say hello to Mack for a second. He's one of us.'

'Hi again,' she says. 'We've already met. He was lovely and held the door for me when I needed the toilet. Hello, Mack, I'm Leslie. Nice to meet you. You look *ve-ry* smart for a young man.'

That was more than enough, thank you very much. Life could have ended then and I would have settled for that.

On the Friday, I went back to Sunderland, mainly because I had to get a letter from school, confirming I'd officially left. I would turn 16 in November. Then, after Christmas, I would have officially left and could return to Quarndon.

'Don't tell yer mam the details, son. Just say you're coming to stay with us for a few weeks,' Brian said. 'We'll just keep extending your stay.'

Because I was so bright, I had been scheduled to take Maths and English GCSEs a year early. But I missed the exams because Dad thought it more important that I went out to buy some lead solder to help his business forging 50-pence pieces – I told Brian I had already passed.

I went back to Sunderland shortly afterwards.

The year 1988 was our last Christmas in Shakespeare Street. It was a hard, strange Christmas. Across the river in Pallion, the last ship had just been launched into the Wear. When the red hull of the *New Heritage* goes into the water, Sunderland's last shipyard closes.

Mam was preparing to leave. In the New Year, she'd be joining Dad, who had gone to live in Harrow. They'd be living in a bedsit. I wondered where I fitted into the relocation. There was never a proper discussion. She said: 'I'm going to London. You're either coming with me or you're not.'

Aaron was still in the army and our Darren's time at the University of Ulster had ended when he spent his full-term grant – and half of next year's – on buying people in his halls of residence clothes and Hi-Fis. It was part of our DNA – whenever we had money, we wanted to share it around.

We didn't realise Darren had money troubles until he came home and told us he couldn't go back to Northern Ireland. One day, he said he was going to the shop for a pint of milk. The next we heard from him was via a postcard sent from France, where he was working on rich people's boats.

Our Joanne had found the man who would take her out of Shakespeare Street. Alan was her law lecturer at Sunderland College. A vegetarian and political activist, he possessed the biggest heart of anybody I ever met. He was in his twenties but looked older. These were two people genuinely in love.

On New Year's Eve, we walked to the bus depot at Park Lane, where I would get the National Express to Sheffield to meet Brian at Hillsborough.

'I'll see you in a couple of weeks, Mam.'

'No, you won't, son. You'll not be coming back.'

Deep down, she knew – mothers always know.

15.

It's a Cracker

18 January 1989

It's early, really early. Outside it's black. We're supposed to be going to Central News to put the papers out.

Central News was to have an increasingly pivotal role in my time with the Cloughs. It was a newsagent's and card shop in Central Avenue in West Bridgford, one of Nottingham's posher areas, near Trent Bridge and the City Ground. As you walk through the front doors, the magazine racks are on the left, the ice-cream cabinet and the cards are on the right. There are two tills, one at the front and one at the back of the shop. The back till is where they sell cigarettes and Spot the Ball coupons; the newspapers are sold at the front.

When I got downstairs to the kitchen, there was nobody there. For once, Brian has slept in. I make him a cup of tea, in the teapot, with the tea cosy on. By the time he comes down, it's cold.

Tonight, Nottingham Forest will play a League Cup quarter-final against Queens Park Rangers. Nigel's a doubt because he strained his groin while gardening, something that has made Brian furious. It doesn't matter that Nigel has so often played when he is not fully fit, played when it hurts. To Brian, this is a ridiculous reason to miss a cup tie.

Nigel's garden has been landscaped, a rockery built, but for privacy, he'd like some trees. 'Son, don't worry about the trees,' Brian had said to him. 'Leave it to us, we'll sort those out for you.'

Brian adored his garden. He would spend hours pruning, watering and talking to his rose beds. At the bottom, there was an orchard and, sometimes, the Forest apprentices would come up to help while Mrs Clough served bacon sandwiches and milk for them. Nigel would sit on the big, petrol-driven lawnmower with his headphones on.

Despite what his dad might have said, Nigel liked gardening and he knew what trees he wanted and they were not the ones Brian was intent on giving him.

After we've put the papers out, we set off in the dog's car to a garden centre in Stapleford called Bardills. Brian marches in and there are eight sequoias ready for the garden centre's biggest and most favourite customer.

The young trees are loaded into the back of the car. We're driving them up the hill and in front of us is a learner driver, grimly determined not to go anywhere near the speed limit. Brian starts gripping the steering wheel tight, muttering to himself. Then, with the brow of the hill approaching, he accelerates past the learner, straight towards another pair of oncoming headlights. Just in time, he swerves the car into its own lane. The driving instructor will now be using Brian's manoeuvre as an example of how *not* to overtake.

The road leading to Nigel's house is narrow with cars

parked on both sides. There's an old boy in his Rover. Brian flashes him through. The old boy recognises Brian and, driving under the influence of celebrity, proceeds to hit the back of a parked milk float. The sound of a hundred milk bottles slamming into each other cascades down the avenue.

The milkman jumps out. 'You stupid old fucker! You shouldn't even be on the road at your age. I've still got half a fucking round to do.'

Brian gets out of his car. 'Hey, young man, this is an elderly gentleman and you should show him some respect. He didn't mean to hit you.'

'What the fuck has it got to do with you?'

'Hey, son, you need to calm down. Now then, how much is this going to cost to fix?'

'I don't know. Eighty might do it.'

Brian rummages around in his tracksuit pockets and hands over 10 x £10 notes. He goes over to the Rover and gives the old man a hug.

It's half seven by the time we pull into Nigel's house and a grey dawn is starting to break over Allestree.

Brian turns to me, finger over his lips: 'Right, Rigor, you need to be quiet. We're going to bed these trees in before Nigel wakes up. I want no noise.'

Half the trees have been placed in the back garden and we're on our way back to get the rest when there's a light, a twitch of a curtain and the silhouette of Margaret in the window.

'Rigor, drop 'em! We've been rumbled! In the car now.'

The sequoias hit the drive. We scramble into the car and screech off back to the safety of Central News.

One of the regular customers was an old woman who came to the shop for her paper but never wore any shoes. This, however, is the first time Brian has seen her.

He stands watching as she pays for her *Daily Express*. Then, without a word, he walks into Ford's, the general store next door where you can buy pretty much anything. He emerges with a pair of slippers.

'Now then, beauty, why don't you put these on? You shouldn't have to come in here in the middle of winter without something on your feet, not in this day and age.'

The woman turns to him: 'Who the hell do you think you are? Do you think you can just tell me what to wear? Are you the kind of person who thinks money can buy everything? I don't care if you're Brian Clough, you've no right!'

'Pet, I didn't mean ... I wasn't trying to be rude now.'

The woman stalks out. Barefoot.

We go to the City Ground, where the lads have a very light training session and some lunch. On the way back, three kids on speedway bikes overtake us and start skidding across the football pitches on the Embankment. Mud flies everywhere. Deep brown scars appear on the turf.

The car stops. Brian gets out: 'Oi, stop that, you shithouses! Those are football pitches, they're for people to play on.'

The boys swing the bikes round to face him.

'Fuck off, grandad!'

When he slides back into the driver's seat, Brian is visibly shaking. We set off back towards Derby and then we're cut up by a BMW on a roundabout. Brian jams his foot down and the dog's car accelerates at a rate it has seldom, if ever, done before.

The road signs say 30. We're doing 50, tailgating the BMW down a country lane. It reaches its drive. The guy must think he's home, that he's safe, but as he gets out of the BMW, Brian runs towards him, grabs him and pushes him hard against the car.

He's a big bloke, he looks powerful. This could easily turn very nasty. Then he looks deep into the face of the man who has hold of him: 'Now, Mr Clough, I'm really sorry. I don't normally drive like that. I was late, in a hurry. I'm sorry. I'm a big fan of yours.' Finally, in a day of confrontations, he has a little victory.

We drive home, straight into the arms of Mrs Clough, who had the knack being able to calm Brian down just by talking to him.

What has been a frantic day has paused for food and, after a bite to eat, we drive back to the City Ground for a League Cup quarter-final. Nigel says he is fit to play.

Forest are electric. They are 4–1 up at half-time. Lee Chapman scores the first two goals. Then, they are awarded a penalty. Nigel is the designated penalty-taker but Chapman is on a hat-trick. The crowd think Chapman should take it, but when Nigel picks the ball up, puts it on the spot, there are boos and the Trent End starts chanting Chapman's name.

Nigel scores.

Brian is livid: Forest fans, Nottingham Forest fans, have booed his son.

Chapman gets his third and then his fourth. Brian starts shouting at him: 'Oi, Chapman, when you score a hat-trick, you don't run to the supporters, you run to me. I'm the one who signed you.'

Queens Park Rangers are beaten, 5–2, and some young fans go on to the pitch, wanting to be with the players. Brian gets out of the dug-out. He's had enough. This is his pitch, his ground, his grass and everybody else can just bugger off. He hits one lad on the back of the head and starts throwing more punches.

Afterwards, Brian is indignant, saying he was stopping a pitch invasion. Everybody else is less convinced. Everybody else thinks this looked bad, *very* bad. He will have to be interviewed by the police.

The corridor to the manager's office is sealed off by stewards. The lights in his office are switched off. Mike Keeling comes to give him a lift home. Brian has been drinking but he isn't obviously drunk, although he is still convinced right had been on his side.

When he told Mrs Clough what had happened, she exclaimed: 'Oh my God, what have you done?' Midnight was approaching but it still seemed a good time for us to take Del for a walk across the common.

He still hadn't come to terms with the fact that the Trent End, where Nottingham Forest's most passionate supporters stood, had booed his own son. Of the fact he had struck his own fans, there was no mention. Most other managers would have spent the walk contemplating the sack. However, Brian's grip on Nottingham Forest was total. The following morning, the chairman, Maurice Roworth, stood on his doorstep and blamed the fans. Brian was given a three-month touchline ban by the FA.

By the time of the Queens Park Rangers game I'd been living with Brian for almost three weeks. In the first year, my life with him would be centred around the City Ground. I had to pinch myself I was going to work with this man, but just as I was always on edge in Sunderland, I was on edge in Nottingham.

It was a schizophrenic existence. In Nottingham, I had unlimited food, plenty of money and decent clothes – everything I had been denied in Southwick. However, as I spent more and more time with the Cloughs, the anxiety grew that my mask would slip. He would see the real me and he would not like the face.

As time goes by and Forest keep winning, I become the sort of person footballers, hardened professional footballers, like to have around. They want me on the team bus, they like having me in the dressing rooms. They think I should watch from the dug-out – they think I'm lucky.

Footballers are superstitious people. Some are first out of the dressing room, some want to be last. Some put their left boot on first, others their right. Always.

Leeds United manager Don Revie was like that. In 1971 he was looking for reasons why his team had lost the title to Arsenal by a point. Then, he glanced at the Leeds United badge. Revie had always thought birds unlucky and now he saw an owl staring back at him. He picked up the phone and ordered the badge to be changed. Immediately.

The following season, Leeds lost the title by a point to Brian, who had also changed the Derby County badge to have the ram facing the other way. Superstition was virtually the only thing the two men had in common. They were born a 15-minute walk away from each other in Middlesbrough. Each won the league title twice but while Revie viewed football as a science, to be plotted and schemed mechanically, Brian saw it as something much more instinctive. To him, it was an art.

The first game after I left Sunderland was at Sheffield Wednesday on New Year's Eve 1988. Nottingham Forest went to Hillsborough twelfth in the table. They had only won four games out of 18. Now, they beat Sheffield Wednesday, 3–0. They beat Everton, Tottenham, Aston Villa, Luton and Arsenal. By 18 March, they are fifth. They have beaten Ipswich, Leeds, Watford and Manchester United to reach the semi-finals of the FA Cup for a second year running. For the second year in a row, they will face Liverpool.

I was as close to living the footballer's dream as you could be without being a footballer. I was in the dug-out, on the pitch, in the dressing rooms, in the manager's office. I was at Highbury, Goodison, Old Trafford, Anfield.

Nottingham Forest are also in the League Cup final. The win over QPR brought a semi-final against Bristol City, who were in the Third Division. The first leg was at the City Ground, where Forest were lucky to get away with a 1–1 draw.

I was back in Sunderland for the second leg. I was playing a seven-a-side game, where I met a lad called Lee Walker, who was the spitting image of Colin Hendry and sold me a Scotland tracksuit for a fiver. He was also a Nottingham Forest fan for no other reason than his dad looked like Peter Shilton.

We watched Forest win 1–0 at Ashton Gate on television. Brian was through to his first major final since the European Cup in 1980. There and then, I promised Lee I would get him and his dad tickets for Wembley. He didn't believe me.

The hotel Forest stayed in for the final didn't exactly fit the occasion. For a Wembley final, clubs would book the likes of Burnham Beeches, a country house hotel in Buckinghamshire, with its own sports pitches and grounds. Forest chose the Posthouse at South Mimms, where the M25 meets the A1. It was a glorified service station but it had a fruit machine and a snooker table, which was all I needed.

We got on the bus at the City Ground. Stuart Pearce and Neil Webb were already on board. Both had been in the papers; there was talk of a move to Manchester United for both of them, where Alex Ferguson would treble the skipper's wages. Now, they were together and I said: 'Stuart, are you staying?'

Pearcey turned to me: 'Son, I've told you before, there are certain things you can't ask.'

'But we're mates. Of course, I can ask. Are you staying?'

'Look, don't tell the Gaffer because we're still having contract negotiations but, yeah, I'm staying.'

'Webby, what about you?'

'I'm not answering.'

Neil Webb left for Old Trafford three months later.

* * *

It's the day of the League Cup final, Sunday, 9 April 1989. I'm nervous. There's going to be cameras on the team bus as we head down to Wembley and I'm wondering what I'll look like on television. It's only when I'm on the bus that I find out they only do the bus broadcast for the FA Cup final.

I'm nervous for other reasons. Brian has given me five tickets for my mates, including a couple for Lee and his Peter Shilton-lookalike father, plus three tickets for Dad, our Darren and one of Dad's mates. Brian's also given me a Nottingham Forest jacket to give to Dad.

We've agreed to meet at a burger van outside Wembley but there are thousands of the bloody things. Burgers, southern-fried chicken, foot-long hot-dogs. We run into each other almost by accident on the steps of Wembley Way. On his way up to the stadium, Dad had been monkey-chanted by a group of fans.

They were supporters of Nottingham Forest. I was wearing a Nottingham Forest tracksuit. What the fuck?

When I hand over the tickets and the jacket, Dad looks me up and down. For the first time I can remember, he seems proud of me.

Wearing the official tracksuit, I go out on to the pitch with the players. I've also got a change of clothes because, before we set off, Garry Parker promised to throw me in the bath if Forest win. As I walk off, a ball rolls to my feet and, from the edge of the box, I launch it into the top corner. There may have been no goalkeeper present but I don't care: I've scored at Wembley.

I thought I'd be with Brian on the bench – they had suspended his touchline ban for the final. Three or four minutes before we're due to go out, Brian comes over: 'Now then, you don't want to watch from the bench. The view's terrible. You'll be better off in the stands.' I found out later that they had miscounted the number of places they had and there wasn't room for me.

Forest are playing Luton, who had beaten Arsenal in last year's final. For most of the first half, it looks as if they will win it again. A header from Mick Harford, who grew up in Sunderland, puts Luton ahead and they should have had more than one goal.

The game turns on a penalty. Steve Hodge is wiped out by Luton's goalkeeper, Les Sealey, and Nigel drives home the penalty. I'm shaking with nerves when he puts the ball on the spot. Nigel was considerably calmer.

Forest seize the final by the throat. Webby scores the second, Nigel the third. They are lovely goals, both made by beautiful passes from Tommy Gaynor, the young Irish forward.

Forest's first game in that season's League Cup had been against Chester. We scored six and Tommy hit three of them. Brian had left him out for the next game, at home to Luton. The game was goalless and, on the Monday, Tommy, who had grown up in Limerick and played for Shamrock Rovers and Dundalk, went to Brian's office to ask why he had been dropped.

I was in the office. Sometimes, when this happened, the player would ask me to leave. Sometimes, Brian would ask me to go. On other occasions I would be ignored and allowed to sit in the corner. This was one of those occasions.

'What do you want, Irishman?'

'I'm sorry, Gaffer. I just wanted to know why you'd left me out on Saturday? I scored a hat-trick on Wednesday. What more can I do?'

'Listen, son, you only scored against bloody Chester! It doesn't count.'

Tommy deflated in front of me, his courage seeping out of every pore. This was the kind of conversation Brian was well used to. Tommy would probably have rehearsed what he was going to say before he knocked, but here in this office, in front of this man, the words he had gone over in his head disappeared. There was nothing left to say.

That night, we walked Del around the cricket ground. 'Now then,' Brian said, 'how do you think I handled young Tommy Gaynor?'

'But, Brian, if you had scored a hat-trick when you were a player and your boss had told you it didn't count, how would you have felt?'

We both laughed at the same time: 'I'd have cut his bloody balls off.'

'You're quite right, son, I would have done just that.'

Tommy played in every one of Forest's League Cup games.

The promise was kept: I was thrown into the big, deep baths in the Wembley dressing rooms. I put on the blue Marks & Spencer sweater Mrs Clough had given me and posed for a picture with the League Cup wearing Brian's glasses.

There is beer everywhere on the team bus as it travels back to Nottingham, beeped and flashed by Forest fans as the North Circular Road becomes the M1. Webby is hammered, walking up and down the bus, shouting: 'You'll do for me, Tommy, you'll do for me!' I'm pretty drunk on the little bottles of Amstel they keep at the back of the bus.

Brian is deeply happy. This is his first trophy in nine years, the first he has won since the split with Peter Taylor. He wanted to prove he could win things again and he could win them without Pete. Now he had.

Brian loved trophies, whatever they were. His first trophy for Nottingham Forest had been the Anglo-Scottish Cup in 1976. Later that month, Forest would be back at Wembley for the final of the Simod Cup, a competition invented to make up for the loss of European football because of the Heysel ban, imposed after Liverpool fans had run amok before the European Cup final against Juventus.

There had been 39 deaths that night in Brussels and the five-year ban on English clubs helped ensure that the last European game overseen by a man who had so improbably and romantically conquered the continent was a 1–0 defeat in Bruges a couple of weeks before I first saw Brian on the beach at Seaburn.

They would win the Simod Cup, beating Everton, 4–3. The year before, they'd beaten Sheffield Wednesday at Wembley to win the Mercantile Credit Centenary Trophy. To Brian, it was all silverware.

When we're dropped off, Brian takes the League Cup and puts it in his boot and we drive to Allestree for fish and chips at Mr Mo's. It's quite late and we buy up whatever he has left: cod, pies, saveloys. Payment is offered but not accepted – 'This is on me, Brian. You've earned it.'

When we get home, Brian takes some fish and chips into the lounge and sits on his recliner, eating them with the League Cup standing on top of the television. Eleven years before, when he won it for the first time, he had done exactly the same.

16.

The Longest Day

Saturday, 15 April 1989

It's a beautiful spring morning. Brian is one game away from the first FA Cup final of his career. Nottingham Forest will play Liverpool, who are league champions and top of Division One. They have won their last 11 games.

Steve Chettle is nervous. He's a brave footballer but this afternoon he'll be in defence, up against John Barnes, and he hates the very thought of it. However, the rest of the lads on the bus are confident as we drive up the M1 to Sheffield.

Of the last 22 games, Forest have lost two. We've just won the League Cup. We're in the final of the Simod Cup. We are motivated, not just because we want Brian to win the FA Cup, but because Nottingham Forest in April 1989 are a very good side. However, when the bus parks up inside Hillsborough's big blue gates, the atmosphere is strange, nasty, brooding. As I get off the team bus, I'm scared – I've never felt like this before.

Sometimes, at Millwall or Leeds, Brian would order the bus to park outside the ground and the players to walk, just to show they were not intimidated. This is different. There's a kind of electricity in the air. Hostile electricity. Vitriol. When I'm given my ticket, I'm told not to show it about.

The ticket takes me to the Main Stand, where I'm sitting alongside Ronnie Fenton, Franz Carr and a young lad called Billy Stubbs. He was one of Brian's hunches. Like Garry Birtles, he was a forward, signed from non-league football, where Billy had been playing for Seaham Red Star. Brian gave Billy £10 to shave off his moustache. Unlike Garry Birtles, the hunch never comes off.

The semi-final begins. Peter Beardsley hits the bar, then some Liverpool fans seem to be invading the pitch. I leap out of my seat and start shouting. Their fans are trying to stop our counter-attack: bastards.

Franz Carr taps me on the shoulder and says: 'Hang on a second, son. Sit down and shut up, this is something different.'

Over to the left, in the Leppings Lane End, Liverpool supporters are being lifted over the fences or being helped up to the second tier of the stand. The game comes to a standstill. Something is going very wrong. I start to panic. Our Darren and some of my mates from Sunderland have come down for the game. Brian had sorted tickets for them and now they're on the other side of the ground, in the Spion Kop.

Are they safe – are they?

We are all ushered down into the dressing rooms. Somebody says there has been a death. Later, we are told five people have been killed. Lee Chapman has played for Sheffield Wednesday. He knows the club's commercial manager, who tells him the gymnasium is being turned into a morgue.

I go back out with a few of the players. There's a line of about 40 policemen who are standing across the pitch with their arms linked. They start marching towards the Kop, where the Forest supporters are – they want to stop the Nottingham Forest fans from invading the pitch and clashing with the Liverpool supporters. That there could or would be a pitch invasion in these circumstances is the product of someone's imagination.

As bodies are carried by on advertising hoardings, I go to the end of the police line and ask what they're doing, why aren't they helping? A policeman turns and says I should mind my own fucking business – they have their orders.

The disaster is being broadcast live by *Grandstand* on the BBC. The cameras catch me walking by the side of the pitch alongside Des Walker, Steve Hodge and Billy Stubbs. I've got the tracksuit top tied around my waist and my skinny arms are showing through a cream T-shirt – that's how Mam knows I'm alive.

We go back to the dressing rooms and mill about. Nobody says the game has been called off, but at six o'clock, Brian tells the lads: 'We're going home. Get your stuff and get on the bus.'

In the players' lounge they have watched Des Lynam on television say there's a possibility that as many as 75 have died. The Nottingham Forest bus, like the Liverpool bus, went home in silence. The only difference was that one had the radio playing softly while the other, returning to a numbed Merseyside, was not allowed even that distraction.

Brian was at the front of the Forest bus, slumped in his seat. The deaths had left him distraught; the early, confused reports that Liverpool fans have stormed the gates and triggered a catastrophe have left him darkly furious.

For a long time afterwards, he was convinced Liverpool fans who had come early to Hillsborough and waited patiently by the fences at the Leppings Lane End had been overwhelmed by a tide of supporters, who had disobeyed every instruction and swept into the stadium: the innocent killed by the reckless.

Usually, words tumbled out of Brian. There were one-liners, there were quotes from Sinatra, there were the exchanges with Michael Parkinson or David Frost that could captivate a television audience. There were the speeches that inspired footballers to win European Cups and there were the dark threats that would chill your blood.

Tonight, there were no words. We walked Del around the common in complete silence.

The next day, I was in the lounge watching *Willy Wonka & the Chocolate Factory*. Even at 16, it's a film I loved because I am Charlie Bucket, the poor, scruffy kid who wins the Golden Ticket and sees a world that would otherwise be barred to him.

I went out to take Del for a walk and I was coming down the drive when someone emerged from behind a clump of trees.

'Who are you?' he asks.

'I'm Craig. I'm taking the dog for a walk.'

'Why have you got Brian Clough's dog?'

'I live here.'

'You live in that house with Brian Clough?'

'I do.'

'I'll tell you what, son. I'll give you 2,000 quid if you'll give me his phone number.'

My head's reeling but I've just been watching *Willy Wonka & the Chocolate Factory*. The film has a villain, Arthur Slugworth, a rival chocolate maker who tells all the children who win the Golden Ticket that he will reward them handsomely if they smuggle out an Everlasting Gobstopper. At the end, you discover Slugworth works for Wonka and this is a loyalty test, one that Charlie passes.

With his thin face and glasses, the guy by the trees even looks like Arthur Slugworth.

This guy works for Brian. This is a test to see how far he can trust me. If I fail, Brian will throw me out.

'I'm sorry, mate, but you've got no chance.'

I walk up the drive and tell Brian, who marches out, looking for the man. For the next three days, there are journalists and photographers in the garden. Some have stepladders so they can take pictures over the fence.

In one sense the Cloughs and the Bromfields were alike. When one felt threatened, they all responded and now Nigel goes to close the gates, telling everyone they are on private property.

Brian has a rifle that is supposed to be used for shooting pheasants, although it has yet to be fired at anything. Now, he threatens to use it on those milling around outside. For those few days, he retreated totally into himself. He was as quiet and as alone as I ever saw him. Those days will be the start of his being dragged down by alcohol.

Nobody at Nottingham Forest wanted the game replayed, but it was – at Old Trafford on Sunday, 7 May. This time I watched Nigel get poked in the eye in the first minute by John Aldridge, who scored twice. I hated him for that. When Brian Laws put through his own net to make it certain Liverpool would win, Aldridge went over and ruffled his hair. I hated him even more.

Just as we had done the year before, Forest had to go to Anfield immediately after being beaten by Liverpool in an FA Cup semi-final. This time, we lost 1–0. Steve Chettle made the mistake for the goal and once more, Aldridge went over to ruffle his hair.

On the bus I asked him: 'Did he go to ruffle your hair?'

'Yeah, he did.'

'Why didn't you just punch him?'

'You know, Mack, I really wanted to do it but can you imagine what the Gaffer would have done if I'd been sent off? He would have absolutely destroyed me.'

'You might not have been able to punch him but I could.'

With that, I got off the bus and marched towards the players' entrance, shouting: 'Aldridge, you fucking cheating bastard! You fucking twat, where are you?' I am 16 and wearing glasses, heading towards a dressing room full of professional athletes.

Fortunately, John Barnes, who was good mates with Des Walker, and Stevie Nichol managed to restrain me and guided me back to the bus.

Aldridge scored again when Liverpool beat Everton to win the FA Cup. Six days later came the final night of the season.

The only way Liverpool would not win the Double was if Arsenal came to Anfield and beat them by two clear goals.

We watched the game on television in Brian's study. Arsenal scored but time was draining away and with a quarter of an hour to go, Brian stood up and said: 'I can't watch this anymore,' and walked out.

He didn't see Michael Thomas score Arsenal's second. He didn't see John Aldridge lying distraught on the turf. He didn't see Tony Adams go over to Aldridge, ruffle his hair and say: 'That's for Brian Laws.'

He did hear me, running around the house screeching in celebration, in a way I have never celebrated any goal scored by Nottingham Forest. That, too, was for Brian Laws.

17.
When I Was 17 ...

When I was 17, it was a very good year
For a small-town boy who lived a dream,
Seeing things he'd never seen,
Watching Brian building his second-greatest team.

I'm behind the counter in the most famous newsagent's in Nottingham. Sometimes Brian would turn up at Central News, handing out charisma with the *Daily Mail*. He could be wonderful around people who didn't know him and had never met him before. At every general election he would go out on the doorstep with Phillip Whitehead, who was the Labour MP for Derby North until he lost his seat in the Thatcher landslide in 1983 – he was a natural.

Whenever he came into Central News, there would always be requests for photographs and autographs. Even when he didn't want to, he would pull on the smile, say the one-liners, laugh along. When it was just Simon behind the counter, they would say things to him they would never dare utter in front of Brian. Sometimes, they would talk at him, rather than to him about players not playing and transfers not made. Why had Neil Webb been allowed to go to Manchester United? Why was John Sheridan not playing?

Sheridan was the biggest talking point. He was a beautiful passer of a football who had joined Forest from Leeds for £650,000. But Sheridan did not play a league game and after a few months of inaction was sold to Ron Atkinson at Sheffield Wednesday for a £90,000 loss.

There was no obvious reason why he did it. Brian liked players who were clean-shaven and Sheridan wore stubble. He liked players who didn't answer back and Sheridan had attitude. Also, he didn't run. Forest wanted a box-to-box midfielder like Ian Bowyer or Steve Hodge. They got a stroller, albeit a graceful one – Brian wanted more.

At first, I was only helping out at Central News. Simon would open up at six after driving to the shop like a maniac because we were always running late. The papers would be laid out, we would break for a cup of tea and then open up.

I would fill up shelves, serve customers. I was good at it, especially the mental arithmetic. We sold a vast array of cigarettes, the brands others didn't. If someone asked for a packet of Gauloises Disque Bleu or Capstan Full Strength, I'd know where they were and what they cost.

Very quickly, I was made assistant manager. Most of the original part-time staff were elderly and soon I would be telling a 60-year-old woman when she could take her break or when she should start filling the shelves. As a teenager, every scrap of power can go to your head; it started to change me.

I'm changing in other ways. I'm getting better at football. I've been practising hitting the bar with Scot Gemmill. I've actually started beating him when we play first to 10, although he smashes me at everything else.

Still tiny, I haven't learned to tackle so AC Hunters, the team that Simon coached, play me on the left of midfield, where I can't do any harm.

I'm giving myself driving lessons whenever I'm waiting for Brian to leave the office. We're in the dog's car and I'm practising changing gear. We've left the engine on to keep Del warm. I'm definitely not allowed to drive – I'm still only 16. But, if no one's watching, I might as well have a quick dash around the car park. Brian's told me not to do it, but Del loves it. His tail never stops wagging and you can see his eyes smiling.

When Brian gets in, he's pissed off because he has to put the seat back.

'Have you moved this car, son? I'm sure we parked facing the other way.'

'No, Brian. I just played with the windscreen wipers, that's all.'

When we pull into the drive at Brian's house, he turns to me: 'Hey, son, I forgot to say well done, all those talks we had are paying off. Simon tells me you're doing really well at work. He says you're good with customers, even though they mustn't be able to understand a bloody word of what you're mumbling. Son, get your bloody head up and look them in the eye while you're talking to them. Make eye contact and keep smiling, you've got a lovely smile – everyone likes someone who smiles.'

Then, we're off, arm in arm, skipping down the lane, laughing and doing Morecambe & Wise-style dancing with his walking stick, tapping his shoes.

By then, I loved Sinatra almost as much as Brian did. I had no choice. Frank was in the lounge, he was in the car, he was on Brian's lips when he walked with Del and me around the cricket pitch.

On the Thursday before we went down to Wembley for the League Cup final against Luton, I answered the door to the postman. He had a telegram for Brian. It was from Frank Sinatra:

Go Get'Em! Win This Thing. All the best, Frank

I can't quite believe I'm holding a telegram from Frank Sinatra to Brian Clough. I can't quite believe Frank has remembered the date of the League Cup final.

When he held the piece of paper, Brian seemed overwhelmed, as thrilled as I'd been when the letter with the Nottingham Forest badge came through the door at Shakespeare Street.

'Weeeaaaahhh, Rigor! Be good, son, be good. I've said it a million times, but that's it, that's all that counts. Whatever you're going to do in life, you've got to try to do it as best you can and then you've got to keep doing it, day in and day out. If you do that, then you've cracked it, son. If you're going to be a football manager like me, you might as well be the best in the business. If you're going to be a teacher, make sure you're a bloody good teacher. Son, you might have no choice but to be a newsagent but it's nice to know you're getting pretty good at it. Keep it up, well done.'

Then, he starts singing: 'Like you'll never get rid of your shadow, Rigor, you'll never really get rid of me. Just me and my shadow, strolling down the avenue. Me and my shadow, we're alone but far from blue.'

Then, we're off home, where Nigel wants to talk to me: he has a surprise. Brian won't tell me what it is, but says I will love it.

There have been plenty of surprises. One was to go with him to the Midlands Football Writers' Dinner in Birmingham.

Mine was a last-minute invitation and, of course, I had nothing suitable to wear. Brian had a wardrobe full of suits, although he didn't like wearing them and especially didn't like tying his own tie. Mrs Clough had to help him do it. He told me to pick out a jacket.

I chose a blue, double-breasted blazer with the Nottingham Forest badge etched in gold. On my frame it seemed massive – I was swimming in it.

Brian was going because Nigel had been nominated as Midlands Footballer of the Year. Just before the ceremony started, he heard that Tony Daley of Aston Villa had won.

'Tony Daley, Tony fucking Daley? Ahead of my boy? You have to be fucking joking!' He was livid.

Brian was not the sort to forget. A year later, in November 1990, Forest were playing Aston Villa. Villa had a new manager – Jozef Venglos from Czechoslovakia, who had replaced Graham Taylor.

Venglos had taken Czechoslovakia to the quarter-finals of the World Cup in Italy and had a big reputation. I was with Brian in the dug-out at Villa Park and all we could hear was Venglos shouting: 'Go, Tony Daley! Go, Tony Daley! Give the ball to Tony Daley!'

Midway through the second half, Daley was substituted and as he walked off, Brian put his hand to his mouth and shouted: 'Go, Tony Daley!'

He seldom told Nigel how highly he rated him, how good a player he thought he was. In public, he called him 'the number nine', 'the centre-forward'. When Nigel's name came up in private, all Brian could talk about was how good he was.

The great fear was that Nigel would leave. Not because he no longer wanted to play for his father but because he was Nottingham Forest's most valuable asset and, with average gates of 20,000, everyone at the City Ground, even the son of its absolute ruler, had his price.

Italy rather than France was now the big draw, where the most money could be made – a few years later, Des Walker would join Sampdoria. Now word got out that Bari were interested in taking Nigel to Serie A.

'Do you think he'll go?' I asked Brian as we walked Del down the drive.

'If he does, his mam will cut my balls off.'

Nigel stayed, but so did the fear.

Graham Taylor, who was still then manager of Aston Villa, had never hidden his admiration for Nigel. 'He is the only footballer in the English game I would buy a ticket to watch' was a phrase he used more than once.

WHEN I WAS 17

Aston Villa were now challenging Liverpool for the title and they had a bigger budget than Nottingham Forest. One winter afternoon, when it was already growing dark, Carole, his secretary, said: 'Brian, Graham Taylor is in the foyer. He says he was just passing and wondered if you'd like a chat.'

Brian knew instinctively who would be the subject of that 'chat'. He leapt up and switched off all the lights in his office. Through the gloom he said: 'Rigor, take the keys and move my car out of its parking space. If Taylor sees the car, he'll know I haven't left.'

I hadn't actually passed my test but I slipped into the car park. Fortunately, because it was less obviously the car of the manager of Nottingham Forest and it was easier to drive, he had taken the dog's car rather than the Mercedes. I nosed it out of the ground and into a side street. I then went back into reception and saw Graham Taylor sitting in the corridor – 'I'm sorry, Mr Taylor, but the manager has already left for the evening.'

Taylor's face registered pure astonishment: he had been in that seat for at least 45 minutes.

The low gates, however, meant Nottingham Forest were always vulnerable. Paul White, who succeeded Ken Smales as club secretary, had a television in his office that was linked to the turnstiles. On matchday, Brian would come up before kick-off and check the attendances.

A couple of years later, in May 1991, he would stand in front of the screen and shake his head. It was clear Forest would not sell out their home game against Liverpool. They had reached the final of the FA Cup and had won their last two games at the City Ground, against Norwich and Chelsea, 5–0 and 7–0.

He turned and shouted: 'What do I have to do to get this lot to watch my team?'

He seldom had trouble selling tickets for the Baseball Ground and always maintained that Derby was 'a proper football city' in a way Nottingham was not.

Nigel possessed a vast record collection and once asked if I liked Billy Joel. I always wanted to please so I said I loved his music. Apart from 'Uptown Girl', I couldn't name a single song he'd written.

I started being given Billy Joel albums, smiling with fake gratitude each time I was handed a copy of *The Stranger* or *Piano Man*. They even took me to see Billy Joel at the Birmingham NEC. By this time I quite liked Billy Joel – I could by now name all his greatest hits. There would also be a ticket to see Paul Simon perform at Wembley Arena.

A month later, I went with the lads from AC Hunters to see Roy 'Chubby' Brown at the Derby Playhouse. As the Derby lads were wiping tears from their eyes and choking on their own laughter, I was staring straight ahead. This was a very different artistic experience from listening to Paul Simon sing 'The Sound of Silence'.

If I wanted to hear some stupidly-dressed bloke from the North-East swearing a lot, I could have gone to any street corner in Sunderland. Mam and Dad had taught us to talk properly and not to swear, which made me the poshest scruffy kid in Southwick. We were always told to pronounce where we lived as 'South-Wick' never 'Suddick', which is what every-one else in the area calls it.

Chubby Brown wasn't funny at all. He just swore like a trooper and my mam could do that.

The North-East comic Brian loved was Bobby Thompson. He was from Penshaw on the outskirts of Sunderland, where in Victorian times they had built an imitation Greek temple. But Bobby wasn't interested in Greek temples, his only concerns were where he could find the money to buy his next pint of Vaux, his next packet of Woodbines or to place his next bet. He was called 'The Little Waster' and one of the themes of his act was forever being in debt.

One of the first jokes Brian told me was from Bobby's routine, when his wife opens the door to the bailiffs:

'Knock, knock!'
'Is Mr Thompson in?'
'Take a seat.'
'A seat? I've come to take the bloody lot!'
'Weeeaaaahhh ...'

When we got back, Nigel was waiting in the kitchen with an envelope with my name on it. He said it was a reward for working so hard at Central News, a once-in-a-lifetime thing – it wouldn't feel right if they didn't take me.

I opened the envelope. Inside, was a ticket to see Elton John at Wembley Arena. With it was a backstage pass with 'May 25, 1989. Access All Areas' written on it. For the next two days, I smiled like an idiot.

We travelled down on a luxury coach with Stuart Pearce and a couple of the other Forest lads, as well as Simon and Nige with Sue and Margaret. Nigel and Margaret were childhood sweethearts who had known each other since they were at primary school. Simon was now married to Sue. When they first met, three years ago, Sue seemed so beautiful inside and out, I knew it would be game over for Simon.

Simon told me that he knew I had to be at work early the next morning, but as long as I promised to wake up on time, they'd be pleased to take me along.

Unlike Billy Joel, I loved Elton John in a way that, as a teenager, you weren't supposed to. I should have been into INXS, Bobby Brown and Guns N' Roses. Instead, I was making tapes with Elton John mixed in with All About Eve.

I had met him a few months before. We had beaten Watford 3–0 in the FA Cup and he came into the changing rooms at Vicarage Road to congratulate us. His cousin, Roy Dwight, had scored for Nottingham Forest in the 1959 FA Cup final and had then broken his leg. There were no substitutes then and Forest had won the Cup with 10 men.

I was standing at the dressing room door when he knocked and asked if he could come in and 'say hello to Mr Clough'.

Brian was in the bath when he came in and I had to pass him his towel sharpish. I shook Elton's hand, but I don't think he will have remembered that.

Simon told me a story of the last time they had gone to see him at Wembley. They were still kids and to reach the backstage area, they had to walk through a massive puddle. Elton had picked Libby up and given her a piggy-back so she wouldn't get her feet wet.

'Don't be scared when you meet him,' he said. 'He's just a really normal bloke.'

As the coach travelled down the M1, I began planning what I might say to Elton. I was doing this a lot more now, trying to think in advance so I didn't stand there like a blabbering idiot. If I was going to move in famous circles, I couldn't show any nerves.

I'd be smiling to myself when I pictured everyone falling about laughing and then imagining how they would fall in love with me for making them smile.

I thought that, when we were introduced, I'd tell him how nice it was he'd given Libby a piggy-back. Not all pop stars would do that. I also wanted to thank him for writing the songs that helped get me through so many tough nights in Southwick.

We had been given our backstage passes and a glass of something and were waiting around, wondering if Elton would say hello to us before or after the concert.

I saw him coming out of the corner of my eye. He was wearing a lilac suit and a brightly decorated trilby.

'Sorry I don't have long, but I just want to say hello before I go on stage. Can't talk much, I'm afraid. We've been going for two months solid and I'm not sure my throat is going to hold out. I don't want to croak during "Crocodile Rock".'

Sympathetic laughter broke out.

He shook hands with each of us, one by one, and spent a couple of minutes talking to Nige and Simon about how horrible Hillsborough must have been before congratulating Nigel on winning the League Cup.

Craig, who was Nigel's optician, took up ages of his time asking Elton where he got his glasses from. Of all the stupid bloody questions.

It was now my turn. I had the question planned.

'Hello, young man,' said Elton. 'We've met before, at the football. How are you?'

'Pppiggy-back, Libby, "Nikita", brilliant ... I mean ... err ...'

Elton John stood there, nonplussed.

Nigel stepped in: 'Er, we were telling him the story about you giving our Elizabeth a piggy-back last time we met, he wanted to tell you he thought it was a nice story.'

'You should have just said. I'm getting a bit old now, but if you want, you can jump on. Come on, hup!'

And so the man who has sold 25 million records was offering me a piggy-back. It would be something I could tell my grandkids. I hesitated.

It was because of what happened when I took Franz Carr into the showers at Old Trafford a couple of months before.

Let me explain. We were playing Manchester United in the FA Cup quarter-finals. Franz often became nervous before games. He had butterflies and didn't want to warm up. So, he and I went into the showers, which like everything at Old Trafford were bigger and grander than anything at the City Ground, and had a little game of one-touch. We didn't put the water on. Obviously.

Franz relaxed and it was his cross in front of the Stretford End that provided Garry Parker with the only goal of the game. When the lads heard about what had happened in the showers, they ripped the piss out of us. Mercilessly.

I was afraid the same thing would happen if they found out I'd had a piggy-back ride off Elton John.

'No, you don't want one? Good job, anyway. I'd probably put my back out.'

Then he was gone. Off to perform 'Rocket Man'.

The concert was electrifying. I cried. I smiled. I sang with my eyes closed. Elton told the audience that some of the Nottingham Forest team that had won the League Cup were there – including Nigel who had scored two of the goals – and could they have a round of applause?

At the end, he addressed the crowd about Hillsborough, dedicating 'Candle in the Wind' to the people who had lost their lives, saying what a tragedy it had been for Liverpool, the city and the club.

The reaction from the crowd was not what he expected. There was murmuring, a few shouts of 'hooligans!' and some boos.

We were in north London and, the following night, Arsenal would be playing Liverpool at Anfield for the league title. Elton was furious. He wouldn't do a second encore and, back-stage, he was still raging.

We got back to Quarndon at half two in the morning. Simon was coming to pick me up at a quarter to six to put the papers out.

Brian woke me up at half ten the next morning with a cup of tea: 'Now then, you daft bugger! Simon came to pick you up this morning. Son, he even threw pebbles at the window, but you didn't get up. I was going to wake you up earlier, but you were snoring so loud, I couldn't get near the bloody room so I thought I'd let you sleep in a bit longer.

'Now come on, get up, get dressed, get on the train to Nottingham and say sorry to our Si for sleeping in. You must have had a good time yesterday, you've not stopped smiling since you got back. Lovely, now come on, get up and get off to work.'

My seventeenth birthday was on 22 November – the day President Kennedy was shot. A couple of weeks before, there had been a knock on the door: it was Nigel, carrying a portable television.

Forest had beaten Crystal Palace, 5–0, in the League Cup and Nigel had been named Man of the Match. The League Cup was sponsored by Rumbelows, who sold televisions and electrical goods – the Man of the Match got a telly.

'There's some good news and some bad news. This is the good news,' he said, pointing to the telly. 'The bad news is that Margaret and me are getting married next month. It's going to be a small wedding, with not many people there.

'We really wanted you to come but you're not family and if I invite you, there will be family members who can't come and they'll be offended. But we're having a party, a couple of weeks after the wedding, and we'd love you to come, Craig. We really would love you to be there.'

I went downstairs, found Del and took him for a walk around the cricket pitch, crying all the way there and back.

When I walked Del with Brian, he would sometimes sing

'Consider Yourself' from *Oliver!* and when he came to the line: '*Consider yourself one of the family*', he would always turn to me. But the thoughts kept sweeping through my mind:

When it came down to it, I wasn't part of the family, was I? This was the first step towards edging me out.

The party was held in a beautiful restaurant on the banks of the Derwent in Darley Abbey. I behaved like a total prick all night, even heckling the hypnotist.

Sue came over to me and said: 'Come on, Craig, this isn't you.'

But it *was* me. It was me getting my own back for Nigel not inviting me to his wedding.

Brian was becoming irritated with me, mainly because of the extra work my untidiness made for Mrs Clough. Only once did he really lose his temper, shouting, 'I've had enough of this! I want you gone. What's it going to take to get you gone?'

'If you want me gone, I'll go.'

I ran out of the house, to the church at the bottom of the common. It was raining. I'd gone so quickly, I hadn't put a proper coat on.

Mrs Clough got into her BMW and came looking for me. Soon, she was ushering me into the passenger seat.

'What's wrong, pet? Where do you think you're going in this weather?'

'I'm sorry, I've had an argument with Brian.'

She brought me back and sat me down in lounge with Brian. She pointed to her husband and said: 'Let me tell you something, son. He'll go before you do.'

18.

The Irishman

It's the summer of 1990. The World Cup summer. It's a beautiful day in July and Kev and me have gone to Sutton in Ashfield to watch Nottingham Forest play in a pre-season friendly.

I'm living in digs on Davies Road in West Bridgford. Brian arranged them for me. Libby was the only one of the three Clough children living at home and I think Mrs Clough wanted time to herself – I could be a messy bugger.

Apart from a couple of teenage tiffs, Kev had pretty much been my best mate since the age of four. I'd asked some of my mates if they fancied coming down to Nottingham and Kev was the only one adventurous enough. He would live with me after the 1991 FA Cup final, but, for now, he was testing the water and travelling down at weekends.

It was great to have someone whom I considered to be a real friend, not someone I'd met through knowing Brian.

At school, Kev's nickname had been 'Tefal', not because he was super-intelligent but because he had such a big forehead. Even as a teenager he seemed to have a receding hairline. He was a decent footballer and, when he went to play for AC

Hunters, Nigel said he had 'the sweetest left foot I've ever seen'. His one weakness was that he would always be attracted to the path of least resistance.

At Sutton, there were a few first-teamers involved but it should be a nice, relaxing game. Archie Gemmill's in charge, although Brian might come and watch.

Brian has ordered Steve Stone, the young, powerful, Geordie winger who has just broken through to the first team, to give us a lift back to Newcastle. Stoney was reluctant because, on the bus to Sutton, Kev's feet reeked and he didn't fancy the idea of two and a half hours in a car back to the North-East accompanied by that smell.

Kev and I had gone for an ice cream. While standing in the queue, I noticed an absolute vision of a girl was pointing at us. She wore a white vest with a tiny pair of denim shorts. Her hair was in a ponytail and she had the loveliest, brownest legs.

Although I was wearing just a pair of shorts and a T-shirt, she had seen us get off the team bus.

The biggest change in my life since I became part of the football scene was that girls who would otherwise have walked on by now found me irresistible(ish). Me and Kev had a double act where, whenever a girl asked our names, we'd say they were talking to Walter and Farquois. Even if they thought we were total cocks, it started a conversation: 'Really, I've never met a footballer called Farquois.'

'Hi, my name's Corinna. Do you want to sit with me and my friend and watch the game?'

She was so lovely, I didn't watch the game, which was just as well since Nottingham Forest, who a few months before had won the League Cup for the fourth time under Brian, were being outplayed by Sutton Town.

I was also trying not to totally ignore Corinna's best mate, who Kev could have.

'Do you have a phone?' I said.

'Yes.'

'Can I call you some time?'

'Yes, that's why I gave you my number.'

I hadn't realised but she had pushed a piece of paper into the pockets of my shorts.

'Would you go to the cinema with me next week?'

'Yeah, love to. Give me a call on Wednesday,' she said.

Fucking hell, a girl has said yes!

I hardly noticed we were losing at half-time. We went for a walk, Corinna and her mate left and me and Kev were celebrating the fact we had a double date next week. Kev didn't really want to come because frankly, he considered Corinna's mate insufficiently attractive, but there was no way Corinna would go to Nottingham on her own from Sutton so she had to bring a friend.

Suddenly, Brian's voice comes bellowing from the stands: 'Hey, Archie! Get the Irishman on.'

The Irishman does not come on. We're still two down and there's only 20 minutes to go. Brian had this thing about measuring players' attitudes in smaller games – you would have thought he was losing a major final.

'Hey, Archie, get your bloody son off and get the bloody Irishman on!'

Archie did as he was ordered and sent on the young,

combative 19-year-old Irish midfielder. He was sensational. We left Sutton with a 2–2 draw.

I went over to Brian: 'Blow me but the Irishman was a bit special.' The Irishman's name was Roy Keane.

A few days later, Forest went to Arnold Town for another friendly. Arnold went into a 3–1 lead and about a thousand people started jeering. Roy took control and scored twice to allow Forest to leave with some dignity. He was only about six months older than me. I'd played snooker with him, felt as close to him as anyone could be to the young Roy Keane.

Roy had come over from Cork for a couple of weeks' trial. They put him up in Colwick Road in one of the two houses Forest owned: one for the first-year apprentices, the other for the first-year pros. It was next to the City Ground and for a while, before Brian found me the place in Davies Road, I lived there too.

I was hanging around with Sean Dyche and Craig Boardman. They were both centre-halves. Craig, whom everyone called Stan after the Liverpudlian comic, was the best-looking player at Nottingham Forest. He always had girls around him, although he never had the attraction of being a first-team footballer – his career would be largely confined to Halifax Town.

Dychie was his partner in central defence and he, too, never played a league game for Forest. He would, however, captain Chesterfield to an FA Cup semi-final.

Sean was rather more academic than the average defender. He absolutely loved his crosswords and was bright as a button. So were his shirts. All the Forest lads were going out to a nightclub in Nottingham called New York, New York. Sean offered to lend me one of his Ted Baker numbers but I thought they were too loud – I'd wear one of Nigel's suits. Whenever you saw pictures of Frank Sinatra in nightclubs back in the fifties with the Rat Pack, they all wore suits.

Suits were cool.

When I turned up, Sean eyed me up and down: 'What do you think you're wearing, Grandad?' The laughter was loud, the embarrassment louder.

A few days later, Libby told me: 'If you're going out with the Forest lads, you cannot wear a suit. You've got to have some fashion sense.'

She took me to Ted Baker in Nottingham to kit me out. The shirt she bought me cost 40 quid. Then it was along to the Birdcage, which had opened in 1965 as Nottingham's answer to the boutiques of Carnaby Street and the King's Road. There, Elizabeth bought me an Armand Basi T-shirt. She was getting Nigel one, so I might as well have one. They cost £65. Each.

It's tough when you're 17, sitting on a bus surrounded by people you idolise. They were there everywhere I looked – Pearce, Keane, Chettle, Hodge, Laws, Walker, Crosby, Gemmill, Carr, Wilson, Sutton, Parker, Wassall, Rice, Chapman. The hardest part was that I never really knew how they viewed me. It wasn't the first time I'd been surrounded by stars, but it was the first time I cared what they thought.

I couldn't ever really tell them how much I loved them. At a game, I couldn't celebrate how a kid would have celebrated. I couldn't get angry like a normal fan would. I couldn't hate players like a fan could.

It was a tough group to survive in. They were winners, leaders, the piss-taking was relentless and, if you couldn't stand on your own two feet verbally, you'd be destroyed. Very quickly, I became very good at sarcastic responses. No matter who you are, no matter where you play, if you're outwitted by a kid, you've got to shut up, sit down and take it while everyone congratulates the young 'un on a great comeback:

'Well done, Mackem. Don't take any shit, sunshine.'

The responses could be brutal. Sometimes, the stick became so bad I wanted to cry. Very early on, Nigel had told me: 'No matter what happens on the bus, you cannot go blabbing to Dad.' Sometimes, I defended myself with a nasty brand of sarcasm, something that wasn't me. Inside, it felt like I was changing.

More often than not, I'd travel to away games on the team bus but this time Brian asked if I wanted to go with him in his car to Anfield. It was a Tuesday night in August, the first away game of the season. We would meet up with the team at the hotel.

'We're leaving at two, Rigor. Make sure you're ready.'

Roy Keane would be coming with us. It would be a great experience for him to come with us, take his boots and get a feel of what it's like to be around the first team.

Mike Keeling came up the drive in his Mercedes to pick up Brian. He'd already been to the ground to get Roy but there was three of them when they got out of the car. Phil Starbuck, a young striker, was also coming along.

Phil was one of those who didn't quite make it at Nottingham Forest. He became a born-again Christian, finding God more easily than he had the back of the net.

'Sorry, Rigor, but we've got to take young Starbuck as well. A couple of the lads are doubtful and he might end up on the bench. Can you go with Simon instead?'

Fucking bastards. Roy Keane and Phil Starbuck have stolen my seat in the car.

Brian was putting out empty milk bottles on the doorstep. When he sees Roy, he goes inside and brings out a full bottle.

'Hey, Irishman, get some of this skimmed milk down yer! It'll keep yer strength up.'

'But I don't like milk, boss.'

'Get it down yer.'

Roy does as he's told.

On the way to Liverpool, I told Simon I thought Roy might play.

'Who is he? Nah, there's no chance, not at Anfield.'

We met Nige before kick-off. He told Simon to put his mortgage on Liverpool – 'We're playing a couple of kids.'

Liverpool are league champions and real nasty bastards right through the middle of the park. You didn't get away with playing kids on their patch.

One of the kids was Roy Keane.

This was a trick Brian had used before. He did not want a young footballer to dwell on the game and allow nerves to seep in. He had done it to Mark Crossley when Forest had played Liverpool in Lee Chapman's debut a couple of years before, where I had become so wound up about meeting Leslie Ash.

Crossley was 18, a big, daft lad from Barnsley. Forest's regular keeper, Steve Sutton, a down-to-earth guy from the Peak

District who played in a Salvation Army band, had been laid low with flu.

Brian phoned Crossley's father and suggested it would be worth his while coming down to Nottingham that night but not to tell Mark he would be facing Ian Rush and John Barnes. Then, an hour before kick-off, he told Mark to put his gloves on.

Forest beat Liverpool and Crossley was on the winning side in the next two games, against Newcastle and Coventry.

Brian then told Mark to come to Quarndon early on Sunday morning. As Mrs Clough served him tea and toast, Brian announced that Mark would be spending the afternoon in goal for AC Hunters. They would be fined £50 for playing a ringer. Brian insisted Mark paid the fine himself.

Two years on, Brian's tactic of not telling a young player he would be starting until the very last minute didn't produce a win. We lost, 2–0, at Anfield, but Roy was sensational.

When we got back, we took Del out for a walk. Brian was impressed with the Irishman: 'He'll be staying in the side for Coventry, that's for sure.' Once in, Keane was hardly ever out of the first team.

Roy was fierce. He would stand his ground on anything. He wasn't exactly looking for a row, but when it was something he believed in, he would stick to his guns. He had a lot of time for fans, especially at away games – 'Fair fucks to them! If they're ready to get their faces painted like eejits and travel round the country for us, they're alright in my book.'

The coach was a great place to be after we'd won, not so much when we'd lost. It was always the skipper who set the tone. If we'd lost, there'd be times when he'd come down the bus and tell the rest of the lads to keep it down.

'Hey, boys, we've just lost a fucking game, we've nothing to be laughing about.'

There had been quite a few lost games at the start of the season. Nottingham Forest had finished ninth in 1990, although we did retain the League Cup, beating Oldham in the final.

When the season began, everyone wondered how Stuart Pearce would be affected by missing the penalty in the World Cup semi-final against Germany – he was that important.

Forest won one of their first five league games. We went to Manchester United on a Wednesday night and Old Trafford began chanting: 'Pearce is a German.' Then, from 25 yards, the skipper sent a free-kick hurtling past Les Sealey and into the top corner.

We were on our way.

The lads would sit in their groups, depending on whether they were in one of the card schools or not. The top-boys table always included Stuart Pearce and Des Walker. The next table might have Nigel, Gary Crosby, Brian Laws and Garry Parker. The game was usually hearts. There would seldom be an in-depth analysis of the game but they'd chat about incidents, especially if something unusual happened.

In April, we were travelling back from Maine Road after a 3–1 defeat by Manchester City. Although we'd lost, the team bus was full of banter. Des had played a pass out to the left and Stuart had taken his eye off a slow, rolling ball and let it go under his boot for a throw-in to Manchester City. Stuart's response was to launch a tirade of abuse towards the linesman.

On the bus, the skipper said: 'I don't know why I did that. I was just so embarrassed, I had to blame someone.'

The digs in Colwick Road were run by John and Liz. John Galley had been a centre-forward for Forest for a few years in the early 1970s and had ended up in charge of looking after the club's young players. Liz was a strong-willed blonde, who would shout a lot. Big on discipline, they had a 10 o'clock curfew. They once tried to get one of the apprentices kicked out for leaving too much talcum powder on the bathroom floor after having a shower – they went to Brian and said he was a disruptive influence, who made too much mess.

Brian said: 'Are you trying to tell me that you want to move a lad out because he's talcing his balls? Get away!'

We would go to Barker's snooker club by the Lace Market and get a taxi back to arrive at Colwick Road as close as we could to 10. Once, we mistimed by four minutes. The front door was locked but in the front room, some lads were watching a video.

The four of us climbed in through the window. I was last and just as I was clambering in, there was John standing over me. He knew I hadn't been out alone. When I wouldn't tell him who else I'd been with, he went to Brian and said I was out of control – my room was a mess, I wasn't pulling my weight. Soon afterwards, Brian found me the place in Davies Road.

But I was becoming tired of being told what to do. At Quarndon, Mrs Clough would hoover the house before the cleaner arrived. She would tell me to tidy my room before it was cleaned. It felt like I was back in Southwick. I thought about what Geoffrey Boycott had told me: that I should remember how lucky, how special I was. I didn't feel that special. I was getting up at God knows what time to open up the shop. I worked hard and was paid not very much. When my mates in Sunderland discovered how little I was earning, they told me Brian was taking the piss.

For about six months whenever I went back to Sunderland, I would stay in Shakespeare Street. The council hadn't been told we'd left. Everything was empty, everything was a mess. After the council realised their mistake, I'd stay with Kev in Roker, one of Sunderland's posher addresses – where Kev lived was the exception.

Whenever I went back to Sunderland, I'd be told that, sooner or later, the Clough family would drop me. They would grow tired of having to look after some nobody from the North-East.

Listing what the Cloughs had given me should have been like John Cleese asking what the Romans had ever done for us. They had not given me roads, aqueducts or public baths. They had given something more precious: an education.

It was something that as a teenager I appreciated less and less. More and more, I was being drawn back to Sunderland and to what I thought were my real mates. When I went there, I had cool clothes and I had money. I had stories people wanted to hear – I wanted to show them I was doing well.

When I was in Nottingham, I felt ordinary. Scot Gemmill had got me a pass for Breadsall Priory, a hotel and country club in Derbyshire that had saunas, steam rooms and swimming pools. Afterwards, we'd go out for a few beers, or in Scot's case an orange juice and lemonade. It was nice of them, but caught up in the middle of their conversations, I didn't feel part of their footballers' talk – it was like being 14 and back in Sunderland.

When I was growing up there, Kev and a kid called Steven Home were two of my best friends. Kev did a milk round, Steven's mam ran a newsagent's; they each had access to cash. When we went out to the leisure centre or to see a film on a Saturday night, we would end up in the Wimpy Bar by Sunderland station.

By this time, I would never have any money. I would watch them tucking into their quarter-pounders. Once, Steven had eaten so much he couldn't finish and asked if I wanted his cheeseburger. As I held out my hand, he took the bun and licked it all over. To him, it was a joke. It was one that crushed me and, from that moment on, I vowed I would never make anyone feel this low.

In the country pubs of Little Eaton, nobody licked their panini or took a slurp from their Peroni before offering it to me but it was the same feeling. Deep down, I thought I didn't belong. I thought I wasn't good enough for these people.

19.

I'm Still Standing

I'm 17, nearly 18. I have met someone. Her name is Trudy. I'd noticed her the first time she came into the shop and not just because of her looks.

She worked at the Halifax and they wore bright green uniforms. Really bright. Really green. She had a beautiful, warm smile. She was tall, blonde, had blue eyes and fair skin. You couldn't miss her when she came in for her chocolate.

She had a friend called Anne, an older woman who had been coming in for the paper for years.

'Should I tell her you like her, Craig? She's lovely, you'd like her a lot. She's met a boy, I think, but he lives on the other side of the world.'

The boy was called Brian and the other side of the world was New Zealand.

Trudy was on her way to the counter. I had to play this cool. I played it really cool – I ran into the back and let someone else serve her.

I was walking down the lane in Quarndon with Brian and Del. It was Saturday night and Nottingham Forest had just beaten Southampton, 3–1. The goals were made up of a superb chip from Nigel Jemson, a Terry Wilson bullet header and a scrappy finish from Jemmo. Stuart Pearce had set the tone with a thundering tackle on their midfield hardman, Jimmy Case.

He hadn't scored, but Brian wanted to talk about his boy.

'Weeeaaaahhh, Rigor, how good was our Nige today? Did you see the way he tackled before Jemson's finish? And you can't teach them that, son. Weeeaaaahhh, that's *my* lad!'

I can't say what made Brian Clough a great manager but the things he said weren't usually complicated. Sometimes, he would have me cringing at some of the things he said after a match. Other times, I would want to cuddle him, he had said something so nice.

During games was where he really stood out. He could spot in a heartbeat who was causing the other team problems, which of the opposition players had 'shot it'. Having seen a weak link, he would try to exploit it. He knew instantly which of his players was performing above themselves.

He would look across the dug-out: 'Hey, Liam, look at that. Bing is murdering them. They can't get near him.' Then he'd be up, hand against the side of his mouth, bellowing, pointing to Gary Crosby: 'Centre-forward, give him the ball! Hey, Harry, get him on the ball!'

We would talk football whenever we took the dog for a walk. It could be early morning on the cricket pitch, late in the evening down the lane or in the car on the way to work. We'd talk about what I thought was the mistake that led to their goal and then he would tell me what really went wrong. We'd talk about who I thought had made our goals and then he would tell me how it really happened. We'd talk about who I thought was Man of the Match and then he would tell me who it really was.

'I'd give it to Bing, he put the cross in.'

'*You* could have put that cross in, son. The skipper made the goal with his challenge on the edge of our box. In fact, the skipper won us the game with that tackle. Superb! You've got no bloody idea.'

Tonight, the subject was family. He told me how proud he was to have such handsome kids.

'Hey, son, I'm including you in that as well. Fair enough, you might not be as handsome as Simon and you don't look *quite* like Beau Brummell, son, but you've scrubbed up well, you're not bad-looking *and* you're funny. How come you're not having much luck with the girls?'

I told him I had met a girl but I hadn't asked her out yet and we could only be friends because she was with someone else in New Zealand.

'Bloody hell, Ronnie! She's ran halfway around the world to get away from him and you're telling me you still won't ask her out?'

He'd given me a new nickname because I'd started whistling a lot. After the war, Ronnie Ronalde was one of Britain's biggest musical stars with an act made up of whistling and yodelling. America had Frank Sinatra, we had a bloke who whistled his way through 'If I Were A Blackbird'.

'Stop whistling! You're not bloody Ronnie Ronalde,' he'd say, pronouncing it Ronal-day as if Ronnie were from Italy rather than Islington. I liked the nickname much better than 'Rigor'.

'I'm scared she'll say no,' I told Brian.

'Give over! She'd be lucky to have you. I'll tell you what, son. All you've got to do to get a girl is tell them you know me,' he said winking and snort-laughing his head off. 'Honest, try it, and if that doesn't work, tell her the shop's yours. Weeeaaaahhh, New Zealand! I'll bloody New Zealand you! Come on, we're getting off home. Hey, Dog! Come on, we're going.'

A couple of days later, I was walking up Davies Road after a game of tennis and I saw Trudy waiting at the bus stop.

This time I was determined not to blow it. I knew I looked alright – I had on my Sergio Tacchini T-shirt and my black Lotto shorts. I couldn't let her go without at least saying hello.

'Hi, I've seen you in the shop a couple of times. My name's Craig, nice to meet you.'

'Hi, yeah, I know. I said hello today, but you'd already walked off. I'm Trudy.'

She lived in Cotgrave, a mining village a few miles outside Nottingham, and had to get the bus home every night.

'Do you have long to wait for your bus?'

'About 15 minutes.'

'I live just up here. Why not walk to the next bus stop with me? I can keep you company while you're waiting.'

'Sure, why not?' She looked me up and down. 'You've got sexy legs.'

I did have good legs. I so wanted to be Stuart Pearce that, when I went to Brian's, I spent every spare minute on the weights machine in the games room, listening to Michael Jackson, Motown or Elton. I'd try to teach myself how to disco dance between two pool cues I'd placed on the floor. When I grew tired of dancing, I'd start the weights – bench-pressing for the thighs and curls for the calves.

Several missed buses and three hours later, I was in love. Then she told me about Brian from New Zealand and I was crushed. I decided to carry on talking.

She would have given me her number but neither of us had anything to write it down with – 'I still remember the telephone number from my first house in Sunderland, Trudy. It's 091 492766. See what I mean? I can even say the alphabet faster backwards than I can say it forwards.'

I got her number.

'Can I call you to check you got back okay?'

'No. God, it's nearly 10 o'clock! Mam will kill me. I'll see you tomorrow morning anyway. I've got to pick up the paper.'

A couple of walks later and we'd agreed a night out together – as friends. I wanted to take her to the Goose Fair, which was the biggest event in Nottingham. A place of waltzers, roller coasters, big dippers and now bungee jumps, it flooded Forest Fields with lights and laughter and people. It was on in a few weeks.

Trudy thought the Goose Fair might be too big. We found another fair, out of town, with about eight rides.

I met Trudy's mam, Cath, and her dad, Bob, a plumber. Trudy won herself a cuddly dog on the darts game. I had tried three times to win it for her but all three darts had to stay on the board and mine kept falling out. We laughed so much my jaw was still aching when I got home.

I would need to work on how to make her more than a friend.

The alarm had an annoying buzzing, beeping noise and I'd already turned on the snooze a couple of times. I was thinking I should post Dad's birthday card, otherwise, even if it went first-class, it wouldn't get there on time. He turns 40 tomorrow.

He and Mam were living in Harrow now. The last phone call I'd had with him had been a ridiculous argument about a plan I'd come up with to live abroad.

'It's not your decision to make, Dad. It's got nothing to do with you anymore. I've been making my own decisions since I was a kid and you didn't care then.'

'Howay, Craigy, be careful, son! I'm still your dad. There's no way you can talk to me like that, none at all.'

I put the phone down and cried. Now, I promised myself I would ring him tomorrow and wish him a happy birthday.

Judith, my landlady at Davies Road, brought me a cup of Earl Grey and told me it was time to get up – 'You can't sweat in bed like that all day. Come on, it's beautiful outside and you're still asleep.'

I'd just got my trousers on when Judith shouted that I needed to come down quickly.

Simon was sitting in the front room. He looked pale and angry. I didn't know what I'd done. Had I forgotten to order something from WH Smiths? I'd had a Ribena Light and a packet of nuts on tick without telling him yesterday. Maybe it was that.

'You'd better sit down, son,' he said, 'I've got some bad news, I'm really sorry. Sit down. Come on, sit here.'

I already knew.

'Your dad's died, son. I don't know the details, other than it was a heart attack. It happened yesterday in Wandsworth. Your mam wants you to get down to London as fast as you can. Is there anything I can do?'

It's his birthday tomorrow. He can't be dead.

'I'm sorry, Craig. Hey, come on, come here. Are you okay? It's alright to cry, come on.'

'I'm not crying, Simon. It's okay. I've got to get to London, it's okay.'

I cannot begin to explain how I felt. Scared. That's the best I can do.

I went upstairs to get ready. Simon had given me £100 in two £50 notes. The first £50 notes I had ever owned, they were big, crisp, greeny-brown with Christopher Wren on the back. They oozed class. The train ticket to St Pancras was only 30 quid but he wanted me to have enough for emergencies.

I told him I would get the bus to Nottingham station.

'I'm not having you getting on a bus when the train station's only 20 minutes away. Come on, son, let's go.'

We drove through West Bridgford quiet as mice.

'Do you fancy some music, Casper?'

Casper was Simon's nickname for Nigel, who when he was young was shy and soft-voiced – a little ghost around the house.

Simon put on 'Mr Blue Sky' by ELO. No matter what kind of personal tragedy you are going through, when 'Mr Blue Sky' plays, you have no option but to sing along. For the first time, Simon handed me his imaginary mike. There was a reason why he put that song on.

'Stay as long as you need,' said Simon as he dropped me off at the station, 'give your mam our love and tell her we hope everything goes well … as well as it can.'

On the train I sat opposite a lovely-looking girl in a white blouse. I put on my Walkman and played 'I'm Still Standing' by Elton John over and over and over again. For the two hours it took to reach London, I cried solidly.

The girl got up and went to the buffet bar. She didn't come back and there was no way she had spent the journey eating – she was skinny as a rake.

'I'm Still Standing' shouldn't have been a song that made me cry, but I was paying too much attention to the words.

He's gone. He was the man who defined us. He made us laugh and he made us cry. He made us walk *a lot*. He was the man who destroyed any chance we had of a childhood. He was the man who hurt my mam so much, she could never have a normal life. None of us could. None of us did. But he was also the man who we all loved. He was the man who was my dad. Stepdad, but you get the drift.

It was over.

I went to see him before they closed the coffin. He looked amazingly calm but they hadn't olive-oiled his hair, which would have pissed him off no end.

I wanted so badly to shake him awake, to say sorry for the argument. I wanted so badly to punch him in the head. I wanted so badly to tell him that, no matter what we had been through, I loved him with my whole heart.

But it was too late. I kissed his cheek and walked away.

Our Dazzy didn't have anything black to wear but I bought him a suit for £45 with the money Simon had given me. I gelled his hair and gave him one of Nigel's white shirts and a dark tie.

There were six of us to carry his coffin: me, Darren and four of his mates. I was responsible for the back-left corner. It killed my shoulder and all I could think about was that I was going to drop it. We put him in the ground in Harrow, a million miles away from Sunderland, a million miles away from home. We didn't have enough money to buy a proper gravestone so there was a tiny wooden cross instead.

We had a wake for him at his favourite pub in Harrow, just off Vaughan Road. All his 'mates' came round to tell us how cool he was. I nearly got in a fight because someone played 'Don't Cry Daddy' by Elvis Presley. I cried while our Dazzy told stories about him from when Dad was in the Merchant Navy, then I promised I would never shed another tear for him in my life.

Dad had suffered a heart attack while walking to work. He had stopped drinking and hadn't smoked a joint in six months. He was going to start saving so he and Mum could move into a different place; he was trying to get himself fit again. Not long before, he had told me on the phone that he was nearly 40 and it was time he got his life back on track – he had wasted so many years.

He was also cheating on Mam. At the funeral, I'd noticed a woman hovering at the back. Nobody knew who she was. I watched her for a bit and while everyone else was walking away, she stayed. When we were gone, she had put flowers and a card on his grave. While Mam was talking to the vicar, I walked over to it.

I read the card: 'To my darling Jerry. I wish we had longer together. I love you so much. Sleep well and wait for me. I'll find you again someday'.

When he died, he was dressed in paint-covered overalls and a thick sheepskin jacket covered in red felt-tip pen; one of the pockets was half ripped off. He had fallen over in the street. The woman who rang for the ambulance said he had been there for a while and she thought he might be a tramp.

He was still breathing when the ambulance arrived. He died on the way to hospital.

What a bastard world. Why didn't anyone stop? Why didn't anyone help?

I went back early to Nottingham on Sunday morning, played for AC Hunters in the afternoon, missed two one-on-ones, trying to lob the keeper both times, even though Brian had told me to smash the next one. Simon had put me on the left wing, probably because it was a place where I couldn't cause my own team any problems.

I played in Nige's boots and somehow managed to score direct from a corner, the only goal I ever netted for AC Hunters. I had practised hitting the crossbar so often with Scot Gemmill that I could pretty much hit it anywhere 25 yards from goal.

Every corner I ever took, I tried to hit the bar. As soon as I struck this one, I could tell it was curling in nicely. The keeper flapped at it and everyone started running towards me.

'Fucking hell, Geordie! Get in there, son! You lucky bugger!'

They had no idea I meant it.

We were winning, 2–1, and I'd played as well as I'd ever done. We got another corner in the last minute. Nige was linesman and told me to play it short.

Fuck that, I'm scoring again.

I floated it in. The keeper caught it, hoofed it up-field and they scored. Straight from my corner. I had heard Brian so many times telling his players not to take any risks in the last minute and I had just cost us the win, trying to be clever.

We went to the Shing Do, a classy Chinese restaurant in Derby, with Libby asking me every couple of minutes if I was okay.

'I'm fine, Lib. Life goes on.'

We went back to The Elms to play Trivial Pursuit. Three teams: Nigel and Margaret, Simon and Sue, Craig and Libby.

Margaret was a trainee lawyer. Nigel had three A-levels. Sue was a nurse who knew a bit about everything – especially when it came to the brown and blue cheese questions. Simon was just Simon. Everything he did, he was good at.

I had left Hylton Red House, a school I had never really attended much, at 15. Libby didn't stand a chance.

All Brian's kids took something from their dad. Elizabeth inherited both his sense of humour and his ability to cut people dead with just one look. She didn't always stay around for the family Sunday evenings. Usually, she would be out with her mates. Today, she stayed.

'You okay, Craig? Do you want to talk about it? Let me know if you need me, it might do you some good to cry.'

I couldn't tell anyone I wasn't going to cry for him anymore. I was just worried Mam wouldn't know what to do – she would have to leave him now.

I'd forgotten to ring Trudy. When I next saw her, it had already been five days since we'd spoken and she thought I had stood her up. I told her I was sorry but something had come up, something I could not control.

We agreed to go to the pictures. We saw *Ghost* with Patrick Swayze and Demi Moore.

I hadn't told Trudy about Dad until the movie had started. I probably should have.

'We can go if you want,' she offered. 'Maybe this isn't the best movie.'

She held my hand so tightly it hurt.

20.

The Cup Final

Brian and I are on the cricket pitch with Del. It's a full moon, the shadows of the trees are falling over the grass.

I say to him: 'Come on, you have to stop drinking. You don't need it. It doesn't make you feel better. It doesn't help the team and it won't bring Pete back.'

He looks at me through eyes that were once sharp and bright and are now dull and cloudy. 'You're right, son. I've got to stop. It's doing me no good, no good at all. Do you know what? I'll stop tonight, this very evening.'

That's how the conversation went in my imagination. That's how it appeared in my dreams. Despite the hundreds of times Brian had told me to be brave, to speak my mind, to say what I thought, I never used that advice to help the man who gave it.

Instead, I became his barman and whenever he wanted a drink, I'd pour him a bit more vodka and a bit less orange because I thought that was what he wanted.

I wasn't the only one who lacked the courage to challenge him about the booze. Not once did Nottingham Forest attempt to ban alcohol in the offices and function rooms of the City

Ground to protect the man who had taken a Division Two club to the peaks of the game.

Drink clouded the memories of many people who encountered him during his final seasons at Forest, but mine never were. I remember a man who seemed to stand a hundred foot tall, carried himself with charisma and charm and lit up any room he walked into. I remember the man who made players visibly grow just by making an 'Okay' signal from the touchline. I remember a man who protected me from everything.

Yes, it was difficult to watch, it was difficult for the family, but, as usual, Mrs Clough's patience and support were unwavering. She was his rock. She loved him so much, she would go to hell and back for him. Sometimes she did.

A few months before, the man who was with him every step of the way from Hartlepools to winning a second European Cup in the Bernabéu was sitting in the foyer that led to the manager's office. He was wearing a cream coloured mac over a suit and his thick grey hair was swept back.

Then Brian came in and as he walked past the man in the foyer, he gave him a spiteful little kick to his feet. Once he was in his office, he sent for Carole, his secretary.

'Who has let him into my ground? I want him out now and I want whoever let him in fired.'

Scot Gemmill, who was with me, said, 'You know who that is, don't you?'

'No.'

'It's Peter Taylor.'

They had achieved everything together. League titles in Derby and Nottingham, European Cups, the kind of money that would have been truly difficult to spend in the England of the 1970s. They had fallen out partly because Taylor had gone off to manage Derby after 'retiring' from Nottingham Forest in 1982 and partly because he had written a book about their lives together. It was called *With Clough by Taylor*.

On neither occasion did Pete inform Brian. When he signed John Robertson, Forest's charismatic winger, again without the courtesy of a phone call, Brian broke off all contact.

With Clough by Taylor begins with Pete describing a phone call from Brian in the autumn of 1965. They had been team-mates at Middlesbrough but had not spoken in four years.

Clough said: 'I've been offered the managership of Hartlepools and I don't fancy it. But, if you'll come, I'll consider it.' Then he put the phone down.

It was a one-sided conversation, but it changed the lives of both men.

Had Brian allowed him another conversation, in his office, that afternoon, his last years at the City Ground might not have been overcome with grief, regret and drink. They did not speak – they would never speak again.

Not long afterwards, a morning in early October, the phone rings. I'm in the breakfast room, Mrs Clough is cleaning. Brian takes the call in the kitchen: it's Ronnie Fenton.

'Pete's gone. He had a heart attack in Majorca.'

Brian doesn't say a word. He drops the phone, which hits the floor with a bang and dangles there on the flex. He leaves the house and says he's going out for a walk – a long walk. Five hours later, he returns.

He's been crying.

Between ordering Pete out of the City Ground to the phone call from Ronnie Fenton, Brian's attitude had begun to soften. He no longer called him 'Taylor' but 'Pete'. There would be more stories about the league titles at Derby and Forest, how they painted the stands at Hartlepools – 'Weeeaaaahhh, could he make me laugh! The times we had together.'

There had been no other reason for Pete to come to the ground than to try to make peace. It would have taken some courage to do that and Brian's realisation of how he had behaved overcame him.

He phoned Pete's family. He went to the funeral. He talked about him in public, warmly and affectionately, calling him, 'my mate'.

It wasn't enough. The void still remained and the booze flowed in to create an endless wake for his lost friend, although 'friend' is too weak a word to describe what Pete was to Brian.

The one trophy Clough and Taylor had never won was the FA Cup. Between them, they'd had three quarter-finals at Derby and Forest and their last cup tie as a pair had been a third-round defeat at home to Wrexham. Taylor had been in sole charge of the team because Brian was in the Derby Royal Infirmary, suffering from chest pains. Taylor said he was 'shot' and in the summer of 1982, they went their separate ways, exhausted by each other.

The road to the 1991 final was tortuous. We needed three games to get past Crystal Palace. In the first replay, Forest were 2–1 up when, in the last seconds of extra time, Roy Keane played a short back-pass to Mark Crossley, who dashed out of his area to clear and drove it straight to John Salako, who chipped him from 35 yards. When the team came back into the dressing room, Brian punched Roy in the stomach.

A week later, Palace were finally beaten. On a bitter February night at St James' Park, we were two down to Newcastle in horrible conditions. Stuart Pearce got one back and then, very late on, Nigel scored. I celebrated like a banshee – I loved it when Forest scored, but I loved it most of all when it was Nigel.

Nigel had taught me to shave. He had bought me contact lenses because he was tired of me being called a 'speccy twat'. When he stroked home goals like these, goals that really mattered, I would go berserk.

We beat Newcastle, 3–0, in the replay at the City Ground. A 1–1 draw at Southampton brought another replay. On a Monday night in March, Nigel Jemson scores twice and then Forest are awarded a penalty. Nige, who is the designated penalty-taker, steps forward to take it and Jemmo wrestles him in front of the Trent End, takes the ball and scores.

As he celebrates, I am standing on the track by the pitch screaming abuse at him. Fans tend to have one member of their team they hate – I could never hate any of Brian's players. However, partly because he was taking the chance of a goal from Nigel, who had been struggling to score, and partly because he usually called me 'Brian's bum chum' and made baaing noises as I got on to the team bus, I made an exception for Nigel Jemson. When he mocked me, I would find myself fighting back tears.

Back home, Brian said to Nigel, 'Why didn't you punch him?'

'Because if I'd punched him, I'd have got myself sent off.'

There was no real answer to that.

Jemson had played brilliantly against Southampton and was a far better forward than he was ever given credit for. He had started to piss me off a few months before at Coventry. Forest were going for three straight League Cups and after 38 minutes at Highfield Road they were 4–0 down. In the space of a few minutes, Nigel scores a hat-trick to make it 4–3 at the interval. Garry Parker equalises and then Jemson only has to square it to give Nigel a tap-in. He shoots, he misses, and at the other end, Steve Livingstone scores to send Coventry through, 5–4.

Jemson's hat-trick against Southampton gave us a quarter-final against Norwich. Roy had taken to celebrating his goals by performing a somersault and Brian had warned if he did it again, that would be the end of him at Nottingham Forest.

On the way to Carrow Road, the talk on the bus was: 'What happens if Keaney scores?'

Keane scored the only goal and when the ball hit the net, he made to do the somersault celebration but stopped himself. Just in time.

The semi-final was at Villa Park against West Ham. They were in Division Two and had Tony Gale sent off for a professional foul on Gary Crosby after 25 minutes. Forest were playing so well at the time that West Ham would have lost whatever happened but probably not by four.

Brian had come out early before kick-off to breathe in the atmosphere, walk around the pitch and shake a few hands. When it was obvious Forest was going to win and all the headlines would be about him making an FA Cup final for the first time, he went back into the dressing rooms to let the players take the applause.

Brian used to say that Lee Glover, a young forward, was the most talented footballer ever to come through the ranks at Forest and he was immense that afternoon. He could have the guts kicked out of him and would still hold the ball up.

Brian admired bravery and, perhaps because his own playing career had been destroyed by injury, he admired footballers like Lee and Steve Stone, who came back from torn cartilages and broken legs.

When they were injured, he would keep extending their contracts. Once, when he was feeling his way back from another injury, Lee asked if he could prove his fitness by playing for AC Hunters. When Brian said yes, he was as thrilled as a child. He didn't hear his manager say under his breath: 'There's no chance whatsoever I am letting him play Sunday League.'

In the build-up to Wembley, Forest were smooth, they were brilliant, they were effortless. Chelsea were thrashed, 7–0. They put five past Norwich, four past Leeds and beat Liverpool.

We would be playing Tottenham, who had beaten Arsenal in their semi-final. Arsenal were a group of well-organised, nasty bastards who would become league champions after only losing one game. The thing was, because Arsenal were champions, we would qualify for the Cup Winners' Cup even if we lost the final – we expected to qualify by beating Tottenham.

I went to Wembley with Trudy, Simon and the family. Brian even invited his next-door neighbour, a lovely old boy who had two beautiful granddaughters. Brian was nervous but not for the reasons people imagined. He wanted to win the FA Cup but it was not an obsession. It was a piece of silverware, not a holy grail. He would have preferred to win the league but he also wanted to shut people up from talking about Brian Clough and the FA Cup. He was nervous because he would be meeting Princess Diana.

Elizabeth had bought him a rosette with 'World's Greatest Granddad', which he wore as he led the team out. He adored Stephen, Simon and Sue's first child and Brian's first grand-child. He called him 'Jackie Coogan' after the little boy who acted alongside Charlie Chaplin in *The Kid*.

All the stars seemed to be aligning. Paul Gascoigne, who is so wired up in the tunnel that he seemed to be on drugs, is carried off, although he should have been sent off for a chest-high challenge on Garry Parker in the first minute, let alone the assault on Gary Charles that rips Gascoigne's cruciate and was fortunate not to finish Gary's career.

Gascoigne would never be quite the same force again and, because of the attention it brought upon him, neither really will Gary Charles. Both men involved in that tackle will become alcoholics.

The referee, Roger Milford, who I'd *never* forgive, is laughing when those tackles went in. Even though Stuart Pearce scores from the free-kick, Spurs should be down to 10 men. Mark Crossley saves a penalty from Gary Lineker.

And then, one by one, the stars start falling from the sky. Paul Stewart – Tottenham's muscular midfielder, who was superb that afternoon – equalises. Nottingham Forest seize up; the passing no longer flows.

The final edges into extra time. Before the restart, Terry Venables is with his players, talking and encouraging, while Brian just sits on the bench. He wasn't trying to be clever. I imagine he thought there was nothing else to be said. The skipper could shout encouragement, he didn't want to fill his players' head with junk – his boys knew what they had to do.

Des Walker, who has never scored for Nottingham Forest, deflects a ball into his own net and it's all over.

There was a post-match banquet laid out. Nobody ate. When we got home, Brian took the dog for a walk.

Had they won, he would have retired. Nobody said it. There were no explicit conversations but there were murmurings in the background. Mrs Clough would have sat him down and persuaded him that the journey that had begun by the North Sea at Hartlepool in 1965 had come to an end. Everything that could be won, had been won.

It was more than this. Once he was outside football it would have been easier for him to stop drinking. Going to work at the City Ground was like going to work in a pub – there was booze in every office and every function room. Every win or every defeat gave him a reason to drink. But Nottingham Forest lost and those conversations proved as imaginary as the ones Brian and I had on the moonlit cricket ground: 'Do you know what? I'll stop tonight, this very evening.'

He still had a good young side who could play beautiful football and who were still capable of winning trophies. He carried on.

21.

A Betrayal

There were many reasons why I loved Scot Gemmill. He was the son of a man who had won the league with Derby and Nottingham Forest and who had scored one of Scotland's greatest goals, but he was completely unaffected by it.

Scot would play football with me after training, he would turn out for AC Hunters. Once, while playing for AC Hunters, he was substituted. When he asked Simon why, the reply was: 'Because you're not giving enough in midfield.' Forest fans would tell him he was only in the first team because of who his dad was.

He'd endured far worse than just taunts or being subbed in a Sunday League game. When he was a teenager in Forest's youth teams, Scot had been knocked unconscious during a training session and taken to the hospital in Nottingham in a coma.

I went to see him with Brian. Archie was by his bed. In the background was a priest. There was a chance Scot might not live and the priest might be needed. Brian was visibly shaking. The priest wasn't required: Scot pulled through.

Scot made his debut a few games before the 1991 FA Cup final. We were playing Wimbledon and I went down to London on the train with Simon and took Kev along. Simon offered him a job working at Central News with me.

Scot's breakthrough came the next season. That summer, Steve Hodge was sold to Leeds. He hadn't been in the starting line-up for the Cup final. He'd played in the two previous league games, the wins over Liverpool and Leeds, while Roy Keane was injured. Brian had a rule: 'If you play well, you keep the shirt' and Harry had played well.

The day before the final, Brian had given Stuart Pearce the team for Wembley to read out on the bus back from Burnham Beeches, where they'd been training. Harry's name wasn't on the crumpled bit of paper but Roy's was: Leeds offered him a three-year contract and a better salary.

Twelve months later, Harry had won the championship alongside Lee Chapman and Chris Fairclough, two others Brian had allowed to go to Elland Road. Nottingham Forest finished eighth.

The Zenith Data Systems Trophy was the last of those competitions designed to replace the European football that was lost after the deaths at Heysel Stadium in 1985.

The final, between Nottingham Forest and Southampton, was played on Sunday 29 March 1992. I was taking some of my mates down to Wembley. It was the day the clocks went forward and none of us noticed. We were lounging around, discussing what time we should set off, until suddenly we realised time was no longer a friend. I drove like a lunatic down the M1. We arrived in time to see Forest win, 3–2. Scot scored the first and the last goal and made the second.

In December, we'd been playing Arsenal and Scot had chipped David Seaman from about eight yards. Sometimes there is a moment when you know someone is going to make it and for those of us watching Scot, urging him on, this was it. Wembley just confirmed it.

Two weeks later came another Wembley final, the last of Brian's career. The League Cup against Manchester United. Every time we went to Wembley with him, we were convinced we would win. Not now. We had beaten them home and away in the league but Manchester United were changing and at Wembley, they won, 1–0.

It was worse even than the 1990 League Cup final against Oldham, which was so bad that Brian had them in for training the next day, even though they'd won. As they trained, Des Walker shouted to him: 'You can run me all you want, but I've got a seven-grand win bonus.'

Del the dog had been given a new car, a white Ford Sierra estate. By now I'd passed my test and if I needed a car, Brian would loan me the dog's car on the understanding I would be driving it to Nottingham or to see Trudy in Cotgrave. Very often I drove it to Sunderland to show it off to the lads, have a bag of chips and then drive it back. Only if he looked at the milometer would Brian ever know.

I was driving with my mates in the back towards the Durham Road through a steep dip called Tunstall Bank. At the bottom there was usually a van with a speed gun. Everyone in Sunderland knew what it was and feet were applied sharply to brakes. Not this foot, not this time, and suddenly there was a police car behind me.

Now I'm panicking. I'm not the registered owner of the car, that is a Mr B. H. Clough, who thinks I'm somewhere between Nottingham and Derby, not 150 miles away in a speed trap.

Right, be calm, be very polite and very apologetic. They might take pity on a young driver who doesn't know the road.

As soon as the policeman approaches the Sierra, Kev winds down the window: 'Afternoon, cunt-stable.'

I get out of the car while they carry out a registration search.

'This car is registered to a Mr Clough of The Elms, Quarndon, DE22. He wouldn't be the manager of Nottingham Forest by any chance?'

'Yes, I know this looks strange but I live with him and he lets me borrow his car sometimes and I've just popped back home to Sunderland. I'm sorry for speeding, I really am.'

'I'm a bit of a Brian Clough fan as it happens, son. Let's see how well you really know him. What's his wife's name?'

'Barbara.'

'How many kids does he have?'

'Three. Simon, Nigel and Elizabeth.'

'He's got a dog, hasn't he? What's it called?'

'Del. Most nights, I take him for a walk on the common.'

The quiz goes on. I don't think he knows all the answers but the copper wants to see how quickly I respond.

'Look, Mr Clough knows I've got the car but he doesn't know I've taken it to Sunderland. If he finds out, I'll be in real trouble.'

'Okay, you can go, but two things. One, slow down and watch the speed limits. They are there for a reason. Secondly, tell your mates that it's probably not a good idea when stopped by the police to call them "cunts". Now on your way.'

I was now living with Kev in a flat on Trent Boulevard. It was a Victorian house, divided into flats and was owned by an Italian, Joe Mascia, who ran a football team called AC Italia. We gave Joe a set of Forest kits in lieu of the first month's rent.

It only had one bedroom but was big enough for Kev to put down a mattress next to my bed. We were both working at Central News, we were a good team.

By now, I had my own car, a Ford Escort 1.4 LX. It was Elizabeth's and she'd given it to me once she got a new BMW. It was immaculate.

At Christmas, I planned to drive down to Harrow to see Mam. I told her not to worry about sweets, I could take care of those. For every away game, we made up a 'box' for the Forest coach. There would be three boxes of crisps, three trays of pop and three boxes of chocolate.

I got a cardboard box and filled it with Mars Bars, Twixes and Dairy Milk. There would be plenty of treats. It was only when I saw the grey chimneys of the Ratcliffe on Soar power station by the M1 junction that I realised I'd forgotten to put the bloody box in the boot! Joanne's kids would be coming round – I had to go back.

The box was on my bed and, to reach it, I inadvertently stepped on Kev's mattress that lay beside it. As I did so, I felt something hard, bulky and scrunchy underneath.

When I lifted the mattress, there were 15 small plastic bags, each of which contained 20 one-pound coins.

I decided to wait for Kev to get back from Central News. He would nearly be finished. I heard him come in, led him into the bedroom and pointed to the bags:

'Kev, what the fuck is that?'

'Yeah, I was going to tell you about that. It's from the shop, I was going to share it with you.'

'Kev, that's fucking ridiculous! You don't think Simon's going to miss 300 quid? You've taken too much. And you had no bloody intention of sharing it with me. I'm supposed to be halfway to London by now.'

I should ring the police. Right now. I should certainly tell Simon. Right now. I don't know why the fuck I told Kev that Simon never checks the till reel.

'Okay, I'll take half.'

I scooped up seven plastic bags. The betrayal had begun.

22.

Sea Breezes

Frank Sinatra had Palm Springs, Brian had Cala Millor. A bolthole in the sun that would always be part of him.

After they had played their last fixture, he had sent Derby to Majorca on the spring night in 1972 when either a win for Leeds at Wolves or for Liverpool at Arsenal would have stopped them winning the title. Leeds lost at Molineux and Liverpool drew at Highbury. In the Bahia del Este hotel, Peter Taylor chain-smoked cigars until he was told the final scores. Brian, who had taken his family to the Scilly Isles, told reporters that only now did he believe in miracles.

Eight years later, before Nottingham Forest played Hamburg in the European Cup final, Brian had taken the squad to Cala Millor. There was only one rule: the lads could do whatever they liked – provided they did not train. Forest won their second European Cup.

Brian went to Cala Millor virtually every year and in the summer of 1992, he asked if I'd like to come. I wouldn't be staying with him and the family but he'd arranged an apartment on the seafront. The building was called Los

Apartamentos Rigo, which given that Brian always called me 'Rigor', he thought was a great joke. I invited Kev, Steven Home, Lee Walker, who was Kev's cousin, and Trudy's brother, Andrew White, because he'd never been abroad. By then I had broken up with Trudy but imagined that taking her brother on holiday would win her back. I was wrong – she was a vegetarian and would leave me for a butcher.

We reached Cala Millor in the early hours of the morning and as I tried to settle up with the guy who ran the block, he waved me away. He would keep waving me away for the next two days until he explained: 'There is no need, it is a present from me to Mr Clough.'

Simon had given me £150 spending money, which was pretty good of him since, just before we flew, he'd asked me to move his car, a beautiful, metallic blue Ford Sierra Ghia. It was tightly parked and when I scraped the side of it down a telegraph pole trying to reverse it out, it was even more so.

There were two options. I could stop, which would mean just a door was damaged, or I could go through with the manoeuvre, which would involve gashing the whole side of the car right down to the bumper. I chose option two.

When Simon surveyed the damage, he said that rather than risk his no-claims bonus, he would pay for it himself. It meant he couldn't give me the £300 spending money he'd planned. That he gave me anything other than a bollocking was an extraordinary act of generosity.

We saw Brian every couple of days. He would arrive unannounced, which kept us on our toes as far as drink, girls and the state of the flat went. The usual time was about seven, when we'd go out for dinner.

His favourite restaurant in Cala Millor was a fish bar in a side street. He told me to take the lads there for a meal but added, 'You're not paying for it, Rigor. When you get the bill, give the owner this.' He handed me a traveller's cheque for a hundred dollars.

Brian had booked the table and after the meal, the owner didn't ask for payment. I didn't quite know what a traveller's cheque was but I knew what a hundred dollars could buy, so I slipped it in my pocket as we left.

When we got back to Nottingham, I felt Sean Dyche was the likeliest to know what to do with a traveller's cheque. I showed it to him and asked if I could just go to a bank and cash it.

'Fucking hell, no! This has the Gaffer's signature on it. If you go to a bank with that, you'll get yourself arrested.'

When he was in Majorca, Brian craved the sun. He would lie on a lounger for hours, eyes hidden behind sunglasses, his face perfectly still. By the end of the fortnight, he would look Spanish.

He was a great talker but not a great reader, although you might find a Dick Francis novel by the sun-lounger or under his arm. He would walk the promenade or drive to the other side of the island; to the sweeping bay at Santa Ponsa or the narrow streets of Soller.

When we went off on our own, he would turn to us and say: 'Remember you're English. You represent England.' He didn't want to hear that we'd been drunk.

And he would have heard. Everyone on this part of the island knew who Mr Clough was. His presence had brought people and money to Cala Millor and, as friends of the Cloughs, we had coffees and beers that did not have to be paid for.

Once we walked into a sports shop that was owned by a cousin of Miguel Nadal, whose defending was so physical he was known as 'The Beast'. Nadal had signed for Barcelona the year before and we were presented with free shirts in the colours of the new European champions.

The Rigo was right next to the Veronica Beach Hotel and we were allowed to use the pool. There were a lot of Germans at the hotel so we outflanked them. We got there early, grabbed the sun-loungers and spread out our towels – we would not be moving.

When I saw a beautiful teenaged girl in a black and white polka dot bikini lying on just a towel on the concrete poolside, I cracked. I grabbed my sun-lounger, raised it over my head and carried it over to her.

I laid it down beside her with words worthy of Sean Connery as James Bond: 'Someone as beautiful as you shouldn't have to lie on the ground.'

We sat and talked for what seemed like hours. She told me her name was Danijela and during the course of our conversation, she revealed she was 'Junior Miss Croatia'.

Since Croatia had been an independent nation for exactly a year and during those 12 months their citizens had been bombed, shelled and shot in the Yugoslav civil war, they had joined the Miss World organisation with impressive speed.

They had also become members of the Eurovision Song Contest. Their government may have been new but it had a sense of destiny.

On the other side of the pool, there was a diving contest going on.

'Come on, Craig, why don't you join them?'

Because I can barely swim. If they have a 20-metre doggy-paddle contest, I'll join in.

'I want to see you dive.'

I could have just confessed, told the truth that I was a lousy swimmer. But she was Junior Miss Croatia. So, I told her a story about how I was traumatised by water after jumping into a pool fully clothed to save a kitten.

'Did the kitten live, Craig? Did you save it?'

'Yes. I gave it mouth-to-mouth resuscitation.'

'That is a lovely story, Craig. I cannot see why that would make you afraid of water.'

'Because … because I forgot about the baby hamster that was in my pocket.'

The pattern of the fortnight had already been set. Kev and Steve would date Esther and Cati, two girls who worked in the bar at the Apartamentos Rigo, and I would date Junior Miss Croatia.

We all went to an English pub called The Buccaneer. There was disco music and a dancefloor. If I couldn't impress Danijela with my diving, I would impress her with my dancing. I sash-ayed forward into the strobe light.

There is an international language of facial expressions and you didn't have to speak Serbo-Croat to realise Danijela's face was registering bewilderment as to why she had chosen to spend a night with this uncoordinated English boy. She left, although we would keep in touch. In time, she would become a model, move to California and marry a brain surgeon. I like to think Danijela got the rougher end of the deal.

By the time we got back to the apartment, all the lads except me were shitfaced, particularly Steve. When I knocked on his door with a glass of water, he had passed out and Esther was sitting on the bed, looking lost.

'I want to go home.'

'Esther, it's three in the morning. You're not going anywhere by yourself. I'll walk back with you.'

She lived in a house inside the grounds of Cala Millor's football club. We had to climb through a gap in the fence and walk past the darkened open terraces. Behind one goal was barren wasteland. That was the way to her home. By the time I dropped her off, I was in love. It was a struggle to see her with Steve for the rest of the fortnight.

When we got back to Nottingham, things were changing. Simon had bought a fruit shop on Central Avenue, which he turned into one that sold cards and stationery, which he called Central Cards, and another newsagent's called Central Cabin: he had his empire.

We moved into the flat above Central Cards and Central Cabin. Kev and I still shared a bedroom but it was so huge, we could partition it so Kev had a double and on my side there was a double bed and a single.

One day, Kev turned to me: 'I've invited the girls over.'

'Who?'

'Cati and Esther. They want to come to Nottingham, they want to find work as au-pairs. I've told them they can stay here.'

'In case you hadn't noticed, Kev, we've got one bedroom.'

'Haway. They're desperate. Once the season's over in Majorca, there's nothing for them. They have to go on benefits. I told them they can stay here for a couple of days. Come on, we can swing this.'

We drove over to East Midlands Airport to pick them up. I tried to be as gentlemanly about it as I could. While Kev and Cati snuggled down on the mattress, I offered Esther the double and went into the single.

In the wee small hours of the morning – to quote Frank – she lay on the sofa and held my hand. Then we went into the kitchen and kissed. For the first time.

23.

Twilight of a God

30 January 1993

I'm at the City Ground. Nottingham Forest are two up against Oldham. Ian Woan, another footballer Brian has taken from the non-league game, has scored both goals. Oldham won't be coming back from that.

I don't like leaving the ground early but I've got a good excuse: it's Esther's birthday. We've only been together for five months but Brian has told his secretary Carole to arrange 'something special'.

Something special turned out to be a chauffeur-driven car to take us down to London to watch *Les Misérables* and a table at Langan's Brasserie. It's the most famous restaurant in London, co-owned by Michael Caine. All I had to do to get a table was to go to the door and say: 'Brian Clough sent me.'

We were being picked up at 4.30. When I got to the flat, Esther had changed into a black ballgown. I put on a suit and outside was a black Rolls-Royce. In the back was a bottle of champagne.

The car glided down to the heart of this dazzling city and dropped us off at Cambridge Circus. In front of us was the backlit, pale-red brick of the Palace Theatre amid the snow. Esther had never seen anything like the spectacle of *Les Misérables*. She had never seen snow either.

Our reservation at Langan's was at 9.30 but there was no sign of the Rolls-Royce. We waited on the steps of the Palace Theatre for what seemed like an hour. When the car pulled up, the driver explained he'd got lost – I knew he'd just done another job.

By the time we got to Mayfair, Langan's was closing. I knocked on the door and said that Brian Clough had sent us. After scanning a clipboard, they let us in and showed us to a table.

I scanned the menu. First, the starters. I didn't know what a soufflé aux épinards was, but I did know it was 10 quid. Poached eggs were also a tenner, although they did come with some haddock.

The main courses did have things I recognised. Steak and mushroom pie and Langan's bangers and mash. The price of the pie dwarfed anything sold at the City Ground. I didn't ask to see the wine list.

'Sorry, I need to take your order, sir. The kitchen will be closing shortly.'

'Could we have a green salad to share and some water?'

'There's no need for sir to be so abstemious, the bill has already been settled.'

'I'll have the pie … and some wine.'

Bernie Bloom's jazz quartet, which played at Langan's every evening, had stopped for the night. Bernie, however, was still in the corner on the piano playing some jazz standards, which only needed Frank's voice to make it complete. On the walls David Hockney's paintings stared down as people came over and told us how lovely we looked. We were love's young dream, everything seemed perfect.

Except everything *isn't* perfect. Everything is falling to fucking bits. The win over Oldham was Nottingham Forest's sixth of the season. We are second bottom. There are fires everywhere and nobody is putting them out.

Des Walker has gone to play right-back for Sampdoria. The skipper is injured. Teddy Sheringham has been sold. Roy Keane is playing centre-half. Nigel is playing in a new position almost every week.

I see a man, more fragile than he once was, but still one of the gods of the game, still with an aura about him. However, too many people say there is a ghost where Brian Clough used to be. He won't look people in the eye any more. His head is down. He no longer shouts instructions from the bench. The players are dismissing words that would once have inspired them.

Too often his eyes appeared dull and distant. Too often his appetite for football seemed to have vanished beyond his recall.

The only time his eyes seemed to sparkle as they once had was when he was with his grandson, Stephen, whom he would balance on his knee, see-sawing him up and down.

Brian had a replacement for Des in Darren Wassall, who was quick and good enough to have played against Manchester United in the League Cup final. But there had been an incident after a reserve game with Rotherham.

Darren was complaining that his hand was injured. Brian had spat on it, rubbed it and said: 'That's better now.' Darren's mam was appalled. He was sold to Derby for £600,000. Nigel and Roy perform heroics at centre-half but it means they're not playing up front or in central midfield.

A deal for Stan Collymore has fallen through because as Brian reckons: 'There is only room for one big head at this club.'

There was, however, room for Robert Rosario. He was big – he stood six foot four – and he would work his nuts off. He was Brian's last signing and he scored one goal. It was enough to give us a win against Tottenham but not enough to prevent Rosario being dragged up as evidence that Brian's ability to spot a player had deserted him.

In November, he had re-signed Neil Webb for £800,000 from Manchester United. When he left for Old Trafford, everyone called Webby 'Fat Wallet' because he would be doubling his money in Manchester. By the time he came back, it looked like he'd strapped the wallet to his belly because he seemed seriously chunky. He had done his Achilles tendon and although he could still pass a football beautifully, something was missing: he wasn't as quick or as sharp as he once was.

Suddenly, people are no longer so keen to play for Nottingham Forest. Too many stories of what the club is now like, what Brian is now like have leaked out. Brian was in desperate need of a central defender, even one like Colin Foster, despite once saying he was so soft, Elizabeth could have tackled him. However, he now wanted footballers he knew and trusted. Colin had anchored the defence alongside

Des Walker for two seasons and was now at West Ham, where he was barely getting a game. Brian asked him to come back to the City Ground. A fee of £400,000 was agreed and then Colin said no. He preferred life on a weekly contract with West Ham reserves. The ingratitude was staggering.

With Brian in a trance, without the skipper and Des, the team is rudderless. It burns and it drifts. The players shrug and stare.

Inside the club, the directors and officials were doing more than shrugging and staring. One director, Chris Wootton, a man who wallowed in all the privileges that Brian had made routine at Nottingham Forest, was telling the Sunday papers the manager was no longer in a fit state to run the club. Brian said if he saw him, he would shoot him.

The directors did not close ranks around him, nor did the supporters. There were some fans who had so lost faith, who had so little memory of the finals, the trophies, the glory that they wanted rid of the man who had brought them there. The arguments provoked fights in the stands. Sometimes, I would join in on Brian's behalf whenever I heard someone say he had lost control.

When it was all over, the stadium would embrace him, press him to their hearts. The Trent End would echo with his name as if he had just won another European Cup but while there was hope, there was a kind of civil war.

There was always a win to give us hope. We reached the quarter-finals of the League and the FA Cup. There was talk Brian might bow out at Wembley – we were beaten by Arsenal both times.

In December, we thrashed Leeds, the defending champions, 4–1 at Elland Road. Forest were still bottom, but we were now just a point away from safety.

In February 1993, we beat Middlesbrough and Queens Park Rangers. Forest were out of the relegation zone on goal difference. They won none of the next five.

In March, we beat Southampton and were a point away from Sheffield United and safety. On a Monday night in early April, we beat Tottenham at the City Ground. There would be no more wins.

I was actually enjoying watching Forest far more than I ever did. I wasn't going with the team, I wasn't going with Simon, I was going with my mates. I could stand and shout. I could go crazy when we scored and wouldn't have to be on my best behaviour.

It was not that the offers to travel with Simon or with the team dried up, it was just that I increasingly preferred being around my own people. However, looking back, it seems I was pushing myself away from the Cloughs.

In April, we all decided to go to Loftus Road to see Forest play Queens Park Rangers. I knew it was in west London somewhere, but as I drove down, I wasn't sure exactly where it was.

By one of those great coincidences, we found ourselves behind a car with a QPR sticker on the back window. We would just follow it to the ground. The car took a strange route before eventually turning into what for many men around here becomes their spiritual home on a Saturday afternoon: the Hammersmith branch of B&Q.

We finally found Loftus Road and squeezed the car into a parking space so tight we had to bounce the Escort into the gap with the steering wheel on full lock.

The game was thrilling and brilliant and summed up why Nottingham Forest were relegated. We scored first, QPR went 2–1 up and Kingsley Black, a young midfielder signed from Luton who did more than anyone to try to keep Forest afloat, scored twice. Les Ferdinand then scored two of his own and we had lost, 4–3.

Nottingham Forest, twice champions of Europe, were bottom, five points from safety with five games to play. In the shit. 'In the clarts' as we would say in Sunderland.

In the bloody clarts.

Nine days later, I was back in London, dressed in a full Forest tracksuit. It was a Wednesday night game at Arsenal. I got there at half six, strolled up to the door and said: 'I'm with the team.' The doorman walked through Highbury's marble halls to fetch Paul White, the Nottingham Forest club secretary.

'Bloody hell, you're getting a bit cheeky, but come on in!'

I went straight to the dressing room. Graham Lyas, the Forest physio, took one look at my trainers, which were expensive Nike Huaraches, and told me they offered about as much support for my feet as a pair of sandals.

I said something sharp to him, something I immediately regretted, and sat down on one of the benches.

Liam O'Kane pointed at me and said: 'What's he doing here?'

Brian replied: 'You're right, he's getting too familiar.'

The game was drawn 1–1. Roy Keane equalised in stoppage time. I never set foot in a Nottingham Forest dressing room again.

It wasn't just Brian's empire that was crashing around us, so too was Simon's little kingdom: Central News, Central Cabin and Central Cards. It was also being destroyed from within. By us – by *me*.

Me and Esther, Kev and Cati were living in the flat. Very often, so were our Dazzy, Steve Home and Lee Walker. We were in and out of the shops, up and down the stairs, and it began to piss Simon off. But that was nothing compared to what was going on inside Central News. A customer would come in and we'd be having a heading contest, sending the ball back and forth across the shop.

We'd shout across: 'Just leave the money on the counter.'

'I've only got a fiver.'

'You're going to have to wait because we're on for the record. We're nearly up to 200 headers.'

Sometimes, they would leave the money on the counter, sometimes they would leave and find another newsagent's where serving customers took priority over heading a football. Sometimes, they would tell Simon what was going on in his shops.

When we were all living in Southwick, there was a news-agent's on The Green where we worked as paperboys. A girl worked there in the evenings and we'd gather in the shop and when she left the counter to go into the stockroom, one of us would shout: 'Take a chance!' Then, we would stuff our pockets with as much chocolate and crisps as we could before she came back.

Now, I was shutting up Central News for the night, putting on the alarm and, as it beeped, someone shouted: 'Take a chance!' Before the alarm could go off, we grabbed a couple of Ripples, a few cans of Fanta and ran across the road, giggling like idiots. However, what started out as a piece of childish fun very soon took on a more sinister turn.

Before too long we were treating the two newsagents as our personal tuck shops. We saw the till as a reservoir of petty cash. Our Darren was smoking 40 Bensons a day, all of which were provided by Central News. Whenever Steven or Lee took anything, I told them I would settle up later. Of course, I never would.

I was treating my mates from Sunderland as Brian had treated me. He was always giving presents to me – of food, money, clothes, opportunities and experiences. In a way, I wanted to do the same for my mates, I wanted them to experience the joy of being given things.

The joy of feeling special.

Only I was doing it with stuff that was not mine to give and my second-hand generosity extended beyond the Southwick lads.

There was an Italian guy who played football with us. At first, we let him off paying for his *Sun* in the morning, then we let him off paying for his *Evening Post* in the afternoon. If he wanted a Mars Bar while he read the *Post*, we'd tell him to help himself.

He soon twigged. At Easter, he would load up with chocolate eggs. He would take armfuls of fireworks as Guy Fawkes Night approached. Boxes of Christmas cards as Advent began.

Increasingly, my mates shared in the experiences of being around Brian Clough. They were treated to his foibles. Lee was wearing an earring when he first met Brian, who told him earrings were worn by either 'poofs or pirates' and unless he was one or the other, he should take it off.

They were also treated to his generosity. There were tickets to watch England, to see Sunderland play Newcastle, to Old Trafford. All it required was a call to Carole, Brian's secretary.

In September 1992, I travelled on the Nottingham Forest team bus for the last time. Kev was with me and we went from a fabulous hotel in west London, where we'd had dinner with the team, to Chelsea.

In the dressing room, Brian was his usual self, telling us to get out there with the team. As we walked around the perimeter of Stamford Bridge, we were presented with programmes and scraps of paper to sign. Eventually, Kev turned to the supporters and announced like a seasoned pro: 'Sorry, lads, I can only do three or four before we have to go.'

I was much more accommodating with my fame, meaning there were some lads in London who would go home from the match – which ended in a goalless draw – trying desperately to match up my signature with the pen portraits of the Nottingham Forest team in the programme.

That I had done it at all really pissed Brian off.

Everything came to a head on Valentine's Day. We had decided to keep the card shop open late. Normally, it would close at half five, but people kept popping in for a Valentine's card before they went out and by eight o'clock we were still open.

Simon was across at Central News, stocktaking. He came over and saw Lee serving behind the counter. Of all of us, Lee Walker was the least culpable. Perhaps it was because he was a Nottingham Forest fan but of the Sunderland lads he seemed to be the only one who seemed to appreciate the experience the Cloughs were offering us. That night, he was serving customers, putting money in the till, giving change.

Simon shouts at him: 'What are you doing here? You don't work for me, I don't want you in the shop! Get out!'

Lee hits back: 'We're just trying to work. You're always having a go at Craig. Get off his fucking back and leave him alone!'

Lee, bless him, doesn't know that the reason Simon doesn't want any of my mates around is because he now knows what's going on. I hate myself for what is going on. Simon, like Nigel, had tret me like a brother. This was his reward and it was something I couldn't summon up the will to stop.

Brian used to have an attitude that you can never not be busy. If there are no customers in, fill the shelves. If the shelves are filled, clean them. If the shelves are clean, hoover the floor. After the argument on St Valentine's night, we cared less and less.

Brian came in and we were outside in the little car park, playing basketball. The shop was empty. I popped my head in.

'Son, what are you doing? Get a grip!'

'I'm on a break.'

'Anybody could have come in. Absolutely anyone.'

He would give me a lecture about loyalty, about deciding which side I was on.

Of course, I'm loyal. I'm bloody loyal. I never discuss what I see in the Nottingham Forest dressing rooms. I avoid journalists. I love you and I love Nige and Simon and I love your family.

But that was not quite what Brian meant. Brian had taken me out of Southwick and presented me with the kind of life that was the stuff of dreams. In return, I had taken Southwick into the very heart of his family.

Finally, Nigel came round to the flat. He asked everyone else to go out for a walk and sat me down: 'Look, Craig, you're not being straight with us. Something's going on. What I need you to do now is not come to work for a week. We'll still pay you but I want you to take some time and have a think about where your loyalties lie and decide who's looking after you and who's not looking after you and make a decision.'

'I don't know what you're talking about. There's nothing going on.'

On the floor was a box full of crisps, a tray of Lucozade Sport and a box of Cadbury's mini-eggs.

'Where did they come from?'

'We paid for those.'

The shops were haemorrhaging money. Eventually, after Brian had retired, Simon paid us off. He said they could no longer afford to keep us on. He gave me and Kev £800 each as a farewell payment – 'There's not enough hours for you now but, here, we don't want to see you out on the streets. This'll be 10 weeks' rent for you both.' Simon did not mention we had stolen from the family. Outwardly, he showed nothing but grace. I got a job at the Trent Bridge Inn by the cricket ground.

I wasn't at the City Ground for the game that saw Nottingham Forest relegated. I didn't see Brian swallowed by the love of the crowd on the final whistle. I didn't see the post-match interviews where he seemed finally relaxed, as if a weight had been lifted from him.

I was in Cala Millor. I had gone with Esther to a wedding in Majorca. Kev must have called me with the result: that Sheffield United had won and we were down.

I went to Ipswich for the final league game of the season. They were all there – Simon, Sue, Margaret and Mrs Clough. I shouted: 'Brian Clough's red and white army' throughout. Nigel scored a penalty, which would be his last goal for his dad. By then, Ipswich had already scored twice. We didn't deserve to lose but again we lost.

There was one more act, one more curtain call. It was the Nottinghamshire County Cup final. Nottingham Forest would be playing Notts County. They came to the City Ground in their thousands for a match they would ordinarily just have glanced at in the following day's *Evening Post*.

Forest won, 3–0, to give Brian the final trophy of his career. I didn't know how welcome I would be, but at the last minute I decided to go. There was a part of me that hoped he wouldn't see me.

Brian took the applause for one last time and then disappeared. I was walking through the foyer until the thought grabbed me that I couldn't just leave. I knocked on the door of his office.

'Can I come in, Brian?'

'Of course you can come in, Rigor. Take a seat, have a beer. We've had some fantastic nights in here, some brilliant memories, haven't we?'

The room was dark. The only light was provided by the misty floodlights peering in through the three slitted windows of his office. His inner circle was inside. Frank Sinatra and the Ink Spots were playing. Amid the music, Brian kept telling people not to cry, not on his behalf. There was a bewildered sadness that it had all come to this.

He sat back in his chair, nursing a drink and his memories. 'Pete should be here,' he said with his eyes closed. 'Pete should be here.'

It's close to midnight. People were trying to get him to leave. Mike Keeling said: 'Come on, Brian, let's get going.'

I was on the floor, back against the wall. 'Knock it off, Mike! This is his last night in this office. He's been here 18 years, he decides when he leaves.'

We stayed another 40 minutes. When he finally got up and walked out, I started crying. Brian turned and said: 'Come on, you can stay with us tonight.'

It was my last night in Quarndon. When we got back, we took the dog out for a walk. We didn't exchange a word. Brian simply stood in the middle of the common, humming away to himself and gazing up at the stars.

24.

The Last Song

20 September 2004

It's a Monday. A Monday in Warsaw. I'm 31 and because I live in Poland, I only know my weight in kilos. It's 74. I'm worried about getting a bit of a pot belly from the Tyskie beer, although I still play football three times a week. I also speak Polish pretty well.

I'm the regional director for a start-up firm that headhunts people across Eastern Europe. I think I look sharp. I've just bought myself a new suit and since the first haircut at John Borrington's in Derby, my hair doesn't get fluffy anymore. My teeth are still big but they haven't been yellow since I was a 16-year-old. I'm good at selling and good with people.

Warsaw still has a look of a Communist capital; the big Stalinist Palace of Culture still towers over the city but it is changing. English is beginning to edge out Russian as the second language. We have just moved into a brand-new office.

Kev phones.

'Hello, mate, it's me. You'd better sit down.'

I already know what he's going to say, I am already crying.

'I've got some bad news, Craig, if you haven't already heard. Brian has passed away. He died today, mate. I'm sorry. Is there anything I can do?'

There are seven consultants in the office, looking at me strangely. I've got to stop crying, but I can't. I am back to being that lonely, terrified 11-year-old boy.

He was buried at St Alkmund's church in Duffield. I didn't go to the funeral, I wasn't brave enough to ask. I took the next flight back to England. I wanted to see Simon; instead, I sat on a bench in West Bridgford for three hours, unable to say anything. Unable even to move.

On 21 October, fans of Derby and Nottingham Forest came together in the rain for his memorial service at Pride Park. The choir of Derby Cathedral sang. Martin O'Neill, who had won the European Cup with him, said he was 'an incredible manager but a better man'. Geoffrey Boycott remarked: 'People who thought he was all talk did not really know him.' Nigel spoke of his 'rare ability to understand human need'.

I had seen him twice in retirement. The first had been in January 1994. Nottingham Forest were heading back to the Premier League. Brian was writing his autobiography that would detail times when promotion to the top flight was not even the first course of the Forest story – it was the bread that's placed on your table while you study the menu.

I was going to Majorca to live with Esther, which none of the family had thought was a good idea, and I wanted to say goodbye. He invited me in and said: 'Just to let you know, Rigor, I rewrote my will this morning and you'll be pleased to know you got a mention.'

'Alright.'

'I said that under no circumstances whatsoever is that thieving little shit to receive a penny.'

Mrs Clough intervened, telling Brian not to talk to me like that.

'Weeeaaaahhh, what are you talking about, pet? I'm only telling the truth.'

He did, however, go to his study and return with 5,000 pesetas to take Esther out for a meal in Cala Millor.

The family were right about Majorca. I turned up in Cala Millor with a couple of suitcases, wanting to surprise Esther. She did not want to be surprised. There were arguments and then a separation.

The last time Brian and I saw each other was where I had seen him the first time. In Sunderland, at Roker Park, not far from the beach at Seaburn. It was November 1994. The book had been published and now he was promoting it.

I was working at an Indian restaurant on Sunderland's main drag, Fawcett Street, for all I could eat and £15 a night.

I went up the stairs to the big room, where he and Ronnie Fenton were sat behind a pile of books. He looked so much better. His skin was clear, his eyes were bright and he was wearing his green jersey and holding court.

He waved me forward: 'Come in, son, sit down.'

Then the conversation veered towards the serious: 'Listen, son, you let us down. You lied to us. You know we had a meeting, me, Nigel and Simon? We were thinking of getting the police involved, but the three of us decided that we'd brought you down to give you a better life and if the police had been involved, that would have been your life over. So, we cut you loose.'

I really wished they had called the police. If they had done, I would have been punished and I would have paid for what I did. Instead, the guilt stayed on me like an overcoat. At any time I could have stopped it. I invited the lads down from Sunderland and at any time I could have told them to leave.

It was a miserable day and behind me was a father and son. The lad didn't have a jacket and looked shivering. Brian went into his pocket and told Ronnie to do the same. Between them, they had about 30 quid – it wasn't quite enough for what Brian had in mind.

He looked at me: 'Son, do you have any money on you?'

I had 20 quid.

'That will do very nicely.' He gave the £50 to the father and told him to go downstairs to the Sunderland club shop and buy his boy a jacket.

'Don't worry, I'll give you the 20 quid next time I see you. Listen, son, we still love you. You could still be anything that you wanted to be. Get yourself sorted and come down to Nottingham and see us all again. Be good and don't be a stranger.'

I would never see him again.

One of the consequences of the chaos surrounding his leaving of Nottingham Forest was that Brian was never able to have a proper retirement party. To say goodbye *to everyone*. Everyone who had meant something to him.

Simon and I would discuss what the last song should be. Naturally, we assumed Brian would want Frank Sinatra singing 'My Way'. Simon went for 'Watching The Wheels' by John Lennon.

There's something bombastic and self-justifying about 'My Way'. East End gangsters have it played at their funerals. 'Watching the Wheels' is more poignant with its line about 'surely you're not happy now you no longer play the game.'

The farewell song at his memorial service was not John Lennon and it was not Sinatra. It was 'Let There Be Love' by Nat King Cole.

Brian was 58 when he left Forest and there was a little part of me that hoped he might return at Wolves or even Chesterfield. But that's how he differed from Frank: he didn't do comebacks and, for that, I'm glad. He was happy, in his way, that he was no longer involved.

I kept running away, always wanting to start again from zero, always thinking I could reinvent myself, be someone different. The parts I thought I had discarded in Southwick, in Quarndon or among the shelves of Central News, always returned to find me.

On an impulse, I gave up a perfectly good, perfectly well-paid job selling computer software to work on a farm in Kent, picking strawberries. The workers, who were nearly all Polish or Bulgarian, were housed in caravans. When, late at night, I made it to the farm, they showed me to my accommodation. The caravan had no electricity and in the middle of the floor was a bucket to piss in.

You were paid £1.20 for every tray of strawberries. Most of the workers reckoned on doing 30 trays a day. In my first three days, I made a total of £4.80. I stayed for three years.

One of the girls working on the farm was called Sylwia, who came from Krakow. She invited me over.

I was hired by a headhunting company. I moved to Warsaw and met someone called Aleksandra. When I was 13, I had drawn a picture of the girl I would marry – she had looked pretty much like Aleksandra, who was incredibly beautiful.

Everything after the Cloughs had been anti-climactic, a disappointment. Aleksandra was not. She was a psychologist, who was interested in the arts and philosophy. The 10 years I spent with her in Warsaw were the happiest of my life.

She had no interest in football and had never heard of Brian Clough. When his name cropped up, she would say: 'He sounds like a very interesting person.'

Brian Clough was, however, a name in Poland. He was the man who had called their goalkeeper, Jan Tomaszewski, 'a clown' before Poland prevented England from qualifying for the 1974 World Cup. That summer in West Germany, Poland finished third.

When an article about Brian appeared in Poland's biggest-selling newspaper, *Gazeta Wyborcza*, Aleksandra's father brought it to me. 'You knew this man?' he said almost with a sense of wonder. Her brother, Grzegorz, became fascinated by Brian and read everything he could about him.

By now, I could speak Polish. I joined in conversations, listened to the radio, the television. I was friends with a lovely guy called Pawel, who spoke impeccable English and, when we went out, he pretended he spoke no Polish and I would have to translate for him.

I was good at my job. I'd been selling things on the streets of Southwick at the age of seven. When you work in sales, the word you hear most often is 'no' or in Polish '*nie*'.

When I was told to piss off while knocking on our neighbours' doors in Southwick, I would say: 'If you don't like this stuff, what do you need me to bring?' Rejection never bothered me and because of that, I was a success. Except that something, somewhere told me that success, a good job, plenty of money and a woman like Aleksandra was something I did not deserve. The way I had left Nottingham and the way I had left the Cloughs was a guarantee of that – I would always carry that weight.

I still followed football or rather, I still followed Nigel. Only once did I go back to the City Ground, for Stuart Pearce's testimonial. It was partly because of the way they had treated Brian and partly because of the way they had treated Nigel.

He had gone to Liverpool in the relegation summer of 1993. He said it had been made pretty clear that it would be best for all concerned if he left Nottingham Forest. The club wanted a clean break with the past.

Liverpool were prepared to pay £1.5 million but Forest wanted more and took the club and a player whose loyalty had run thickly through his veins to a tribunal to squeeze another £1.25 million from the deal.

Five years later, Nigel joined Burton Albion as player-manager, although gradually he stopped playing. I would go over to watch them, sometimes I'd sponsor a match.

Brian would often come to support his son. Eton Park had a maximum capacity of 4,500 so if I wanted to see him, he wouldn't be difficult to find. I always told myself I would go over and thank him for what he had done for me but the longer you leave a conversation, the more difficult it is to have it. I told myself I had nothing he would want to hear. Sometimes, I would hide to avoid his gaze.

After his death, I did approach the family, one by one.

I saw Mrs Clough at a Burton Albion game. I said: 'Mrs Clough, can I have a word?'

'Of course, you can.'

'The first thing is that I'm sorry. I think you know that.'

'I do, pet. I do.'

'I also want to say thank you. Thank you for everything you did for me. Thank you.'

'All Brian wanted to do was to give you a better life than the one you had. Yes, you fell off the waggon for a little while, but he would be proud of what you've done.' Then, the steel entered her voice: 'But you know us, son. Once you're out of our circle, you're out of our circle.'

I talked to Simon in the shop. Central News had moved, although it was only three doors down. Central Avenue had changed. It was now pedestrianised and gentrified; full of upmarket bars and cafés. The flat above the shop, where me and Kev once lived, was now a very posh restaurant.

He was checking the stock, arranging magazines on the shelves. He said he didn't have time to talk.

'Simon, I'm not leaving until we've had a proper talk or until you kick me out. What I'm expecting you to do is punch me in the face.'

I could understand if he did. I really could.

We started talking football and we talked for two and a half hours. In the end, Simon said: 'Craig, I never thought I would say this, but it has been really good to talk to you. Really good.'

I found out he had not told his wife, Sue, or anyone else outside the family the reason why we had fallen out.

It's a Tuesday night in April. It's 2018. I had been working with Kev in Nottingham until we fell out and he fired me. Nigel is back managing Burton. They have long since moved to a neat new stadium. Nigel has promoted them to the Championship.

When he first came across Burton Albion 20 years before, they were in the Southern League. He's had League Cup semi-finals with Derby and Sheffield United. It's not quite two European Cups and a couple of league titles but for a manager who has never been given proper money to spend, it's a record to be proud of.

It's a hard night. Burton are being pummelled by Hull. Some people in the crowd, who presumably haven't considered how a club with an average gate of 4,600 might survive in the Championship, are shouting: 'Clough Out!' and Nigel's body language seems weary and defeated. They are going down but before they do, they will win at the Stadium of Light to relegate Sunderland.

Hull have won, 5–0, and I thought Nigel might quit that night. I hung around the stadium for an hour before he emerged. I approached him as he walked to the car park.

He said: 'I'm sorry to hear about your brother.'

'What?'

'Don't tell me you don't know.'

A shake of the head, a pause.

'I'm really sorry to have to tell you, Craig, but Aaron's died.'

I immediately start talking football. 'Nigel, I know you and you shouldn't resign. You've done astonishingly well. Nobody expected Burton Albion to be in the Championship in the first place.'

He turns and says: 'Craig, you don't know me. You knew me 25 years ago but you don't know me now. The last person who said he knew me was the chief executive of Derby just before he sacked me. I'm going nowhere.'

Burton's next game was against Derby. They would win, 3–1.

Aaron had left the army and had been working for British Rail in Colchester as a ticket inspector. One day, he'd been called a nigger and had done what Dad would have done: he lamped the guy.

But Aaron was an alcoholic. He'd been drinking and British Rail fired him for assaulting a customer and for being drunk on duty. From there, Aaron's life drifted out of control. He was on antidepressants. One night, he took his medication, had a few beers, forgot he had taken his medication and took it again.

The combination killed him.

Three or four days before he died, Aaron had tried to phone me. However, the only number he had for me was my company phone, which I had returned to Kev.

All Aaron heard was a request to leave a voicemail.

It wasn't suicide. He hadn't intended to take his life. At heart, Aaron was still an army man and his clothes were laid out, neatly pressed, ready for the next day.

A day that never came.

He was 47 and left a daughter and two granddaughters of whom he was touchingly proud. I shared something with him. An inheritance from our parents; the feeling that we did not deserve to be loved.

I wished he had spent more time with Brian. I wished he had come down to Nottingham with me. When we went to the City Ground, he was the favourite with the lads. He was so willing to help, he smiled so easily, that they all loved having Aaron around – Des, Harry Hodge, even Archie. In the years after he joined the army, the first question I was always asked was: 'How's your brother?'

25.
The Cycling Man
20 July 2020

They say no man is an island. But I am. Since Aaron died, I've cut myself off. I haven't worked, I've barely gone out. I'm as isolated and alone as Easter Island, South Georgia, St Helena.

I've bounced back from everything since I was a kid. It was something in my blood. I'm a fighter and a survivor. That's the one thing my parents gave me, or perhaps it's the only thing they couldn't crush.

Brian Clough wasn't my dad. He wasn't responsible for me. He wasn't tasked with bringing me up as a better person or even a decent human being, he didn't have to do any of it.

I've been trying to capture what Brian Clough meant to me. I am part Bromfield and part Clough. I begged, stole and borrowed the Clough part.

I am lucky enough to have walked or pushed myself into the life of a special man and an incredible family. All they ever wanted was a better life for a kid, who before they encountered him, had no real life at all.

When I hear people talk about Brian, I don't quite recognise some of the descriptions. He was supposedly a tyrant who terrified grown men, who ruled through fear. Maybe, but the overwhelming emotion I received from him was love.

The legacy he left was a testament to the person he was. Caring, confident, sometimes self-conscious, funny, lovely, occasionally nasty, but above all, he was a genius. He taught me how to be a good person. I didn't learn quickly enough but, eventually, I learned. I don't miss the football, I don't miss the lifestyle but I do miss the people. I would give everything for one more walk on the common. One more talk, one more jokey piss-take.

I've rented a beautiful cottage in the countryside near Alfreton. On a Sunday, I would walk two and a half hours to his grave in Duffield to talk to him. When I first went to St Alkmund's, it took me 45 minutes to find it.

I thought I would be confronted by a monument but there is just a small plaque that says 'Brian Howard Clough 1935–2004' and 'Barbara Beatrice Clough 1937–2013. Walking Together in the Sunshine'. It was in reference to a saying of Brian's: 'Always walk on the sunny side of the street. I can't understand anyone who wants to walk in the shade.'

I've decided I'm not going to walk, I'm going to cycle as far as I can. Perhaps around the coast. Who knows where I'll end up? The only things I have are a bike, which I bought a few days ago, a tent and a personality. The only decisions I have to make along the way are: Do I stay in the tent or do I go?

The country had just emerged from the hibernation of the first lockdown. The first day took me to the Travelodge in Alfreton, which I discovered was still closed because of Covid.

That left Alfreton Park, which runs alongside the A61 to Chesterfield and Sheffield. I was woken by a dog pissing on my tent.

Invariably, I would be woken by a dog walker, who would usually gaze down on me with a look of contempt as if I were a hobo. Then, when you started talking, the cold looks would melt away.

I had no map. I'd intended to go east, to reach the coast at Skegness, but I went west: from Burton, to Crewe, to Nantwich. Once I did 30 miles in driving rain but in a complete circle. When I realised I'd come back to my starting point, I was wet, cold and laughing.

At Shrewsbury, a family called me over to have a beer with them. They said what I was doing was an inspiration. It made me want to push on into Wales. The life I'd lived before I disappeared meant nothing. I talked to everyone I could, stayed in people's houses. Everything became about the present. I realised I was someone good.

I had wanted to fall back in love with myself on the trip, but as the bays, the mountains, the hills and the fields passed by, from Tenby to Robin Hood's Bay, I fell in love with my own country.

Always, I was surprised by the kindness of strangers. Later on in the journey, I was in Dorset, lost and nursing a puncture, and hauled myself into a village called Winfrith Newburgh. There was a pub, The Red Lion, owned by a Polish couple.

'*Czy masz dzis wolny pokoj?*'

'Yes, we have a room for tonight. Are you Polish?'

'No, but I used to live there. First, Krakow, then Warsaw.'

They served me vodka and food and refused payment for any of it.

I cycled through Wales to Machynlleth, on the edge of the Snowdonia National Park, and then reached the sea at Aberystwyth. Eventually, I was among the cliffs and bays of Pembrokeshire and the thin valleys of South Wales.

Without knowing whose land this was, I pitched my tent in the grounds of Clovelly Manor. I was disturbed by the sight of a man marching towards me dressed in a Barbour jacket, pink trousers and a cricket sweater. He was the lord of this particular manor and unless I made a donation to the RNLI, it was land he wanted me to leave. I gave him £25, which was £10 more than it would have cost to camp, and as we talked, his manner softened and he became more than a character in a Harry Enfield sketch.

By the time I reached Devon, I'd decided to get this book published, but before I did, I needed to phone Simon. To see if he'd be okay with it, to see if he wanted the past raked over one more time.

This might be a tricky call to make. The family had hated *The Damned United*, the novel about Brian's 44 days at Leeds. Johnny Giles had sued for libel.

I had just taken a ferry across the River Dart to Kingswear, the kind of village that has a steam railway with trains bearing names like *Esmerelda*. It also had a wishing well, where Ellen MacArthur had put in a pound for good luck before she set off to sail alone around the world. She had apparently made two wishes: to complete her voyage and to get married. Both came true. I only wanted to make one wish so I put in 50p and sent Simon a text.

It was answered as I rode on to Torquay's seafront. Simon phoned: 'I know you'll do it right,' he said. Then, as we always did, we talked football. About games we'd seen, about agents, about Nigel.

I flew into Torquay.

I kept riding. The goal was to reach Seaburn on 19 October, to mark the anniversary of my first meeting with Brian. On the 13th I had reached Lowestoft, where the back wheel snapped.

It was a Chris Boardman racing bike, it was never meant to take a tent on the back. Without having the money to repair it, I took it to Dunx's Cycles, which claimed to be the most easterly bike shop in the United Kingdom.

It was run by Duncan and Rikki, who had once built a bike and boat combination capable of crossing the Atlantic. In comparison, my back wheel was a straightforward operation. What was not so straightforward was that when I told them about my trip, they suggested I stay the night. When I woke up, they had stripped down and replaced everything on the bike except the frame. There was no charge.

I had 280 miles to cover. I did it in six days. By the end, I had covered 2,500 miles. I could have cycled to Moscow and still had change.

When I reached Middlesbrough, I went to Albert Park to see the statue of him that Mrs Clough had unveiled. He is 24, his boots are slung over his shoulders. He has just been capped by England and the world is in front of him. He looks the image of Nigel when he started playing for Nottingham Forest.

There are three statues of Brian and this is the family's favourite, partly because a café by Albert Park was where Brian and Mrs Clough had met over coffee and a strawberry milkshake. The café was owned by a relative of the rock star, Chris Rea, the third most famous person to come from Middlesbrough – Captain Cook was born there in 1728.

My destination was the seafront at Sunderland. Tony Irwin, whose mam, Marlene, had always come through for us when we were kids, called: 'I think you should end this journey by staying at the Seaburn Hotel. I've paid for two nights.' Since I had spent three quarters of my time sleeping in a tent, this was a wonderful prospect.

When I was a child, in Southwick, the doors to the Seaburn Hotel had seemed like the gateway to another world. A world that was hard to glimpse and impossible to imagine. It was a world in which Brian Clough became my guide. Now, I pushed through the doors once more.

I went on the beach, the same beach where I had first encountered him, his collar turned up against the wind. Where I'd asked: 'Hello, Mr Clough, can you tell me if Kenny Swain is up yet?'

Where I had begun the games of my life.

Acknowledgements

I want no epitaphs of profound history and all that
type of thing. I contributed. I would hope they
would say that and I would hope
somebody liked me.

Brian Clough

You were not just liked, Brian, you were loved. I would like to dedicate this book to the Clough family, without whom I would never have lived a life worth writing about. To Simon, Nigel and Elizabeth, to Sue and Margaret, thank you for everything.

I would like to acknowledge the love and support I have received from my mam, Gillian, my brother, Darren, and my sister, Joanne, in what were sometimes very bleak years.

This book has been 17 years in the writing. It began life as a letter to Mrs Clough that I started writing when I returned to England after Brian's death in September 2004.

I kept writing and writing. I sent the first three chapters to Ilkka, a guy in Finland whom I had met on Derby County fans' forum, where he posted under the name of 'Cisse'. He helped convince me the story was worth persevering with.

I sent another two chapters to Dave Armitage, the Midlands footballer writer for the *Daily Star*, who has written several books about Brian. He, too, urged me on.

A friend of mine in Nottingham, Ian Rafferty, read everything I wrote and let me live in his house rent-free when I was at my lowest ebb and gave me unconditional support while I wrote. He put effort and dedication into every aspect of my life. When I met him, I had thrown the USB with the original manuscript into the Trent. Without Ian, I might not have survived.

There were some words of encouragement that were important because of where they came from. Alex Dunne is an ex-public schoolboy, who is a man of few words. Hearing praise from him and from Paul Fairclough meant a very great deal.

Lee Walker, too, has been an unbelievable friend and supporter. So, too, has Darren Quinn, whom I knew at Hylton Red House School in Sunderland and who messaged me that he had not stopped laughing and crying since he started reading the manuscript.

Richard Smith, who was my first boss in Poland and my confidant ever since, has been there whenever I was troubled with doubts about the book.

There were times when it seemed there would be no book. One of the themes of *Be Good, Love Brian* is the kindness of strangers. Once, in a pub, Kieran Fitzpatrick overheard me talking about it. I was thinking of trying to publish it myself. He gave me £1,100 to help it on its way.

Perhaps the most significant act of kindness I received from a stranger was from Kenny Swain, without his intervention on the front at Seaburn, none of this could possibly have happened.

Steve Cummins, who moved from Nottingham to Andorra, played an instrumental role in the book's journey. In the years when the momentum to have this story published had waned, Steve told me I could not let the book die and contacted the literary agent, David Luxton, who propelled it forward.

Ewa and Jurek Kubicka were my parents in Poland while I dated their daughter and even after Aleksandra and I parted, mainly because I immersed myself so much in this book, continued to support me. Watching him up close had taught me how a father should behave.

Jen Parberry, a massive fan of Michael Sheen, who played Brian in *The Damned United*, got in touch with me through Twitter and supported me throughout the bike trip that makes up the final chapter. Although she lives a world away, on a cattle farm in New South Wales, Jen became a close friend and supporter. Despite the geographical distance, she provided me with weather reports every day of the ride. It is her drawing of me and Brian on the common at Quarndon that appears on the back cover.

I would like to thank my agent, David Luxton, and Jack Fogg at HarperCollins for their considerable help in steering this book towards publication.

I owe a huge debt to Daniel Taylor. There is no way that without Daniel's influence and brilliant writing that this book would have been resurrected. Daniel is a Nottingham Forest fan with a brilliant sense of humour but he is also a journalist who has a deep understanding of what makes a story worth telling. It was his article in *The Athletic* and the extraordinary response to it that paved the way for HarperCollins to agree to publication.

I would also like to thank my co-author, Tim Rich, who spent four years working for the *Sunderland Echo* and gave the book its structure and flow. There have been certain stages of the book which I thought I could not get through emotionally and Tim has been part-friend and part-psychologist. Because of the pandemic, we have yet to meet.

Craig Bromfield,
Sunderland, August 2021